Applied Econom

John ...

Head of Soc ... ...er High School for Boys, and Econ ... Master
S. Michael's, ... Park.

Dennis J. Iles, B.Sc.(Econ.)

Principal Lecturer in Business and Management Studies, Farnborough Technical College

Brinley Davies, M.A.Cantab.

Head of Economics Department, Worthing High School for Boys

Edward Arnold

First published 1972
by Edward Arnold (Publishers) Ltd
25 Hill Street, W1X 8LL

ISBN: 0 7131 1745 1

Printed in Great Britain by
Butler & Tanner Ltd, Frome and London

Contents

Introduction

This book is intended for students studying economics in Technical Colleges, Sixth Forms in Secondary Schools and Sixth Form Colleges and for those preparing for professional examinations at the intermediate level. The object, therefore, has been rather to stimulate thought and encourage the searching out of facts and figures than to present a comprehensive statistical documentation of the selected topics. Throughout an attempt has been made to fit the necessary descriptive material into a clear analytical framework so that students will be led to appreciate the fundamental importance of basing all their own work on analysis. The value of studying Economics lies in developing a scientific approach to relevant problems and not in learning a selection of "correct" answers to them.

The lack of factual background which must characterise the age-group for which this text is intended has made it seem wise to temper a strictly analytical approach with more descriptive matter than would be appropriate at higher levels of learning. This necessity of adjusting both method and content to suit the market invites the criticism of falling between the two stools of "descriptive" and "applied" economics, but too narrow a definition of these terms seems unjustifiable at this stage. Our object is not to offer something which will entirely satisfy the standards of those who have crossed over this streamlet of knowledge—it is to help over those who are just beginning to make the crossing.

Applied Economics is the using of economic theory to throw light on, and to suggest answers to, human problems. The fact that we are dealing with human problems which have other than economic aspects must be kept continually in mind, not to distract us from strict analysis but to make us aware that our conclusions are not comprehensive. If people are to reach wise decisions they must have at their disposal the best advice that the various social sciences can offer: each discipline can claim that it is foolish to ignore its findings but is not justified in claiming any priority over the others. An economist must indicate the results of any course of action or the ways towards any objective as suggested by his science but he endangers his integrity if he becomes emotionally involved in his recommendations. Thus we may discern certain paths to faster economic growth but whether or not society chooses one of them or prefers a slower rate or even stagnation is of no significance to us in our role as economists—as individual members of society we are, of course, as interested in the decision as anyone else.

In writing about economic problems it is easy to give the appearance that the conclusions drawn are those universally accepted by economists. On the other hand too much attention to the differences of opinion which exist can only be confusing to relative newcomers to the subject. Therefore, whilst some major points of difference have been discussed, the usual procedure has been to draw clearly the conclusions which analysis suggests to each writer. This is intended to underline the nature of economic thought and not to suggest that students should share the specific conclusions. In fact, our advice would be that none of our conclusions should be accepted without undertaking a careful check of our facts and analysis. Our intention is to display the use of analytical techniques and not to advocate our own deductions.

The bibliographies at the end of the chapters are not meant to be complete. They consist of books which are presently available and generally within the scope of students at the relevant level of study together with some particular sources found useful in preparing the work. All students should keep in touch with current trends through *The Economist*, the *British Economy Survey* (Oxford), the quarterly Bank Reviews and the *NIESR Statistical Review*.

The questions appended to each chapter are intended to be used as the bases of discussions as well as for essay titles. Writing and talking are the ways in which thought can be crystallised and refined and there is a little danger that the growing use of the objective testing of knowledge may mislead students into imagining that the hard work of essay writing is of diminishing importance.

Finally, why a traditional textbook and not a series of pamphlets as is the vogue? There is undoubtedly a place for these latter as additional stimulus material but there remains a very important place for the basic text which can avoid the necessity of appearing right up to date with its descriptive material and can concentrate, therefore, on analysis. It is, also, re-assuring and convenient for students to have one book with them at all times irrespective of the varying supply of supplementary material that their particular educational establishment or they themselves can afford. From the teacher's point of view there is also much to be said for having an anchor for any course.

Midhurst 1972.   J.C.P.

1 Economics and social values

As society endeavours to increase its control over the pattern of life it finds itself dealing more and more with economic factors and relationships. This explains, to a large degree, the great increase in interest in Economics as a subject in schools and colleges. It is felt that development of this science and a wider understanding of what it has to offer is a necessary pre-condition of defining and attaining social and political ends. Only too often Economics is cast in the role of the ogre who denies the fulfilment of those ends, and economic considerations are denounced as inhuman and unworthy of people dedicated to improving the quality of life. A careful analysis of the economic aspects of safeguarding or improving our environment is a frustrating delay to those who want quick action to seize the anticipated fruits of a higher quality of life. In the eyes of those who prefer to cling to the comforting shape of the present, the same economic analysis seems an unrealistic exercise resulting in estimates of potential but unquantifiable benefits and disadvantages. Yet, in the last analysis, it is the economic factors which set the seal on what is possible and what is not. Perhaps it is an awareness of this that leads to the derision and even venom which sometimes greets the considered opinions of economists. Most of us have our own dreams of a better world, few of us can accept limits to the realisation of those dreams without some feeling of annoyance. Let us look at some dreams and see what economics has to say about them—not a traditional introduction to Applied Economics but one which may help us to achieve a clearer perspective of the inter-relationships of the social sciences.

Humanising industry

Who wants to be a cog in an impersonal industrial machine? Who wants to live tied to a conveyor belt or an office desk? Who wants a higher standard of living in a new technological world in which we have lost all individuality and become merely animate ciphers? George Orwell's nightmare is one which will always haunt mankind and one's reaction is to shout out against the gradual grinding of liberal standards beneath the tracks of that industrial juggernaut named "Efficiency". Before we go any further, however, we must stop to consider to what extent this nightmare is realistic. Does the pursuit of higher standards of living demand that men should sell their souls? In the early days of industrialism the Luddites vented their frustration on the machines which seemed to them to be the inhuman, implacable source of their miseries, but men have grown to live with and benefit from the use of machines. The nineteenth-century socialists could see no hope of bridling the capitalist monster whose extirpation could only be achieved by revolution, but men have made peaceful progress in controlling the centres of industrial power.

It is quite natural, and to be expected, that people will find new developments difficult to assimilate. Economic change must always take the social and political setting that happens to exist at the time by surprise and the course of ensuing history is the story of adjustment to a changing social and economic environment. In this process there will be conflict between those whose interest lies in preserving past forms, those whose traditional ways of life are being destroyed and those whose interest lies in the changes or who catch idealistic glimpses of the future. Many, during transition, will be impatient at the slow rate of change, some because personal hardship lasting, perhaps over a lifetime, is seen to pass unheeded in the scramble and some because power and influence, self-confidence and arrogance seem to lie with the traditionalists. Does one blame economic forces for human reaction to them?—or does one turn to economic analysis to seek a better understanding of what is happening so that it can be controlled to the advantage of Mankind? The latter course is one of the wider concepts of Applied Economics.

Specialisation and the economies of large-scale production have been discerned as the root factors of industrialisation ever since Adam Smith thrust his "Inquiry into the Nature and Causes of the Wealth of Nations" on to the unsuspecting but receptive world of 1776. Every elementary Economics textbook lists the benefits of specialisation and the advantages of large-scale production and hints at their disadvantages. A careful look at Smith's proverbial comment that "the division of labour is limited by the extent of the market" indicates one very clear escape from the fear of an economy dominated completely by a few giant corporations. Highly organised industrial processes can only operate economically where there is a large market. Where markets are small the small operator makes the most efficient use of resources and will continue to thrive unless the legal and social framework of society is loaded against him. This is borne out by the continued growth of small firms in Britain during the present era. If there is economic progress the markets for some goods and processes will expand and be invaded by large enterprises but the increasing wealth of the community will find expression in the demand for new goods and new personal services the provision of which can provide ample scope for small firms. There may be some markets which shrivel but do not disappear e.g. rural bus services, which become candidates for transference back from large to small operators. The extent to which new small firms can come into being and thrive depends, in part, upon the existence of an adequate, suitable capital market and also in part upon a strict control of the use of monopoly power. Industrial states are only just starting to come to grips with this latter problem and much water is likely to flow under bridges before a pattern of society giving full rein to new, small firms emerges.

Large firms, giant firms, international firms are likely to grow wherever there is a commensurate market for standardised goods. Need these firms be inhuman? Unconcern for the dignity of others is not the prerogative of big business. The worst cases of savage intolerance of the rights of others are to be found, in the pages of history, among the households of aristocrats and local gentry, nineteenth-century mill owners, Dickensian offices, and political tyrannies to mention but a few instances. Even to-day large firms are by no means characterised by being less humane than small ones, nor even is private employment recognisable as being less humane than public employment. Is it perhaps just that "the terms of employment", the legal and social aspects of employment themselves often contravene the individual's desire for dignity? Is it having one's daily life and, maybe, one's very employment dictated by the whims of a "boss" which frustrates and angers sensitive individuals? This would fit the course of history from such hopeless explosions as the Peasants' Revolt in 1381 to the "unofficial" strikes of to-day. Again, our analysis of the situation leads us to a question of socio-legal status, not one of inexorable economic forces. There is no economic factor which specifies that owners and/or management must make decisions without consulting the labour force, nor is there one which suggests that such consultation will detract from efficiency. Many experiments have been, are being and will be carried out in establishing patterns of commercial organisation consistent with the aims of efficiency and humanity. Co-operatives, profit sharing schemes, forms of co-ownership, worker ownership and management, consultative schemes such as Works Councils—all represent endeavour in this field. Economists watch these developments with great interest and their particular contribution is to analyse them in the light of their science: to test the workability of ideas, as it were. This application of our study is important in that it can both encourage experiment with what seems feasible and discourage the adoption of measures which seem very unlikely to succeed.

In terms of intellectual satisfaction and securing effective action, the substance and methods of economics provide the soundest of approaches for dealing with many problems resulting from the continuing evolution of human society. However, since the collection of data and its analysis are bound to be a slow process and since interpretation of analysis and the formulation of policy are bound to leave much room for differing views, we must not be surprised if people often prefer the emotionally satisfying pursuit of will-o-the-wisps supposedly leading from unpleasant, harsh reality into one mist-enshrouded utopia or another.

Pollution

The defilement of our environment with domestic and industrial waste is, at last, beginning to attract serious public attention and is frequently and quite wrongly attributed to the narrow pursuit of economic ends. If we were to substitute "commercial" for "economic" in the last sentence the accusation would have some substance and this common failure to use words carefully can itself prevent the proper analysis of a problem. Thus, if pollution is thought to be the result of economics in action it would seem to be pointless to listen to the advice of economists on how to deal with it. If, however, we accept that it results from the self-interested activity of industries and households we can recognise that the science which studies "human behaviour in relation to the material aspects of life" may well have something valuable to say on the matter.

Pollution might well be thought of as a post-industrialisation Malthusian check to population. Students of the subject tell us that the ever increasing discharge of filth into the air and water on which human life depends could render much of our planet uninhabitable within the foreseeable future. On a somewhat lowlier plane, others draw attention to the decline in the quality of life and the strains put upon us by urban sprawl and the spoliation of the countryside. Economists will tend to emphasise the opportunity cost approach: the defilement of the environment is one of the costs of using resources in particular ways which has been largely ignored; now that its significance is being realised methods of including it in our accounts must be devised.

The first step must be to work out some way of measuring the costs of each type of pollution and the costs of preventing it. Until we have done that we cannot devise a rational policy. It is no use just being hysterically "against pollution": all living creatures would destroy their environments if not checked by others. Man's problem is that he does this more effectively than other animals and manages to control or destroy the checks on himself. We may now be beginning to realise what we have been doing but we cannot put the clock back: our environment is man-made and no-one wants to return to the "nasty, brutish and short" life which Hobbes described as Man's lot in a state of nature. "Civilisation" will advance under the inexorable pressure of Man's search for ever higher material standards of life; the generation of power for aircraft, vehicles, ships, industrial plants and our homes will continue to produce noise and effluent; manufacturing processes will continue to rip materials out of the earth's crust and create vast quantities of waste; households will continue to dispose of empty containers and other domestic rubbish. What we need to know is i) the effects of different degrees of the various types of pollution and ii) the costs of different degrees of abatement, so that priorities for action can be determined. A considerable amount of work has been done already in connection with air pollution, water pollution and noise but less on the spoliation of the countryside by open-cast mining, conventional mining's coal tips, industrial slag heaps, rubbish dumps, gravel pits and other forms of land pollution.

Costs of pollution and its prevention

There have been two national surveys on *air pollution* i) the Beaver Committee on Air Pollution which reported in 1954 (Cmd. No. 9322 H.M.S.O.) and ii) in 1971 *Science Policy Implications of Air Pollution* by P. M. S. Jones (Res. Policy and Planning, 2). Air pollution costs include the corrosion of building fabrics, damage to textiles, the loss of output resulting from, and the hospital services to deal with, respiratory illness.

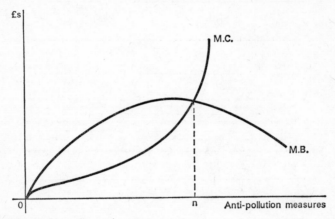

Fig 1.1 Marginal benefits and costs

It has been estimated that in 1971 these costs must have been in the order of £400m.[1] and that the average annual expenditure on prevention was in the order of £57m. The costs of preventing air pollution can be estimated fairly accurately in terms of the supply of smokeless fuels to domestic burners, the adapting of vehicles and aircraft to emit less fumes, the installing of waste consumers in industrial processes and the building of high chimney stacks to disperse industrial gases and dusts. The marginal costs of all these measures rise as their effectiveness increases: a clear case of diminishing marginal returns. Equally, as the degree of pollution is reduced the advantages of a further marginal diminution lessen: viewed either as the diminishing marginal rate of substitution of cleaner air for other things or as the diminishing marginal utility of clean air.

This argument can be illustrated by considering the marginal benefit and marginal cost curves in Fig 1.1. The curve M.B. (marginal benefit)

[1] Craig Sinclair "The Economic Consequences of an Anti-Pollution Programme for the U.K." in *The Pollution of Our Environment*—Liberal Party Publication.

indicates that as resources are used to abate any form of pollution each successive "dose" may yield more highly valued benefits for a time but that sooner or later the stage will be reached at which not only do physical returns diminish but also the degree of inconvenience has so lessened that an extra measure of cleanliness is not valued as highly as previous ones.

The curve M.C. measures the marginal cost of anti-pollution measures and this reflects again the fact that beyond a certain point it becomes increasingly difficult to lessen the remaining degrees of pollution. Thus, when an overhead urban motorway is built it pollutes the environment of nearby houses with noise, fumes and loss of light. If modestly high

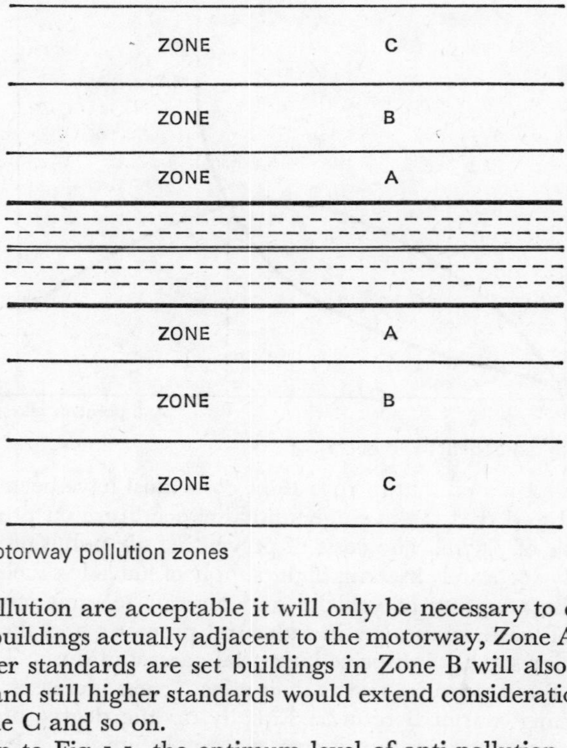

ZONE	C
ZONE	B
ZONE	A
ZONE	A
ZONE	B
ZONE	C

Fig 1.2 Motorway pollution zones

levels of pollution are acceptable it will only be necessary to demolish or "protect" buildings actually adjacent to the motorway, Zone A in Fig 1.2, but if higher standards are set buildings in Zone B will also qualify for treatment and still higher standards would extend consideration to buildings in Zone C and so on.

To return to Fig 1.1, the optimum level of anti-pollution measures is where On resources are used for them. If fewer resources than On are used marginal benefit exceeds marginal cost and the community will consider itself better off if more is done to tackle pollution. If resources greater than On are used to fight pollution, the community will consider the marginal improvements in the environment obtained to be not worth the cost of obtaining them. At On, however, the community assesses the marginal benefit received to be matched by the cost involved, a situation upon which it cannot improve.

To push anti-pollution measures beyond the point at which their marginal cost equalled the marginal benefit to society, assuming that society is properly versed in the matter, would be a misallocation of resources. The assumption that people know what they are doing is critical: society must be educated in an understanding of the results of pollution before it is able to judge the gains from anti-pollution measures and weigh those against other uses of the resources involved.

Water pollution caught the public eye in the 1970's and for many years groups of people have been concerned about the indiscriminate use of rivers as common sewers, about the use of the sea as a dumping ground for coastal towns' sewage, ships' rubbish and oil, industrial and military poisonous waste. In all such cases there is a reasonably obvious but often much more expensive means of disposal and this does to some extent make this aspect of pollution more amenable to measurement.

For rivers the first task must be to agree on the tolerable level of pollution. One day when humanity is both wealthier and less selfish it may be possible to contemplate the vast expense of so controlling the use of water that none is returned to the rivers contaminated in any way. However, as we have already noted, the marginal costs of successive anti-pollution measures rise and the marginal benefits decrease and the line of approach most likely to be successful at present is one that is based on an acceptable scientific definition of "clean water". This would accept such small quantities of effluent as were in no calculable way harmful to life.

Noise might be considered as a nuisance rather than a pollution but in so far as excessive noise is harmful to health and destroys the quality of life it must be included in any comprehensive approach to safeguarding or improving our environment. It is probably fortunate that noise stimulates resentment and anger so that anti-noise groups have become quite a force in shaping the course of events. At present most attention is concentrated on aircraft noise, particularly jet engines and super-sonic bangs, but it is already moving to vehicle noise in the main street and industrial noise has been under study for some time. The volume of noise can be measured in decibels and considerable research has been done on tolerable levels of noise. Thus control of this pollutant begins with some advantage of established, quantified targets although this does not mean that there is any easy way of translating these into money equivalents.

Since the sources of noise are readily identifiable the question of who should bear the costs of suppression rarely arises in public discussion. If an airline wants to operate large, fast aircraft the public is in little doubt but that it should incur the costs of operating them reasonably "quietly". The owner of a vehicle is responsible for its avoidance of excessive noise. The noise of construction and demolition machines is the responsibility of particular operators. The noise producers fight back against control as the increasing marginal costs involved damage their commercial prospects, particularly if they are in competition with operators elsewhere who are not subjected to the same controls.

Land pollution, being of its nature localised, trails behind in the interest of the general public. If there are slag heaps in the old coal mining or iron and steel areas, mountains of waste around quarries and huge water-filled holes in sand and gravel pits, one can avoid them. Urban sprawl and slum areas are also treated as the problems of those who live near them. Local opinion is rarely a strong enough force on its own to get anything done. By their very nature these areas are occupied by the poorer sections of the community or by those whose livelihoods are tied to the continued commercial success of the polluters. Not only would the immediate benefits of treatment be mainly local but also they would be very difficult to quantify. How much is it worth to convert the Wigan Alps into a play-park? What would it be worth to landscape or remove the slate heaps in North Wales? How much would we value the filling in or landscaping of the gravel pits around Chichester? Look around your own vicinity and list the examples of land pollution and then consider trying to fix a price that it would be worth paying for their removal.

Can one hear the cry: "there goes the economist again thinking that everything can be reduced to base, monetary terms. We are talking of priceless objectives; come on, let us turn our backs on this nonsense and proclaim our anti-pollution crusade."? It is very irritating to realise that even anti-pollution measures have an opportunity cost and that the diversion of resources required involves incurring a monetary cost. But this is fact and the economic approach is, as already emphasised, to try to match the cost against the benefit so that the best use of resources, in the eyes of the community, is achieved. The application of economic reasoning to this subject emphasises the necessity of trying to measure i) the costs to the community of continued pollution ii) the costs of anti-pollution measures and iii) the benefits to be realised from the application of such measures. This is not an argument for procrastination: it does not suggest that no action should be taken until all costs and benefits have been quantified and allocated. Where there is cause for immediate alarm, e.g. the careless dumping of dangerous chemical waste, instant action is necessary. There are many cases of obvious, extreme pollution but these are relatively easy to deal with. The real problem is a lasting one and our concern in economics is not to outline crash, emergency action but to provide for a long-term course of treatment and prevention.

The problem has rarely arisen out of sheer lack of concern by polluters. In our form of society firms and government authorities have never been required to take the social cost of their activities into account. A coal mine, whether privately or publicly owned, has always felt perfectly at ease in dumping its spoil on "its own land". "It's its own land, why shouldn't it?"—goes the argument. "If it does otherwise its costs will rise making it uncompetitive and then it will have to close down and that will throw people out of work." But the fact remains there is a social cost in despoliation of natural beauty and even in destruction and death as at Aberfan. A water authority such as Manchester Corporation floods valleys in the Lake District as around Haweswater because that is the cheapest way of increasing its supplies, the private cost is lowest. How can one cost the permanent loss of large tracts of beautiful, secluded valleys to both present and future generations? Yet, this is the exercise which should be undertaken before "keeping the water rate down" assumes final authority.

Are slag heaps and reservoirs of the same kind? Can they both be classified as pollution? It would be very difficult, as has already been indicated, to draw any distinction between pollution and just spoiling the environment. We do best if we take them together and think rather in terms of private and social cost and benefit.

QUESTIONS
'Modern industrialism may produce wealth but it destroys the quality of life." Discuss.

Must the pursuit of economic ends result in anti-social behaviour?

How much should society spend on curbing pollution?

Consider "opportunity costs" as a guide to anti-pollution measures.

To what extent is some knowledge of Economics necessary for the fulfilment of a citizen's obligations in a free society?

EXERCISES
Construct a production possibility curve indicating the choices open to a community between using resources i) for output of goods and services and ii) for anti-pollution measures.

Discuss the impact on this range of choice of a) idle resources within the community and b) economic expansion.

REFERENCES AND FURTHER READING
J. K. Galbraith: *The Affluent Society*, (Penguin 1970)
E. J. Mishan: *The Costs of Economic Growth*, (Penguin 1969)
N. Lee and J. A. Luker: "An Introduction to the Economics of Pollution" in *Economics*, Summer 1971.

2 Index numbers and their uses

An index number is a statistical device for measuring relative changes in a variable. In Economics such a variable may be an average price, an average cost of producing a given commodity, the volume of the flow of production of some commodity, the volume of trade, the average earnings of workpeople and so on. Some of the most well known index numbers in use in Great Britain are the Index of Retail Prices, the Index of Weekly Wage Rates and the Terms of Trade Index. All such indices set out to measure changes in the relevant variable by comparing its magnitudes at different times, relating each to a common base date. If the base date is 1962 it is shown thus: 1962 = 100. The significance of any move in an index depends upon the accuracy with which the methods used in compiling it indicate what is really happening and it is always important to check this carefully. Usually an isolated small movement of an index can be discounted as having no significance—one must look for fairly clear trends before one can be at all sure about the course of events. Failure to be awake to the limitations of statistical devices renders them useless and misleading: it is this fact which lies at the root of the belief that 'statistics can be made to mean anything you want'. This is only true when they are used by people who don't understand them or, of course, by people who are merely parading figures to make a well-established prejudice appear reasonable. Such misuse of statistics does not condemn them, it condemns the people misusing them.

Statistics are essential for the formulation and assessment of economic policy. We must know what is happening as accurately as possible before we can decide on the lines of policy and we must be able to see whether the policy applied is having the right sort of effects. Thus Statistics and Economics go hand in hand. In this chapter we shall confine our attention to the use of index numbers but this must not be taken to suggest that we think that such a brief excursion into Statistics is all that students of Economics need. It is hoped that it will whet their appetites and lead them to specialised books on the subject.

Index of Retail Prices

a) Averages

One often hears people say "the cost of living has gone up" and one's reaction should be to ask not only "what do you mean by the cost of living?" but also "by how much has it gone up?" Certainly governments must formulate answers to these questions as the bases of policies to control fluctuations in price levels.

There can be no single "cost of living" in a community. It will vary from family to family according to their differing patterns of expenditure. If the prices of pork, beef, mutton and chicken all double there will be no change in a vegetarian family's cost of living. If the costs of foreign travel go up they will not directly affect the cost of living of people who spend their holidays in their own country. Every individual pattern of living will have a different cost and since the prices of the constituent items are unlikely to move in the same degree, the cost of living in each individual pattern will vary in different proportions. This situation calls for working out an average pattern of living so that we can measure changes in its cost. Averages are dangerous things, they can be positively misleading. If a person said that he had just been to an interesting meeting attended by 100 people whose average age had been eighteen years you would have a clear picture of the gathering and you would feel that you had been deceived if you were then told that those present had been 50 mothers in their 37th year each carrying a baby a few weeks old.

What is an average pattern of household expenditure? It is certainly not the expenditure of an average household because we can be quite certain of one thing and that is that there is no such thing as an average household! When we set out to measure the way in which people are affected by changes in the value of money to them we must accept that we are seeking to give numerical values to variations in an abstraction. This is by no means as pointless as it may seem at this stage. Governments cannot usually devise separate policies for separate groups of the population, much less for separate families. They act to deal with inflationary and deflationary pressures as they occur and as long as their measures are calculated to offset the aggregate pressures they can achieve their objectives. An increase in aggregate monetary demand unmatched by a similar increase in the flow of goods and services will tend to push up the prices of most goods, some more than others but in such a way that a measure of the average impact of the rise in prices on each household will be a useful indicator, in conjunction with others, of what is happening.

b) Survey of expenditure

The calculation of an average pattern of household expenditure is based on a survey. Not all households are included as that would take so long that the information would be useless by the time it was published. A random sample of households is selected which means that in the process of selection each household has an equal chance of being included in the sample. Random sampling is a fascinating aspect of statistics and readers would do well to follow it up in one of the reference books listed at the end of the chapter.

Each selected household is asked to keep a detailed record of all its expenditure during specified weeks during the year and from this survey an average pattern of expenditure is calculated. Sometimes the recorded figures are at variance with those established fairly accurately from other sources and are adjusted accordingly. In the U.K. recorded expenditure on alcoholic drinks, tobacco and confectionery is noticeably inaccurate: husbands and wives hiding from one another their spending on themselves? Of course, this raises the question of other figures being falsely inflated but there are no other estimates by which to check and correct them.

c)   *Selection of a base year*

However, a standard pattern is calculated and as this is going to be used as the basis for measurement for some time ahead it is important that the year in which the survey is taken should not be unduly influenced by abnormalities.

One way round this particular problem is to adopt the current procedure in the U.K. whereby the pattern of expenditure used in any year is the average of the patterns thrown up by surveys over the previous three years. Thus in 1971 the basis of the index is calculated from surveys between June 1967 and June 1970. This linked index also avoids another weakness of the more traditional type, *viz*, that the representative pattern of expenditure may become less and less representative as time passes. Thus the average pattern of household expenditure in 1962 is hardly likely to be that of 1972 but without having a moving base the index measures the cost in 1972 of living in the 1962 pattern. The concept measured by the linked index is more vague than that of the traditional index but in this sense it is more realistic: the more we try to find something cut and dried the more do we depart from the abstraction of "changes in the average value of money".

d)   *Choice of commodity prices*

A final weakness in the figures on which calculations are based in the U.K. is associated with the question "what is the price of a commodity?" It is easy to see that it must be the average of prices found by random checks but what do we do about such things as "2p off", "special reduction", and trading stamps? In fact, it is the prices charged to the general public which are recorded and no account is taken of trading stamps and discounts to special customers. The more one looks into the complications of the market the more does one realise that anything approaching accurate, detailed measurement of price changes is impossible, that the very idea of "an average change in price" is considerably divorced from the minutiae of reality even though it satisfies our common-sense feeling that there is a reality which it will be useful to measure.

These remarks will serve to underline the importance of limiting the use of any index strictly to the particular data on which it is based. Thus the U.K. Index of Retail Prices is designed to measure changes in the value of money as experienced by the bulk of the working population and does not use the Family Expenditure Survey records of households whose main income is an old age pension and relatively well-to-do households (defined, in 1972, as those whose head received an income of over £70 per week). The survey is based on a fresh annual sample of 11 000 households and the items included are classified into eleven main groups *viz*:

Food
Alcoholic Drink
Tobacco
Housing
Fuel and Light
Durable household goods
Clothing and footwear
Transport and vehicles
Miscellaneous goods
Services
Meals bought and consumed outside home.

e)   Price relatives and weighting

The prices of items in the index are collected regularly. Altogether some 120 000 price quotations are obtained each month from shops deemed to be typical of those where most households make their purchases. The shops are selected from different geographical areas and, as already mentioned, the prices noted are those actually charged. Changes in the quality of goods provides a problem which is got round rather than solved by making adjustments to the index.

It will be apparent that a given percentage change in the price of one commodity may be of different significance to households than a similar percentage change in the price of something else. This is dealt with by allocating each commodity and, therefore, each group a weight according to the percentage of average expenditure upon it. This latter calculation changes each year, weights being calculated on the results of the surveys for the three years ending in the June previous to the year in question. The sum of the weighted price relatives so calculated is divided by the total of the weights to give the index number for the relevant date. This can be expressed in the formula

$$\frac{\Sigma\, xw}{\Sigma\, w} \text{ to one decimal place}$$

where the Greek letter sigma has its usual meaning of "sum of", where x indicates the price relative of each group and w its weight.

f)   Using the index

The index is calculated monthly in respect of a Tuesday near the middle of the month. The base date is January 16th, 1962, but since March 1970 has been re-based on 18th January 1966. It is published in the Department of Employment Gazette and also in the Economic Progress Report.

The process whereby each year's index with its revised weights is linked back to the base year to form a coherent series is one of simple multiplication. Let us assume that the price index for January 1967 based on January 1966 was 105 and that the price index for June 1967 based on January 1967 was 102 then we can link June 1967 with January 1966 by the following calculation:

$$\frac{102 \times 105}{100} = 107 \cdot 1$$

This would indicate that there had been a 7·1 per cent increase in retail prices in the relevant eighteen months. Equally we could say that the price index had risen 7·1 points during the period. Yet again it could be said that money had fallen in value, that £107·1 was needed in June 1967 to buy what could have been bought with £100 in January 1966 (rather a dangerous interpretation of the figures unless the concept of an average measurement is kept very clearly in mind). Perhaps an even more risky interpretation of a price index is the common practice of saying "the pound to-day is only worth, say, 80p". Unless a base date is clearly specified and checked for being a fairly normal one for its period such expressions can be confusing rather than enlightening. Moreover, unless one is aware of the statistical details of the index being used to substantiate the allegation one cannot be at all sure of its meaning, e.g. does it mean that £1 would be needed to-day in order to buy a basket of goods typical of household expenditure in the base year which could be bought then for 80p or does it mean that a basket typical of current patterns of expenditure which now costs a £1 could have been purchased at the earlier date for 80p?

Consumer Price Index

Changes in the purchasing power of the pound *from year to year* are calculated by a Consumer Price Index currently based on 1958: the Index of Retail Prices being used for changes *between* these annual calculations. From the table on page 15 we can work out the change in the purchasing power of the pound between 1961 and 1965 by the equation

$$£1 \times \frac{\text{index for 1961}}{\text{index for 1965}}$$

$$= £1 \times \frac{104 \cdot 4}{117 \cdot 8} = 88 \cdot 6p \text{ (i.e. 89p)}$$

Consumer Price Index (1958 = 100).[1]

$$
\begin{array}{ll}
1960 & 101 \cdot 4 \\
1961 & 104 \cdot 4 \\
1962 & 108 \cdot 2 \\
1963 & 109 \cdot 6 \\
1964 & 112 \cdot 8 \\
1965 & 117 \cdot 8 \\
\end{array}
$$

The Consumer Price Index covers all consumers in contrast to the Retail Prices Index and it includes a somewhat wider range of goods.

In the annual blue book *National Income and Expenditure* total expenditure on consumption is estimated both at current prices and at constant prices.[2] The division of the former by the latter gives us the Consumer Price Index thus:

$$
\text{Consumer Price Index 1970} = \frac{\text{1970 consumer expenditure at current prices}}{\text{1970 consumer expenditure at 1963 prices}}
$$

Other price indices which are regularly published include those for separate commodities including materials and fuel, one for farm prices, some for selected broad sectors of industry and one for general wholesale prices.

Some uses of price index numbers

i)   *Measuring economic growth*

Price indices are useful in assessing short period trends, i.e. in calculating rates of inflation or deflation and therefore assist in designing and checking the effectiveness of corrective policies. They also help in wage negotiations in so far as they remove from dispute the change in the cost of living to be taken into account: this is not to say that wages should fluctuate with the cost of living: that is a matter outside the context of this chapter. Taken together indices of retail prices and of wages can indicate by comparison whether the average standard of living is likely to be rising or falling, i.e. what is happening to *real* wages.

In the modern world a great deal of attention is paid to comparisons of countries' *growth rates*. These are measures of the rate at which real income per head, i.e. national income divided by the Consumer Price Index and the result divided by the total population, is increasing in each country. Their significance lies in their cumulative effect which is a matter of compound interest. The number of years which it will take the standard

[1] Source DEA Progress Report, 17th June 1966.
[2] At present, 1963 prices are used.

of living of any country to double can be worked out from the formula for compound interest.[1] This shows us that Japan's growth rate of 9·7 per cent between 1960 and 1965 would result in a doubling of the standard of living in a little over seven years whereas Britain's rate of 2·6 per cent for the same period would result in it taking some 27 years to double. Such comparisons must not be taken out of context of the existing standards of living of countries but they are useful indicators of the shape of things to come.

In many ways *economic progress* is a more meaningful concept than growth. It is possible to make progress in the face of odds in the form of a rising tide of dependent population, those too young or too old to work, but for that progress to be too slow to result in a rising standard of living. This situation is demonstrated by the following table:[2]

Year	Population (millions)			Real National Income (£million)	Real Income per head (£s)	Real Income per head occupied population (£s)
	Occupied	Dependent	Total			
x	60	40	100	12 000	120	200
x + 1	40	60	100	10 000	100	250

The occupied population is defined as all those people of working age who are at work or seeking work. In the illustration the population remains stationary between two dates but there is a turn-about in its age-distribution which results in a decline in the standard of living from £120 to £100 annual real income per head in spite of the increased productivity which raises real output per head of the occupied population from £200 to £250 per annum. This sort of discrepancy between progress and growth can be important in interpreting the effects of economic policies in countries such as the U.K. with its increasing numbers of retired people and such as India with its increasing numbers of children.

ii) *Comparisons between countries*

There is one use of per capita real income figures which calls for very careful attention, *viz* the attempts to use them to compare standards of living in different countries. Thus, in 1970, at the time of the floods in the delta region of East Pakistan the extreme poverty of the afflicted peasants was often emphasised by statements that their average annual income per head was only £15 and that for East Pakistan as a whole the average was only £35. In so far as such figures do convey a sense of poverty so intense

[1] *vide* J. C. Powicke, *Economic Theory*, p. 295. (Edward Arnold 1968)
[2] From J. C. Powicke and P. H. May's *An Introduction to Economics*. 2nd Ed. (Edward Arnold 1969)

that we cannot imagine it they do serve some useful purpose but they can be very misleading when used in isolation. How can a U.K. citizen consider a figure meaningful or accurate when it would in fact be utterly impossible to maintain life on such an income in his or her own country? It is clear that comparisons between countries can only be tentative and many other factors must be borne in mind when using them. Housing conditions; diets; medical, educational and other public services; expectation of life and many other such factors are relevant to the concept of the standard of living and they cannot be expressed adequately in one figure.

National income statistics vary in accuracy and meaning from one country to another. Since the basis of such calculations is, correctly, only paid work traditional peasant communities would appear much poorer in real terms than they actually are but if we add estimates of the value of their produce in terms of what it would earn if sold we will underestimate differences when we don't make similar additions for monetary economies.

How do we account for armaments and prestige projects? They are included in the national income and so our figures do not draw any distinction between guns and butter nor between palaces and bread. One community may appear to be better off than another whilst its people starve under a crushing burden of taxation to support a pompous, authoritarian regime whilst the other country's population enjoys a modest degree of personal comfort. Or again one country may be sacrificing current consumption so that it may be richer later as the result of an intensive programme of capital formation whilst another country with the same average real income per head is enjoying a much higher level of current consumption but making no provision for the future. The more one looks into it the less satisfactory does a simple comparison of income per head seem. In some communities the divergence between rich and poor is much greater than in others so that the average figures have quite different meanings. Climatic differences create differences in the amount of personal expenditure required to obtain the same degree of comfort. Averages which are not adjusted for taxation and draw no distinction between the satisfaction of personal and collective wants can only give blurred images for comparison.

The calculation of each country's per capita income is made, naturally, in terms of its own currency. How can these figures be reduced to a common base for comparison? A simple answer would seem to be 'by reference to current exchange rates' but these are determined by the flows of goods, services and capital across frontiers, by the activities of such bodies as the Exchange Equalisation Account, by impediments placed on the free flow of trade, by speculative flows of 'hot money' and by the controlling activities of central banks and the International Monetary Fund. Sometimes a country's currency is over-valued on the foreign exchanges and other countries' currencies are under-valued. There is certainly no clear connection between the relative domestic purchasing powers of different currencies and their foreign exchange rates. This apparently intractable problem is dealt with by calculating a price index based on a common basket of the goods and services more generally encountered in all the countries concerned. The price levels in each country can then be expressed as percentages of that ruling in the selected base country. The average income per head in each country is then multiplied by the index number to arrive at a common standard for comparison. This looks very neat and is as accurate an indication of what we are trying to measure as is likely to be achieved but it does not obviate the real difficulties arising when the differences between patterns of living are so great that it is impossible to select a representative basket of goods for the price index.

iii) *Changes in real wages*

In the same way that changes in the National income can be converted by price index numbers into changes in real income so can changes in wages, thought of either as wage rates or as earnings, be expressed in real terms. Real wages, i.e. wages in terms of the goods and services they can buy, are important concepts when studying the effects of price changes on the people in different occupations. The calculation:

$$1971 \text{ wage} \times \frac{1961 \text{ Index of Retail Prices}}{1971 \text{ Index of Retail Prices}}$$

measures the change in the real wage of a particular person or occupation between 1961 and 1971.

Unit value and volume indices

A country's terms of trade are determined by the relative price changes of its imports and exports. If the average prices of its imports rise in relation to the prices of its exports then the terms on which it is trading with other countries are deteriorating: each unit of exports pays for fewer units of its imports. Conversely, a rise in average export prices in relation to average import prices will mean that fewer units of exports are needed to pay for any given number of units of imports. The relative movements are expressed as percentage changes from a base year and they are very important for interpreting changes in a country's balance of payments, in its experience of income fluctuations and in industrial trends.

An immediate problem that is encountered in trying to calculate the terms of trade is that it is difficult to identify prices in such a way that they can be used as the basis of an ordinary price index. Goods flow through the ports in very large quantities and there is great diversity in the volume of separate transactions: what unit for pricing should be adopted? However they are calculated, prices vary with each transaction, with shifts in exchange rates and from one point of entry or exit to another. Therefore the practice is to take the aggregate value of each commodity exported or imported and divide this by the quantity involved. This gives us the *unit value* of each good and the weighted arithmetic mean of the unit values of exports or imports is then related to a base year in the normal manner. As a last step the export unit value index for any year is divided by the import unit value index for the same year, thus:

$$\text{U.K.'s terms of trade index } 1971 = \frac{\text{export unit value index } 1971}{\text{import unit value index } 1971}$$

In the U.K. 1961 is used as the base year for this index which is published in *Trade and Industry*.[1]

It is sometimes helpful to look at the purely physical flow of goods and goods and services. Although money, in its function as a measure of value, enables us to make useful comparisons it is sometimes the case that we can obtain a truer picture of what is happening if we look at the underlying realities. This can be done by calculating indices in measures such as "tons" for goods and "man-hours" for services but such measurements are only of use if one is looking at a single homogeneous commodity: we are up against the simple fact that one cannot add apples and pears together without running into trouble. If the exports of a country rise by 100 million tons, what effect will this have on its balance of trade? If the export of some low-priced bulky goods has expanded at the same time as fewer expensive but light in weight commodities has been sold to other countries an index in terms of "tons" would be misleading. Therefore, in order to measure volume changes, we have to fall back on constant price indices of the form of either:

$$\frac{1970 \text{ exports} \times 1961 \text{ prices}}{1961 \text{ exports} \times 1961 \text{ prices}} \times \frac{100}{1}$$

or

$$\frac{1970 \text{ exports} \times 1970 \text{ prices}}{1961 \text{ exports} \times 1970 \text{ prices}} \times \frac{100}{1}$$

In the first case we are calculating changes in terms of base year (1961) prices, in the second case in terms of the reference year (1970) prices. The former practice is the more usual one. The result is known as a "Volume index number" and in the U.K. Volume Index Numbers for imports and exports based on 1961 are published in *Trade and Industry*.

The same journal also publishes another volume index, the "Index of Industrial Production" based on 1963 which, as its name indicates, measures changes in the flow of industrial output.

[1] Formerly the *Board of Trade Journal*.

Standardisation

The process of adjusting figures to a common base is called "standardisation". Thus, in the National Income and Expenditure Blue Books, items in the various calculations are shown both at current prices and also standardised at 1958 prices. As we have seen, this latter practice enables us to identify changes in quantity. The standardised value of any variable indicates what its value in each year could have been if the base year prices had persisted throughout the period covered. Thus the effect of price changes is eliminated and the changes in volume disclosed. If the standardised values arrived at in this way are divided by the value of the variable in the base year, volume index numbers of the variable are obtained:

$$\frac{1970 \text{ Gross national product at 1963 prices}}{1963 \text{ Gross national product at 1963 prices}} \times \frac{100}{1}$$
$$= 1970 \text{ Index of G.N.P. } (1963 = 100)$$

Standardisation can enable index numbers to be used between places and occupations as well as between points in time. When we seek to compare *land rents* in different parts of a country we must adjust the actual rents observed to allow for the different sizes of holdings which prevail in different areas, i.e. a standardised rent for each area is calculated on the assumption of land being held in the average pattern of the country as a whole. A series of standardised rents can then be converted into an index number by dividing each item by the average rent for the country as a whole.

A moment's reflection will show that a crude comparison of *earnings in different industries* would be very misleading. Calculations must take into account differences in the age and sex distributions of the employees before we have a meaningful figure. The figures must therefore be standardised according to the average pattern of age and sex distribution.

Population changes are often discussed in terms of natural increase or decrease, i.e. the relationship between *birth rate* and *death rate*. These are respectively births per 1000 of the population and deaths per 1000 of the population. Although they give us simple, easily understood explanations of why population has risen or fallen and provide quantitative indicators of the change, they do not throw much light on causatory factors nor are they much help for estimating developments in the near future. In the basic form already noted they are known as "the crude birth rate" and "the crude death rate".

These crude rates have to be adjusted for differences in age distribution before they can be used to compare changes over time or from one place to another. To standardise death rates we first of all calculate *age-specific mortality rates*, i.e. the death rate in each age group, thus:

$$\frac{\text{number of deaths in age group}}{\text{population in age group}} \times \frac{1000}{1}$$

Using the age distribution as weights for each age-specific rate these can now be averaged to calculate the standard death rate for the community:

$$\frac{\Sigma\, SR}{\Sigma\, S} \text{ deaths per 1000}$$

where S is the standard percentage of the population in each age group and R is the age-specific death rate. (Σ being the customary statistical sign for "sum of").

It will be apparent that when comparing one part of the country with another differences in age distribution are very important: one would expect the crude death rate of Worthing with its large number of retired folk to be much higher than that of Wolverhampton with its fairly large number of younger immigrants. A straight comparison could easily suggest that Worthing was the less healthy place to live in. To secure comparable figures we take the death rate for each local age group and multiply it by the number of people in that age group in the country as a whole. These weighted age-specific rates are added up to give the number of deaths there would have been in the town if there had been a standard age-distribution of the population. The local standard mortality rate is then divided by the death rate for the whole country, giving us an index of mortality for the locality. This calculation for each district can be summarised as follows:

1 local age-specific death rates $\times$ country's population in each age group

2 $\dfrac{\text{sum of local standardised deaths}}{\text{population of country}} =$ local index of mortality

Variations between districts in this index will indicate factors relevant to the mortality rates and not the influence of differences in age-distributions.

In tracing trends in population we are particularly concerned with birth rates. Again we want to eliminate factors relating to age-distribution and we calculate age-specific fertility rates, i.e. births per 1000 of each age group in the same manner as we calculated age-specific mortality rates. In this case, of course, sex distribution is of vital importance and we eliminate males from our calculations. *Reproduction rates* are expressions based on the average numbers of girls born to women between the ages of 15 and 45. The gross reproduction rate is a straightforward expression of the number of such births per 1000 women between these ages and indicates the potential growth factor in the population. The actual rate at which a population is likely to grow depends also upon the age-specific mortality rates of girls and women and, in particular, on the infant mortality rate of girls. The sum of the differences between the age-specific reproduction and mortality rates is the *net reproduction rate* which is an index of the rate of expansion or contraction of a population.

Conclusion

An understanding of the meanings and limitations of index numbers is essential to the use of economic theory in throwing light on problems in the world around us. We must be able to measure what is happening before we can make any sensible assessment of what action to take—and we must be able to measure the impact of that action so that we can assess its validity. Finally, by way of reiteration, index numbers are valuable measures if used wisely and that means they must be used in an awareness of the purposes for which they are designed and of their limitations.

QUESTIONS

Is there any precise meaning in the phrase "the value of money"? Relate your answer to devices designed to measure this concept.

What do you understand by "measuring a variable at constant prices"?

Discuss the difficulties encountered in constructing and using the Index of Retail Prices.

What is meant by a country's "growth rate"? How can it be measured?

What is a country's "terms of trade"? Discuss the problems of measuring changes in the terms of trade.

What is meant in statistics by "standardisation"? What is the relevance of this concept to death rates?

Are comparisons of birth and death rates the best means of indicating likely changes in the size of a country's population?

Why has it been said that "there are lies, damned lies and statistics"?

REFERENCES AND FURTHER READING

W. J. Reichmann: *Use and Abuse of Statistics* (Penguin, 1970)
R. G. D. Allen: *Statistics for Economists* (Hutchinson, 1966)
R. Loveday: *Statistics. A First Course* (Cambridge University Press, 1961)
G. G. Bamford: *Arithmetical and Statistical Methods* (Ginn, 1969)
Central Statistical Office:
   National Income and Expenditure
   National Accounts Statistics—Sources and Methods
   Monthly Digest of Statistics
   Economic Trends

3 Wage determination

Marginal productivity

The theory of marginal productivity is an attempt to show how wages (or the rewards to other factors of production) would be determined under conditions of perfect competition and full employment.

The theory considers the employment of additional workers in a firm when plant and equipment are fixed in amounts. The extra output per unit of time attributable to an additional employee is called his marginal productivity. After a point, this marginal productivity will decline, so that each extra worker will bring about a smaller increase in output. This results from the "Law of Diminishing Returns", and can be represented graphically (Fig 3.1) or in the form of a table (Table 1).

Table 1   Diminishing Marginal Productivity

Labour Force (numbers)	Total Output (units) per week	Marginal Output (units)
10	2000	—
11	2200	200
12	2450	250
13	2680	230
14	2870	190
15	3110	140
16	3210	100
17	3300	90
18	3380	80
19	3450	70

Plant and equipment is considered fixed in amount. From the table it appears that marginal productivity (or output) rises at first, but begins to fall with the employment of the 13th worker, and thereafter falls steadily as more workers are employed.

So far we have dealt only with physical output. If we consider also the value of that output, we substitute "marginal revenue productivity" for "marginal productivity". The marginal revenue productivity of an additional worker per unit of time is the extra revenue derived from employing him. An individual firm in conditions of perfect competition cannot influence the price of its products. It must accept the market price

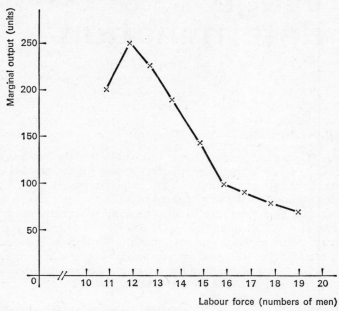

Fig 3.1 Diminishing marginal productivity

The graph above illustrates the data listed in Table 1.

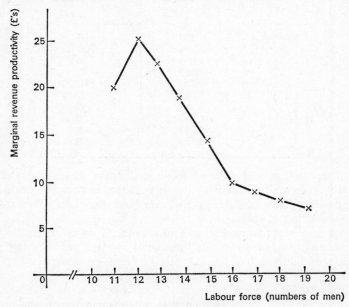

Fig 3.2 Diminishing marginal revenue productivity

and sell what it can at that price here assumed to be 10 p per unit. In such conditions the marginal revenue productivity curve (Fig. 3.2) will be parallel to the marginal productivity curve (Fig. 3.1). The shape is the same; the difference is merely that the units have changed.

(If the firm is producing in conditions of oligopoly, it will only be able to sell extra output by lowering its price. This will mean that MRP falls more rapidly than MP, but we need not concern ourselves with this complication here).

The firm under perfect competition will employ more men per week so long as the extra revenue they produce is greater than the extra cost in the form of wages. Such a firm must take into account that wages, as well as prices, are fixed by market forces which, by itself, it cannot alter. If marginal revenue productivity is greater than the going market wage, it pays a firm to employ extra men. If marginal revenue productivity is less than that wage, a firm will lose more than it gains by employing extra men, and it will benefit by cutting down its labour force. The argument is illustrated in Table 2 and Figure 3.3, and shows that a firm will expand its employment of workers up to the point where MRP of the last, additional worker, is equal to the wage paid.

Table 2   MRP = Wage

Price of Product (pence)	Labour Force	Marginal Output	MRP (£'s)	Wage (£'s)
10	10	—	—	14
10	11	200	20	14
10	12	250	25	14
10	13	230	23	14
10	14	190	19	14
10	15	140	14	14
10	16	100	10	14
10	17	90	9	14

Total Revenue (£'s)[1]	Total Costs (£'s)[2]	Balance (£'s)
200	140	60
220	154	76
245	168	77
268	182	86
287	196	91
311	210	101
321	224	97
330	238	92

[1] Col. 2 Table 1 × Col. 1 Table 2.
[2] Col. 2 Table 2 × Col. 5 Table 2.

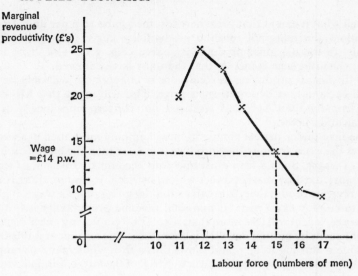

No. of workers employed=15

Fig 3.3 Employment in perfect competition

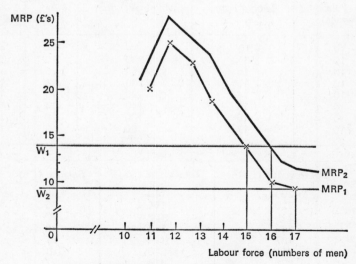

At W_1 with MRP_1 15 men are employed
At W_2 with MRP_1 17 men are employed
With MRP_2 and wage W_1 16 men are employed

Fig 3.4 Changes in wages and marginal productivity

The employment of 15 workers gives the most profitable output, that is, the greatest excess of revenue over costs. This is also the point at which marginal revenue productivity is equal to wage.

It can be shown, by referring to Figure 3.3, or by further calculation, that at a wage of £19, 14 men will be employed. At a wage of £10, 16 men will be employed, and so on. In fact, the downward sloping part of the MRP curve is the individual's firm demand curve for labour. It shows how much labour would be employed at particular rates of pay. If the market wage fell to £9, 2 more men would be employed. If the MRP rose, either through a rise in physical output (productivity) or through higher product prices, more men would be employed provided the market wage remained unaltered. (Fig 3.4). The industry's

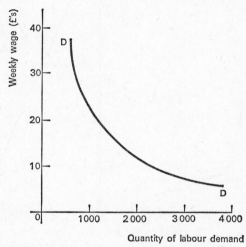

Fig 3.5 Industry's demand for labour

demand curve for labour can be derived from that of individual firms, by adding together the individual demands at particular wage rates and allowing for a fall in product price if the whole industry expands its output. Since it has been argued that wage is equal to, or is proportional to, marginal revenue productivity, it is sometimes suggested that MRP determines wages. From this it is a short step to assert that trade unions are unable to affect wages. An employer will only pay a worker the value of his MRP. If the unions endeavour to raise wages above this level, it will no longer pay an employer to engage so many workers. Some workers will be dismissed, and this will cause MRP to rise until it once again becomes equal to the wage level, i.e. all that unions do, by attempting to affect wage levels, is to cause unemployment.

But the marginal productivity theory is not really a theory of wages at all;

B

it is a theory of derived demand. It indicates what number of workers would be employed at a given level of wages. If the wage level rises, fewer will be employed. If it falls, more will be employed. (Figs 3.6 and 3.7).

To determine prices, however, the two forces of supply and demand are equally needed. The marginal revenue productivity theory is concerned only with the derived demand for labour. It argues that a firm will only pay a man what he is worth to it. It suggests that, if productivity rises, a firm is prepared to raise wages. It implies that trade unions cannot affect

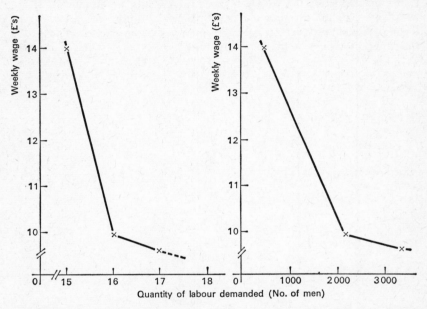

Fig 3.6 Demand for labour (One firm)   **Fig 3.7** Demand for labour (Industry)

the demand for labour. All these are reasonable propositions. But the marginal revenue productivity theory says nothing as to how the market wage is determined in the first place. It does not deal with supply. It is therefore quite possible that unions can influence wages by affecting the supply of labour. Before considering this proposition, however, we must examine some further criticisms of the marginal productivity approach. Here we shall concentrate on those points directly relevant to the argument so far.

Limitations to the application of MRP theory

1   Marginal revenue productivity theory assumes perfect competition. This means that there is one market wage for one kind of labour, and that, through perfect knowledge and perfect mobility, workers are fully aware

of it and able to prevent any deviations from it. The labour market, however, is imperfect in many ways. Perfect knowledge certainly does not exist. Individual workers know very little about the earnings of other workers, even in their own factory, and certainly not in other factories or other industries. Trade unions can help to redress the balance by acting for individual workers in an effort to standardise wage rates throughout an industry. Agreements are often negotiated at national level, so that a basic wage for the whole industry is fixed and publicised. Where differences exist, as in different assembly plants in the car industry, for example, unions can pinpoint such differences and fight to remove them.

But even the unions can lack fundamental knowledge in wage negotiations. Unless the trade unions are aware of a company's financial position, its profit and loss situation, its order book and its reserves, negotiations must take place without proper knowledge. One of the objectives of industrial relations reform, from Barbara Castle's "In Place of Strife" onwards, has been to give union officials more information of this kind for use in wage negotiations.

2   Another premise of perfect competition is that of perfect mobility. In the labour market this certainly does not apply. Even if we accept that there are many homogeneous groups of labour, operating in separate labour markets, mobility within these markets is still far from perfect. Between the groups there are natural barriers—barriers, for example, of talent. A job requiring a high level of intelligence or a great store of learning is not open to workers of low intelligence or with inadequate knowledge. Employment which depends upon certain physical properties —looks in the case of models, height in the case of policemen, strength in the case of many manual workers—is not open to workers who lack these qualities. An occupation which demands the ability to get on with people, or to handle children well, or to speak pleasantly, is unlikely to be open to those workers who can do none of these things. It is true that training, or determined effort, may help some workers to surmount the barriers; but training facilities may be inadequate or too expensive.

There are other hindrances to labour mobility. The factor of ignorance is important. Many workers do not move to better opportunities because they are unaware of their existence. The unions often restrict mobility, by setting up barriers to entry, such as demarcation lines drawn between one task and another, by regulations on dilution, and by stringent entry qualifications. Housing problems restrict mobility—the lack of suitable housing, or the expense and inconvenience of moving even when housing is available. Social factors are important—unwillingness to leave established friends and to give up the membership of groups, combined with the difficulties of establishing one's self socially in another area. Educational difficulties include the reluctance to move children who are half way through their schooling. Other factors which narrow the scope for occupational mobility are occupational pension schemes, which penalise the man moving from a pensionable post to a non-pensionable one, or to a pensionable post in another industry with no transfer of pension rights; and the unwillingness of management to take on older workers who are seeking fresh employment.

It is a moot point whether trade unions make the labour market more or less competitive. They certainly equalise the relationship between powerful, knowledgeable employers and individual, less knowledgeable employees. They can force the market wage closer to that justified on the grounds of marginal productivity. They help to establish a national rate for the same work throughout an industry. But unionism tends to divide the labour market into compartments. Rules applied by the unions to apprenticeships, or by professional bodies to membership; customary differences between skilled and semi-skilled or unskilled workers; the regulations which govern the allocation of work between different grades; all limit the ease of transfer. So does industrial action designed to keep workers indefinitely in their existing jobs when redundancy threatens. Furthermore, the trade unions tend to impose a regular pattern on any movement between occupations that does occur.

3 A further consequence of the assumption of perfect competition is that all firms are assumed to be earning only normal profits. If a union attempted to raise wages by reducing profit margins, profits would fall to a sub-normal level and firms would leave the industry. The reduction in employment would restore the equality of MRP and wages, as we have already agreed.

In reality many firms have a monopolistic or semi-monopolistic position. They earn profits well above the "normal", that is that level of profit necessary to keep a firm in the industry in preference to transferring elsewhere. Such firms could be "squeezed", their profit margins could be reduced, without affecting employment. Unions could play a part here. They could extract higher than equilibrium wages from monopolistic employers. The strength of the union would tend to affect wage levels. With a strong union and a firm earning super-normal profits, wages might be raised considerably. But where a firm is earning normal profits or below, a union, however powerful, cannot force wages much above the competitive level—except in the inflationary circumstances described below. And where a union was weak, a firm could continue to enjoy supra-normal profits although wages were below the competitive level.

4 Perfect competition, on which the theory of marginal productivity is based, assumes *ceteris paribus*,—other things remaining equal. In particular, if prices for a product rise, then demand will fall. If it is possible for the firm to pass on higher wage costs in the form of higher prices without affecting demand, then there is no reason why the demand for labour

should fall. In an inflationary situation, incomes rise as prices rise, demand remains buoyant; other things do *not* remain the same. The net result is that demand remains the same although prices have risen. In such a situation, unions can force up wages without facing an inevitable fall in demand for labour. They can regard the demand curve for labour as inelastic, and therefore can virtually ignore the effects of rising wage levels on the employment of their members.

The supply of labour

The supply of labour is a direct function of the size and age distribution of the population. The larger the total population, the greater the potential working force. The bigger the proportion of the population in the "working-age" group, say between 16 and 65, the larger the potential supply of labour. But the actual supply depends, of course, on participation rates—to what extent the possible working force is actually employed. Among the factors affecting this rate of participation will be the proportion of young people continuing their further education beyond the minimum school leaving age; the number of older workers retiring early, or postponing their retirement beyond the usual age; the number of women at work; and the extent to which the labour force can be swollen temporarily by students on holiday, pensioners returning to work for a season or housewives in temporary employment. Net migration will also play an important part, particularly in developing countries such as the United States of America in the nineteenth century or Australia at the present time.

Much more important to the present argument is the supply of labour in a particular occupation. We have already examined[1] the hindrances to mobility, both between occupations and within a particular occupation. Supply to one specific job is initially limited by intelligence, skill, length of training and entry requirements. Transfer between jobs is hindered by these and other factors such as demarcation rules, objections to dilution, and geographical factors.

Trade unions can thus affect the supply of labour in a number of ways. In so far as they succeed in restricting the supply in particular cases, they are able to push wages above the level they would otherwise reach. The extreme example of a strike shows the unions withdrawing the supply of labour completely in an attempt to force wages to a higher level. By showing the importance of labour to a firm or an industry, the unions hope to compel employers to raise wages above their previous level.

Wage differentials

Under a system of perfect competition, the forces of supply and demand would ensure that, for a homogeneous labour supply, wages would be the

[1] Page 29

same throughout the market. For, if certain groups of workers earned more than the market rate, they would be joined by others seeking to benefit from the higher wage, and this increased labour force would cause the marginal revenue productivity to fall, and with it, the wage. In the case of a group earning less than the market rate, workers would leave in search of higher wages elsewhere. This contraction of the labour force would cause the marginal revenue productivity to rise, and with it, the wage. In both cases the forces of supply and demand would tend to restore the market rate throughout the labour force but this process would be hindered, of course, by the imperfections in the labour market.

The lesson to be learned is that high wages in a particular job will not automatically cause a movement of labour into that job to depress those wages. The supply may be limited by one of the barriers to mobility—natural or otherwise—so that an increased supply is unlikely.

The existence of wage differentials may be explained by the large number of separate labour markets which exist side by side, kept separate by natural and other barriers which prevent the free movement of labour between them.

Another reason for the persistence of wage differentials, even where mobility is less restricted than we have supposed, is the presence of non-wage factors which either increase the net advantages of a job (and thus enable a lower wage to be paid) or decrease the net advantages (and thus force the payment of a higher wage). Such non-monetary factors include the status of a job (a barrister may accept a drop in money salary to become a judge); the conditions of work (sugar-cane workers in Queensland need very high wages to compensate for the unpleasant conditions); promotion possibilities (a dead-end job may well offer more money than one in which the career structure is clearly defined); fringe benefits (such as pension rights and holiday provision).

In theory, in perfect competition, the forces of supply and demand would cause net advantages to become equal within the same market. In practice, the imperfections in the market, and in particular the lack of mobility of labour, ensure that differentials are preserved even within one market.

Equal pay for women

A special case of wage differentials arises where men and women are paid different rates for the same job. Until the First World War women were paid much less than men in similar occupations. But in medicine, in the Civil Service and in teaching, equal pay has already been established, and the general application of the principle of equal pay is now scheduled, by legislation, for 1975.

The short term effects of equal pay are likely to be:

1   A higher wage bill, particularly in women-intensive industries such as clothing and retailing.

2 In consequence, the substitution of capital for labour wherever possible. This movement has already progressed rapidly in, for example, office work.

3 The substitution of men for women if employers are persuaded that men will do the job more effectively.

In the longer term, one would expect to see:

4 A reorganisation of the use of casual, part-time, or young workers to compensate for the higher cost of female labour.

5 An attempt to produce better-trained, more highly motivated female workers able and willing to contribute significantly to the development of a business.

6 A growth in female unionism.

There will also be profound social changes, particularly in families where the woman becomes, as a result of equal pay, the chief "breadwinner". In short, although it is hoped that the introduction of equal pay will remedy a social injustice and enhance the status of women, it is by no means certain that all the changes will be to their benefit.

Local differences in wage levels

Occasionally we find that individuals who appear to be doing the same work are paid at different rates. The reason for this is either that, as individuals, they are carrying out highly specialised tasks which need individual consideration—many highly paid executives or consultants would fall into this category; or that a very small work force or lack of union organisation means that cases are considered individually, for example office staff in a small business or assistants in a small shop. In the latter cases, lack of knowledge of differences prevents unrest, and the lack of a union means that there is no concerted pressure for uniformity in wages.

Of much greater importance, however, is the existence of local variations in wage levels. Such variations may be between one district and another or between one firm and another. The district variations may arise because of different market conditions and persist because of the immobility of labour. In the South-West, for example, demand for labour is not high, as there is little industrial competition for workers. The supply, however, is relatively large, so that wage levels tend to be low. The ultimate answer would be for labour to move from the South-West to high wage areas in order to redress the balance. But this movement is hampered by the geographical immobility of labour, explained by the attractions of the South-West, housing difficulties, and sheer inertia. Similarly, between town and country, or between a city centre and peripheral areas, the difference in wage can often be explained in terms of the cost of transport, the higher cost of housing in the city centre, and the non-monetary disadvantages, in terms of time, fatigue, and so on, incurred if one lives in the country and travels to the town each day.

Local differences arising between firms employing the same types of labour may be the result of special bonus schemes or overtime arrangements within a firm. Higher rates may be offered specifically to attract labour from rival firms. And union organisation within one firm may be traditionally stronger than in another. Free transfer between firms exhibiting such differences may not be possible because of geographical differences, or because training may present problems, or because of other obstacles to transfer.

The application of supply and demand to specific cases

We have seen how the basic marginal productivity theory of wages is subject to all kinds of modifications and conditions to allow for imperfections in the market and the particular conditions in special cases. The procedure can best be illustrated by taking some specific cases and applying supply and demand arguments to them.

1 Teaching

The simple argument would run that there is a great demand for education; that the supply of possible teachers is limited; therefore teachers' salaries should be high. In fact, it is common knowledge that they lag behind comparable salaries in other occupations.

One possible explanation is that there are a number of non-monetary advantages in teaching which compensate for lower salaries. Among the most commonly mentioned are long holidays, short hours, and pleasant working conditions. Of these we can dismiss short hours, since extra-curricular working is very common, and shorter hours in other occupations are becoming the rule rather than the exception. Pleasant working conditions exist in a number of schools, but the average teacher works in conditions inferior to those of his counterpart in business. We are left with long holidays, undoubtedly a non-monetary advantage which many teachers value.

It could then be argued that, when non-monetary advantages are included, the remuneration of teachers is roughly in line with that expected from the supply and demand analysis. However, the whole supply/demand structure can be questioned here. The supply of teachers is manipulated by accepting a low entrance qualification (many Colleges of Education accept candidates with 5 "O" Levels only). And although the three year training period is a deterrent to many, the supply can still be manipulated by employing part-time staff and by increasing the size of classes. The shortage of teachers, in other words, is not reflected in a higher salary. On the demand side the vague "demand for education" needs a close examination in the light of hard fact. Members of the public do not demand education in the economic sense. With few exceptions, they are not prepared to pay for it. The demand then becomes a transferred demand—the demand of local authorities in their efforts to meet public wishes and government policy. The salary becomes an administered wage reflecting, not demand conditions in a free market, but local authority and government policy, economic necessity, and a variety of other factors. We can conclude that the forces of supply and demand have little to do with the salaries paid to teachers.

2 Acting in repertory companies

At first glance, it would appear that the supply of dramatic talent would be severely limited by the paucity of natural ability to act; by the rigours of training, which takes a number of years; and by the hard work involved in constant movement around the country, the learning of new plays at the rate of at least one a week, and the hours of work. By application of even a moderate demand to this restricted supply, remuneration should be high. In practice, wages are low; in some cases, very low. The answer lies in further analysis. Despite the difficulties outlined above, a plentiful supply of labour is always forthcoming. The glamour of the profession and inherent faith in one's own ability spurs on a large number of young hopefuls. Turning to the demand side we must admit that the assumption of "even a moderate" demand is too optimistic. Demand for repertory is low, in the sense that few people are prepared to pay to go to see a play. It is often artificially boosted by aid from local councils or from national bodies, but even so it remains low and may even be declining. The combination of an abundant supply and a limited demand helps to explain the low wages earned by actors in repertory. The existence of substantial unemployment confirms the analysis.

Wage determination in practice

One of the major criticisms of the supply/demand hypothesis outlined above is that wages are determined purely by institutional forces. As developed by some writers, e.g. Barbara Wootton in *Social Foundations of Wage Policy*, this is known as the "socio-institutional hypothesis". Even if this hypothesis were completely true, economic theory would have something to say about the consequences of wage levels set through collective bargaining. We now examine briefly the institutional arrangements in the U.K. for wage determination.

Such arrangements come under the general head of Collective Bargaining, which includes Negotiation, Conciliation and Arbitration. Before collective bargaining can take place, each side must recognise the other for negotiating purposes. From the viewpoint, therefore, of the trade unions, recognition is fundamental for their purposes.

Most negotiating machinery is at present[1] voluntary rather than statutory. It can be ad hoc or permanent in nature. A rough division of employees into various categories of negotiating machinery would leave about 5 millions uncovered by any machinery and would divide up the rest as follows:

a)   7 million employees covered by national machinery which makes the main agreement on an industry basis. The national agreement is then closely followed at company or local level. Examples are the whole of the public sector, the retail co-operative societies, and shipping.
b)   6 million employees covered by national machinery which makes a main agreement, which however, is supplemented by company bargaining. Almost half of these workers are in payment-by-results schemes. Examples are found in engineering, shipbuilding, and the steel industry.
c) 4 million employees covered by Wages Councils.
d) 1 million employees in companies where the main agreement is made at company level. This is the practice in a number of large companies such as Ford, Vauxhall and I.C.I.

In many industries voluntary collective bargaining developed with very little help or encouragement from the Government. In others, Whitley Councils, or Joint Industrial Councils, were set up as a result of reports during the First World War. There are approximately 200 such Councils now in existence, varying in size from 12 to 100 members. They are strong in local government and in central government departments. They vary considerably in powers and activities, but most play an important part in the settlement of disputes.

Wages councils had their origins in the Trade Board Act of 1909, which fixed minimum wages and set up a wages inspectorate for a number of "sweated trades" such as tailoring and chain making. The Wages Councils Act of 1945 was amended in 1948 and further consolidated in 1959. The objective was to establish and encourage collective bargaining in industries where conditions are bad and the level of organisation is low. The Councils fix minimum rates and conditions of work and their proposals, once approved by the appropriate Minister, are legally enforceable, with an inspectorate to aid enforcement. There are now over 50 Wages Councils operating in such areas as retail distribution, catering and clothing manufacture.

Conciliation and arbitration are for use only when the two sides have been unable to reach a settlement. The overwhelming majority of difficulties are settled by negotiations which lead to agreement between the two sides. The important Acts in this field are the Conciliation Act of 1896 and the Industrial Courts Act of 1919.

The Conciliation Service exists to explore the attitude of the two sides and to find whether there is an acceptable basis for settlement. The service

[1] 1972.

is staffed by permanent officials of the Department of Employment. Separate talks are held with each side, and then, if appropriate, a joint meeting is held under the chairmanship of the official. There is no legal compulsion, either to go to conciliation or to accept the results on either employers or workers. Nevertheless, over 400 disputes every year use the conciliation service.

A dispute may be referred to arbitration by the Minister, providing both parties agree. Among the possibilities are:

a) The Industrial Court

This was set up in 1919 as a permanent arbitration tribunal. It comprises representatives of employers and workers, and independent members. It is not a court of law, and its decisions are not legally binding. But they are almost invariably accepted by both sides. The Terms of Conditions of Employment Act, 1959, gives organisations of workers and employers the right to invoke, through the Minister, the adjudication of the Industrial Court on claims for the observance of recognised terms and conditions.

b) Individual arbitration

A representative chosen by the Department of Employment will act as arbitrator between the two sides.

c) A Board of Arbitration may be set up with one or more representatives of the employers, the same number for the workers' side, and an independent chairman nominated by the Minister.

d) A Court of Inquiry

For major disputes, the Minister may set up a court of inquiry, comprising an independent chairman and equal numbers of representatives of employers and unions. The court will ascertain the facts and the underlying causes of dispute. It will report to the Minister and its recommendations usually form a basis for a settlement.

In addition, there exists machinery for voluntary arbitration in a considerable number of industries, e.g. the nationalised industries.

Workplace bargaining

One interesting feature of collective bargaining in recent years has been the increasing importance of workplace bargaining—negotiations at local, rather than national, level. Industry-wide agreements on minimum wages and conditions are supplemented by factory agreements which may have a considerable influence on actual earnings. During conditions of full employment, a high demand for labour results in the offer of local differentials which seek to attract more labour. The system is strongly developed in engineering. The Engineering Employers' Federation pointed out, in their evidence to the Royal Commission on Trade Unions, that national negotiations are concerned with national minimum rates, length of the working week, holidays and similar basic conditions of employment. Workplace negotiations determine piecework rates, merit payments, and detailed hours of work. Actual wage earnings at local level may be 50 per cent or more above the national minimum level.

Productivity bargaining

The purpose of productivity bargaining is to relate increases in pay to specific changes in the method of work. The more efficient use of resources will afford opportunities for wage increases and productivity bargaining (usually associated with negotiations at factory level) settles the share of the workers concerned. Productivity agreements are still the exception rather than the rule in British industry. However, at the factory level they suggest a link between the marginal revenue productivity of a worker and his wages; at the national level they offer one method of reducing inflationary wage settlements by linking wage increases with increases in productivity from which they can be met.

QUESTIONS

Are there any sound economic arguments for government regulation of wages?

Can you suggest the possible outlines of a state wages policy?

To what extent should men and women be paid equally for equal work?

"Full employment and free wage bargaining are incompatible." Comment.

Why are some dirty, unpleasant jobs paid less than some comfortable ones?

What factors determine average earnings in any given occupation?

Does the inequality of wages serve any economic purpose?

Discuss the relative merits of national and local wage bargaining.

To what extent can trade unions determine wage levels?

Can marginal productivity theory make a useful contribution to the study of wages?

"Wage determination is so complex in practice that any attempt to bring order into the present chaos is bound to fail." Discuss this argument.

REFERENCES AND FURTHER READING

A. Flanders: *Trade Unions* (Hutchinson, 1968)
M. Dobb: *Wages* (Nisbet and Cambridge, 1956)
B. J. McCormick: *Wages* (Penguin, 1969)
J. M. Jackson: *Wages & Labour Economics* (McGraw Hill, 1970)
J. R. Hicks: *The Theory of Wages* (Macmillan, 1963)
E. H. Phelps Brown: *Economics of Labour* (Yale U.P., 1962

4 Trade union organisation and reform

In 1970 there were in the United Kingdom about 10 million members of trade unions—less than half the total number of employees. Organisation is much stronger among male workers (55 to 60 per cent are union members) than among female workers (25 per cent). Young workers under 21 are less organised than older workers.

The number of unions has shown a fairly sharp decline over the years, but there are still 500 separate unions. The individual unions vary enormously in size. The three largest—the Transport and General Workers Union, (T.G.W.U.), the Amalgamated Union of Engineering and Foundry Workers, (A.U.E.F.W.) and the National Union of General and Municipal Workers (N.U.G.M.W.)—contain between them one-third of all union members, the Transport and General Workers Union alone having a membership of almost $1\frac{1}{2}$ millions. The eight largest unions—the three mentioned above together with the National Union of Mineworkers, the Union of Shop, Distributive and Allied Workers, the Electrical Trades Union, the National Union of Teachers, and the National Union of Public Employees, organise more than a half of all union members, and the 35 largest unions contain over 80 per cent of all unionists. On the other hand, more than a half of all unions have less than 1000 members. Trade Union conferences have many times urged a reduction in the number of unions. The 1924 Trade Union Congress at Hull resolved that the number of unions should be reduced to a minimum. In the following year Walter Citrine, in a memorandum to the Scarborough Congress, referred to the undignified competition among unions for members. Many mergers in recent years have been the result of Congress influence. The whole question is considered in more detail in the section on Trade Union reform.[1]

The extent to which workers are organised in unions varies considerably from one industry to another. In coal-mining, shipbuilding and the ports, practically every manual worker is a trade union member. Non-manual workers in coal-mining and shipbuilding are also well organised. Industries with a high degree of membership include iron and steel, cotton and the railways. On the other hand, only a small proportion of workers are organised in agriculture, distribution and the food and drink industry. Between these extremes lie engineering, building and construction, and the

[1] Page 43 and ff.

Table 1   The Largest Unions in U.K. (1969)[1]

Transport and General Workers' Union	1 476 000
Amalgamated Union of Engineering & Foundry Workers	1 072 000
National Union of General and Municipal Workers	798 000
National Association of Local Government Officers	373 046
Electrical, Electronic & Telecommunications Union	364 000
National Union of Mineworkers	344 000
National Union of Teachers	318 000
Union of Shop, Distributive and Allied Workers	311 000
National Union of Railwaymen	254 687

[1] Source: D.E.P.

public utilities, gas, water and electricity, with a moderate level of organisation.

With the changing pattern of industry in Britain, the distribution of trade union membership has altered considerably since 1945. Coal-mining, the railways, and cotton textiles have declined. Engineering, transport other than rail and the public services have expanded. Two results have been the growth of the Transport and General Workers Union, organising members in a wide variety of industries and occupations; and expansion among white collar workers.

In 1851, less than 1 per cent of industrial employees were clerical workers. At present about one-quarter of all industrial employees are white collar workers in administrative, technical and clerical occupations, and this proportion is growing. The expansion of national and local government services, the banks, insurance and similar services have given an additional stimulus to this movement.

Types of union

It is usual to divide unions up into three or four types and examine each separately. Any such division, however, applied to British unions can only be approximate. There is a tremendous variety of forms of organisation in this country, and any analysis should be read with this important fact in mind.

The craft union

Craft unions consist of skilled workers following the same trade. Historically, they were among the first trade unions to be formed in Britain. Current example of craft unions are the Associated Society of Locomotive Engineers and Firemen, organising engine drivers and firemen on the railway; the Sheet Metal Workers' Society and the Operative Spinners. The

A.U.E.F.W.[1] has been formed by successive amalgamations of a number of craft unions.

The craft unions have contributed much to the development of the trade union movement, particularly the traditions of industrial peace and solidarity. But they have certain weaknesses. As industry changes, old crafts decline and new ones develop. The distinction between craftsmen and unskilled labourers becomes blurred. The divisions which gave rise to craft unions disappear, and although new crafts develop to take the place of the old, the traditional basis of many craft unions is undermined. This form of organisation is too inflexible.

Another weakness is the concentration on skilled workers to the exclusion of unskilled. However strong a union is, it must eventually have regard for other workers in its industry. Their conditions and their welfare will ultimately affect the members of the union. In fact, the craft unions themselves have been modified considerably in the light of modern development. Amalgamations with unions catering for related trades have led to such unions as the Amalgamated Union of Building Trade Workers. The admission of less skilled workers in the same industry is exemplified by the A.U.E.F.W. Nevertheless, craft unionism has not in recent times proved a satisfactory form of organisation for the majority of unionists in this country.

The industrial union

An industrial union aims to organise all the workers within a given industry. This is the type of pattern which German trade unionism has generally followed. In Britain, however, there are no unions which can be described as pure industrial unions. But among those whose main strength lies in one industry are the National Union of Mineworkers (N.U.M.) and the National Union of Railwaymen (N.U.R.).

The great advantage of industrial unionism is that all employees within an industry are represented by a single union. This aids collective bargaining procedures, reduces the likelihood of demarcation disputes, and stresses the common interest of all workers within an industry.

Unfortunately it is impossible to define exactly where one industry ends and another begins. For example are engineers employed in railway workshops in the railway industry or in the engineering industry? The borderline between industries affords plenty of scope for disputes. Nevertheless, the idea of representing the collective interests of all workers in the same industry is sound—there are a large number of firms which can be grouped together and whose workers share a common interest.

One other problem of industrial unionism is that it may not adequately represent the interests of particular groups; clerical workers, for example, in the railway industry or technicians in any manufacturing industry.

[1] See page 39.

Table 2

The Number of Trade Unions, U.K.[1]

	End Year										
	1959	1960	1961	1962	1963	1964	1965	1966	1967	1968	1969
Number of Unions:	668	664	646	626	607	598	583	574	555	533	508
Number of members											
under 100	134	130	120	121	116	110	113	111	111	99	94
100 " 500	171	176	170	154	148	145	136	134	122	123	119
500 " 1 000	59	56	58	60	60	58	57	60	61	56	59
1 000 " 2 500	110	107	104	103	98	99	90	85	81	80	67
2 500 " 5 000	68	67	66	58	58	61	63	62	60	58	54
5 000 " 10 000	34	35	32	31	31	29	30	28	29	29	29
10 000 " 15 000	18	18	20	23	21	22	19	20	20	17	11
15 000 " 25 000	26	26	22	22	22	20	18	18	17	18	23
25 000 " 50 000	12	11	16	18	18	19	18	19	18	15	14
50 000 " 100 000	19	21	21	18	17	17	19	19	17	19	16
100 000 +	17	17	17	18	18	18	18	18	19	19	22

[1] Source: Department of Employment.

Table 3

Membership of Trade Unions, U.K.

	Year End (Thousands)										
	1959	1960	1961	1962	1963	1964	1965	1966	1967	1968	1969
TOTAL	9 623	9 835	9 897	9 887	9 943	10 079	10 181	10 111	10 033	10 034	10 304
MALES	7 756	7 884	7 905	7 860	7 859	7 936	7 973	7 890	7 785	7 713	7 843
FEMALES	1 868	1 951	1 992	2 027	2 075	2 143	2 208	2 221	2 248	2 321	2 461

The N.U.M.[1] does not organise the clerical employees of the National Coal Board. Such specialists groups may well prefer to be organised in their own craft union.

The general union

General unions are very strong in British trade unionism. As the name implies, the general union seeks to organise workers in a wide variety of industries. The T.G.W.U.[2] is well organised in docks and in road transport but it also recruits from a wide variety of other occupations particularly where industries are small. The N.U.G.M.W.[3] is the third largest union in Britain and is based on the public utilities. The Union of Shop, Distributive and Allied Workers (U.S.D.A.W.) draws its basic strength from the Co-operative movement. It is the sixth largest union in Britain.

General unions have enabled organisation to extend into industries which would otherwise have remained essentially non-union. The N.U.G.M.W. pointed out, in its evidence to the Royal Commission on Trade Unions and Employers' Associations, that horizontal organisation (across many industries) suits the structure of British industry, and in particular the growth of large multi-industry firms. The unions which have grown most rapidly in recent years have this general, rather than an industrial approach.

The problems associated with general unionism are the diverse interests represented, which may lead to internal conflict, and the overlapping of membership which occurs in particular industries.

Trade union federations

One answer to the problem of different unions within an industry lies in the formation of federations. These federations exist to serve the common interests of all the unions within one industry. Examples are the Confederation of Shipbuilding and Engineering Unions, covering 40 unions in this field; the Printing and Kindred Trades' Federation covering unions in printing and publishing; and the National Federation of Building Trades' Operatives. The authority of the federation varies considerably from one industry to the next. And even where there are no formal federations, unions usually co-operate for the purposes of collective bargaining, holding regular informal meetings for joint negotiations.

The Trades Union Congress

The Trades Union Congress is the national body representing the British trade union movement. Ninety per cent of all trade union members belong to organisations affiliated to the T.U.C. Affiliation is voluntary, but the number of union members affiliated has grown steadily while the number

[1] See above   [2] Page 39   [3] See page 39.

of unions affiliated has dropped. In 1927, for example, 205 affiliated unions had a membership of 4 164 000. In 1957, 185 unions represented 8 305 000 members. In 1962 the T.U.C. had 182 affiliated unions. By 1966 the number of unions, through mergers and amalgamations, had dropped to 170, but membership was up to 8 707 000, of whom over 7 millions were men.

The T.U.C. depends for its authority on the support of affiliated unions. Its power cannot be clearly defined, but its main duties may be described as representing the collective views of the trade union movement to the Government, to other organisations and in legislative matters; to aid member unions in the settlement of disputes, should a breakdown be threatened on such a scale that large numbers of unionists may become involved; to promote the settlement of disputes between affiliated unions, and to rule on a dispute where a union has referred the matter to the T.U.C.; to represent the British trade union movement in international matters. The so-called Bridlington rules laid down a standard procedure to prevent the "poaching" of members of one union by another.

The Trades Union Congress meets annually, each affiliated union sending delegates roughly in proportion to its membership. At each congress, a General Council of 39 members is elected. This General Council used to be broadly representative of the various trade interests in the unions, but it does not represent current union importance, being based on nineteenth century union strength. For example, the "mining and quarrying group", with 370 000 members, stills holds 3 seats, while "transport (other than railways)" representing 1 600 000 unionists, only has 4 seats. "Public employees" (860 000 members) have only 3 seats, while "Civil Servants" (634 000) have 2 and "Printing and Paper" (384 000) has only 1 seat.

The General Council of the T.U.C. carries on the affairs of the T.U.C. from one annual congress to the next. It meets once a month and conducts most of its normal work through committees such as those for economic affairs and organisation. The Council presents an annual report to the Congress.

Shop stewards

The shop steward is essentially a trade union organiser at the shop floor level. The growth of the shop steward's influence and importance has been rapid in recent years, despite the fact that the union rule book often places severe restrictions on his power. The union branch often meets in the evenings away from the place of work; the shop steward is at the centre of things. He will therefore collect union subscriptions—his major official role. He will also represent the union at the shop floor level. He may well play a leading part in factory level negotiations. There may be a committee of shop stewards from the main unions represented in the factory, and such a committee will help to overcome inter-union disputes. Shop stewards often play a major part in unofficial strikes, those, that is, which are not officially called by the union or unions concerned. The Donovan Commission in 1968 pointed out that full employment, multi-unionism and the actions of management have all helped to increase the power of shop stewards.

The reform of trade unionism

One major problem of British trade unionism is the multiplicity of unions. This "multi-unionism" has to some extent been modified by important mergers in recent years under the stimulus of the inquiry inaugurated by the T.U.C. in 1962. Examples can be found in printing and in engineering. The Trade Union (Amalgamations) Act of 1964 facilitated progress, and 24 Conferences between related unions were held between 1964 and 1966. The Donovan Commission pointed out that there was scope for many more mergers between unions and suggested, for example, one union for the printing industry and one or two unions for craftsmen in the engineering and construction industries. Another possibility explored by the Royal Commission was that where unions were in competition for members they should conclude agreements on the rights of representation in negotiations.

The solution of industrial unions[1] was suggested by a T.U.C. resolution of 1924, which set up an enquiry into the establishment of comprehensive industrial unions. In 1927 the General Council reported that their task was impossible. Any attempt to compel unions to conform to the principle of industrial unionism would destroy all hope of co-operation among the unions. The inquiry which started in 1962 reached a similar conclusion. After considering the arguments for and against industrial unionism the General Council reported that it would be undesirable to attempt, even over a period of years, to reform the movement along the lines of one union for each industry.

The Donovan Commission reported that while industrial unionism would have a number of advantages, there were theoretical difficulties and decisive practical objections, such as drastic upheavals in the structure of almost every major union in the country and a reversal of the natural pattern of growth in recent years.

Other major problems will now be studied in the light of four different documents published in recent years.

The Donovan Commission

Among the major recommendations of the Royal Commission reporting in 1968 was the suggestion that an Industrial Relations Act should be

[1] See page 41.

passed. Companies above a certain minimum size should be compelled to register collective agreements with the Department of Employment and Productivity. An Industrial Relations Commission should be set up with powers to investigate, upon reference from the D.E.P., cases and problems arising from the registration of agreements. The I.R.C. should also deal with problems of trade union recognition.

An employee should have the right to belong to a trade union, and any stipulation in a contract of employment that an employee is not to belong to a trade union should be void in law.

On restrictive practices, the Commission argued that their removal was but one element in the major problem of securing the efficient use of resources. Its proposals for the reform of the collective bargaining system would help considerably.

The present system of craft unions was held to be most prejudicial to efficiency.

Although the Commission recognised the problem of unofficial strikes and the damaging effect they can have, it rejected the idea of compulsory strike ballots, which, it argued, would have to be confined to major official strikes. There is little evidence, it stated, to show that workers are less likely to vote for strike action than their leaders; and American and Canadian experience shows that strike ballots usually go in favour of strike action.[1] It proposed a greater number of enquiries, particularly into unofficial and unconstitutional stoppages, and suggested that remedying specific grievances, for example over recognition and dismissals, would help considerably.

The Royal Commission came out against the legal enforcement of collective agreements, although the I.R.C. could keep this matter under review. The existing industrial tribunals should be renamed "labour tribunals" and have their jurisdiction extended to cover disputes over contracts of employment. Such labour tribunals would have a primary duty to promote the amicable settlement of disputes by means of conciliation.

The possibility of prohibiting the closed shop was rejected. Under proper safeguards a closed shop can serve a useful purpose, and the disadvantages can be overcome with suitable arrangements. It is unlikely, the report went on, that abuse of power by unions in relation to individuals is wide-spread; but it does happen, and a member unjustly expelled, or an applicant for membership who is unsuccessful should be able to appeal against the union decision. The rules of trade unions should be revised to ensure better safeguards for individual members. An independent review body should be set up, attached to the office of the Registrar of Trade Unions.

Other points recommended by the Donovan Commission included the provision of constitutionally recognised committees to carry out work now performed unofficially by shop stewards' committees; the basing of union

[1] Cf. rail strike in Britain, 1972.

branches on the place of work; the appointment of more full-time union officials; and no change in the law relating to contracting out.

In Place of Strife, January 1969

This white paper recommended the setting up of a Commission on Industrial Relations, first as a Royal Commission, and finally on a statutory basis. The Commission was in fact established soon afterwards, thus following the Donovan Commission's Report. The C.I.R. was not to have legal powers, but it was to be regarded as a "disseminator of good practice and a focus for reform by example".

A further suggestion was that the Secretary of State would have discretionary powers to require a 28 day "conciliation pause" in unconstitutional strikes and those where adequate joint discussions had not taken place. The Secretary of State would have further discretionary powers to require a union to hold a strike ballot among its members when a major official strike was threatened. This second proposal had been specifically rejected by the Donovan Commission.

A new Industrial Board would be set up with power to impose financial penalties on an employer, union, or individual striker. No such proposal was made in the Royal Commission report.

Other particular recommendations of the white paper were:

1   that in the case of restrictive practices, which "restrict the effective use of resources", penal powers would be of no value. Existing instruments would be the best way of tackling this problem.
2   the Industrial Relations Bill suggested by the white paper would lay down the principle that no employer has the right to prevent an employee from belonging to a trade union. The employer could also be required to recognise and negotiate with a union.
3   the T.U.C. should take positive initiatives to deal with inter-union disputes. The proposed C.I.R. could also play a useful role.
4   Trade Unions need to be reformed and extended, with fewer areas of overlap, more amalgamations, additional officials, more adequate contributions and funds. Grants and loans should be made available for modernising the trade union movement.
5   the Industrial Tribunals should be widened to enable them to deal with complaints of unfair dismissals, and legal disputes.
6   a Registry of Trade Unions and Employers' Associations would be set up. Trade Unions would be required to register and draw up rules dealing with prescribed subjects.

Industrial Relations Bill: the Labour version

This was the Labour Government's sequel to "In Place of Strife". It is of academic interest only, but it does show many changes from the original

White Paper. Largely as a result of T.U.C. opposition, the conciliation pause in unconstitutional strikes and the strike ballot for major official strikes were dropped. The Commission for Industrial Relations was to be converted into a statutory body, with £5 millions to spend on a development scheme for trade unions. The C.I.R. would also research into the improvement of collective bargaining and deal with problems of unfair dismissal and non-recognition of trade unions.

Industrial Relations Bill: the Conservative version

The Conservatives, returned to office in June, 1970, had advanced plans ready for a new Industrial Relations Bill. A Consultative Document was published in October setting out the principles and main proposals which were incorporated in the 1971 Act. The principles included the right of every individual to join or not to join a trade union, as he wishes; the right to negotiate collectively; and the right to strike. A code of Industrial Relations Practice was to be and has been drawn up, to encourage the development of collective bargaining, to promote the freedom and security of individual workers, and to develop trade unions and employers' associations as representative bodies.

A new National Industrial Relations Court (N.I.R.C.), equivalent in status to the High Court, was set up by the Act and Industrial Tribunals were given new functions and expanded. Legal cases about industrial relations, including such problems as breach of contract and unfair industrial actions are, in general, to be heard by these new bodies. Industrial tribunals were to deal with individual matters while the National Industrial Relations Court was designed to deal with collective issues and very complex or important cases. Both bodies are able to award compensation, to make orders, and have decisions enforced through the N.I.R.C.

The C.I.R. was put on a statutory basis and was to continue to be responsible for the reform of industrial relations. It was given additional responsibilities, such as the power to inquire into the establishment, abolition or modication of a wages council.[1]

A new office of Chief Registrar of Trade Unions and Employers' Associations was created, with the task of ensuring that trade union rules conform to standards laid down in the legislation, that unions observe their rules and are properly administered.

The Industrial Court was renamed the Industrial Arbitration Board, with functions substantially unchanged.

The Act gave statutory safeguards against unfair dismissal, with a right of appeal to an Industrial Tribunal. Longer periods of notice under the

[1] Between its establishment in January, 1969 and late November, 1970, 29 references had been made to the C.I.R. It had published, as well as its annual reports, 9 individual reports, 2 on the general state of industrial relations and 7 on trade union recognition.

Contracts of Employment Act, 1963, were established for long service employees.

Legal status as a trade union (or employers' association) is given to organisations which register under the Act, and registration gives substantial new rights to such bodies. Immunity from actions in tort in respect of actions arising from an industrial dispute remain. Members of a registered trade union are intended to enjoy equal rights to participate in the affairs of the organisation and to receive fair treatment in their relations with it. The rules of registered organisations must deal adequately with admission, discipline, disputes between unions and their members and the conduct of business. All but the smallest unions must appoint professional auditors.

Any written collective agreements made after the Act were intended to be legally enforceable unless there is an express written provision in the agreement itself. Actions about alleged breaches of a legally binding agreement would be heard by the N.I.R.C. or the Industrial Tribunals.

Claims for recognition by a union are entrusted to examination by the C.I.R. which must have regard to the extent of support for the union and its resources. Recommendations of the C.I.R. can be made enforceable by the N.I.R.C.

The Code of Industrial Relations Practice gives guidance on the disclosure of information by employers to the unions, where such information appears necessary for the conduct of negotiations.

The "pre-entry closed shop", which can exclude an individual from entering certain employments if he is not a trade union member, was abolished. The "agency shop agreement", in which a registered trade union represents all the employees in a particular establishment, was to be encouraged, subject to a ballot of employees if this is called for. An employee can be required after a time to join the appropriate union or pay a regular contribution in lieu of the union's membership subscription.

Where industrial action, actual or threatened, is likely to deprive the community of the essentials of life or seriously endanger the national health, security or economy, the Secretary of State can apply to the N.I.R.C. for a restraining order against a union or employer. The N.I.R.C. can then make an order, effective for a maximum of 60 days, restraining named organisations or persons from calling, inducing, or financing a strike.

Secret ballots can be ordered in special cases if the Secretary of State makes application to the N.I.R.C. in order to determine whether or not a majority of the workers concerned are in favour of industrial action.

An assessment

The existence of no fewer than four documents dealing with Industrial Relations illustrates its topical importance. Major areas of agreement which emerge concern the Commission for Industrial Relations, to be established as a statutory body dealing with the reform of industrial relations; greater emphasis on the rights of individual workers, for example to join a union, or in the case of unfair dismissal—although differences of opinion are found here; the registration of trade unions with stress laid on the adequacy of rules and their observance. The latest measures and trades union reactions to them reveal deep differences of opinion over the strike ballot, the "cooling off" period, and the closed shop. There is also strong disagreement about the renewed emphasis on the legally binding nature of collective agreements.

Problems which remain largely outside the scope of the latest proposals include restrictive practices and their effect on the economy; the adequacy of union finance; and the standard and number of union officials.

Another problem is that, since 1900, the trade union movement has been closely linked with the Labour Party. The unions provide much of the Party's finances, and the "block" union vote tends to dominate the Labour Party Conferences. In 1963, there was a total of 120 Union M.P.s. This close relationship can be regarded as a mixed blessing to both Labour Party and the Trade Unions.

QUESTIONS

"Trade unions are an anachronism in an advanced industrial society". Discuss.

Discuss the case for "one industry, one union" in Britain.

Why doesn't the T.U.C. exercise stricter control of the trade unions?

Discuss the recommendations of the Donovan Commission for the reform of industrial relations.

What changes were introduced by the 1971 Industrial Relations Act and why were they introduced?

Is there a valid economic case for making strikes illegal?

What are the arguments in favour of collective wage bargaining?

"Industrial peace depends on a much deeper rooted reform of industrial relations than that provided by the 1971 Act." Discuss.

Are there too many Trade Unions in Britain today?

Should the T.U.C. be separated from the Labour Party?

Distinguish between official, unofficial and unconstitutional strikes.

REFERENCES AND FURTHER READING
H. Williamson: *The Trade Unions* (Heinemann, 1970)
A. Flanders: *Trade Unions* (Hutchinson, 1965)
E. L. Wigham: *Trade Unions* (Oxford, 1969)
R. M. Grant: *Industrial Relations* (Ginn, 1970)
J. E. Mortimer: *Industrial Relations* (Heinemann, 1968)

J. Henry Richardson: *Introduction to the Study of Industrial Relations* (Allen & Unwin, 1954)
J. M. Jackson: *Wages and Labour Economics* (McGraw Hill, 1970)
Hunter & Robertson: *Economics of Wages and Labour* (Macmillan, 1969)
B. C. Roberts: *Trade Unions in a Free Society* (Hutchinson 1963)
The Royal Commission on Trade Unions and Employers' Associations (The Donovan Commission, 1968)
Department of Employment Industrial Relations Handbook, H.M.S.O.

5 Housing policy in Britain

House rents as a market price

It is possible to divide the supply of housing in Britain into four main sectors: owner-occupied flats and houses; private accommodation hired by tenants at rents which are controlled by the state; private accommodation hired at uncontrolled rents; and council houses and flats built and maintained by local authorities at controlled rents. Now although this is a complicated structure it is fair to say that its evolution has been decisively influenced by one factor, namely, the state's policy of enforcing a maximum ceiling on the rents which most private landlords may charge their tenants. Let us begin by testing the economic validity of this proposition.

We may regard house rent as a price which, under free market conditions, would be determined by the forces of supply and demand. If rents were "too low" the demand for dwellings would exceed the supply, and some families would be homeless; while if rents were "too high" the demand would fall short of the supply and some dwellings would remain empty. Given a free market in which there was competition between tenants and between landlords, the market rent for any particular category of dwelling would tend to settle at a level where the supply of, and demand for, "house room" were in balance.

In terms of interference with a price mechanism, what effect therefore does an officially controlled maximum price (or rent) have? We may start with some graphical analysis.

In Fig 5.1 D_1D_1 is the market demand curve for house-room and S_1S_1 the market supply, while the equilibrium price which clears the market is OP_1.

A decrease in the supply of house-room as a result for example, of wartime destruction together with the deflection of building resources to the war effort can be illustrated by the shift from S_1S_1 to S_2S_2. In a free market the effect of this decreased supply would be to raise market rent to OP_2. This higher rent may be thought undesirable on social grounds and the government may seek to control rents by keeping them at OP_1. This policy will prevent sitting tenants from being exploited if they are also given security of tenure but it does not help poorer sections of the community seeking rented accommodation and now quite unable to obtain it. Some form of rationing has to be introduced to prevent a mad scramble creating a black market in which the pressure of demand on a very limited supply will force prices up to very high levels indeed. Rationing in the U.K. after 1945 took the form of housing lists in which applicants for local authorities' houses were given points and, therefore, orders of priority, according to entirely arbitrary criteria. A parochial view of a family's claim to a rented house or flat usually outweighed any concept of "need".

In Fig 5.2 the effects of continuing rent control after the return of peace are indicated. The inability of landlords to obtain economic rents for their properties led to their selling them as soon as they became vacant or,

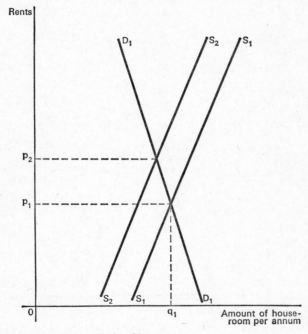

Fig 5.1 A decrease in the supply of house-room

alternatively, putting enough old furniture into them to qualify for the legal status of furnished accommodation which was not strictly rent controlled. In either case the supply of rented unfurnished house-room in the market decreased and this tendency was re-inforced by the almost total drying up of new rented property in the private sector. S_2S_2 is replaced by S_3S_3 and this trend has continued. On the other hand an increasing population and a rising standard of living meant an increased demand for house-room (from D_1D_1 to D_2D_2 and so on) pushing up the market level of rents (OP_3). In the following pages the story of successive governments' belated and grudging recognitions of the necessity to let rents rise to economic levels will be traced. It is sufficient here to note that the results of this "policy" have been i) increased pressure and higher prices in the owner-occupier markets making many people live under the strain of very heavy debts, ii) the creation of a privileged class of sitting tenants and iii) the continued existence of a housing shortage over 25 years after the end of the war.

In the long run controlled rents prevent the expansion of supply to meet increasing demand. Allowing short-run conditions in the market to

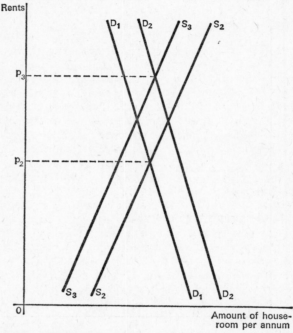

Fig 5.2 A continued decrease in supply of, but an increase in demand for, house-room

push up rents is likely to yield supra-normal profits to landlords and thus induce an increase in the supply of rented accommodation. The long-run impact of this increase in supply will be the elimination of supra-normal profit and a tendency for rents to fall.

A sharply rising price for a socially necessary good or service can present an acute dilemma of policy: price control will protect the position of the poor in the short run (assuming there is no black market); but in the long run it will injure their interest by stifling the price mechanism and preventing the inflow of new production resources. On the other hand, a free market will in the long run be in the interest of all consumers, since it leads to increased production and supply at, possibly, a lower price.

Is there a way through this dilemma? One possibility is for the state to allow short-run profits and prices to rise and to provide poorer consumers with free income (out of the general tax revenue) to enable them to compete in the market for the product. In the long run, as the industry expands and the price falls, this assistance could be progressively removed. This approach might well present some practical difficulties, but at least it would leave the price mechanism, and the re-allocation of resources, undisturbed.

Rent controls and state housing

Another possibility is for the state to impose a maximum price (rent) control, but to stimulate the long run inflow of resources by means of a subsidy to firms which enables them to sell increased output on the market at less than short-run average cost. This type of approach has in fact been the central point of housing policy in Britain since the First World War, and so we can now analyse its consequences directly in a historical perspective, and against the background of the price theory we have been examining.

We must begin, however, by pointing out that the housing market has some special and important characteristics which distinguish it from most other goods and services and which make it more difficult to apply the lessons of the free price mechanism to it.

On the demand side the special factors are these. First, flats and houses are immobile and have a very long life, so that people have been reluctant or unable to buy their own dwelling and instead pay rent as the price of a service: the hire of house-room. Secondly, the demand for accommodation tends to be inelastic in relation to its price (rent), both because changing accommodation and landlord is an expensive and difficult business, and because rent is a contractual payment which generally takes first claim in the family budget. The income elasticity of demand for rented accommodation is also, for similar reasons, low. Even so it is important to remember that as incomes and rents change, and as families go through the cycle of child-rearing to retirement, there will at any given time be a significant group of "marginal consumers" which does provide an elastic element in the demand for housing.

The supply of house-room also tends to be unresponsive to price changes. First, since dwellings are immobile, a shortage of housing in, say, Birmingham, cannot be relieved by drawing on an excess supply in, say, Cardiganshire. Secondly, house-building is a complex capital goods industry whose output depends not only on market price, but also on the availability of capital resources in the industry. Thirdly, and most important, the output of new dwellings is small compared with the stock of dwellings built in past years. So if rents fall, the existing stock of dwellings will continue to be available for a long time, thus placing landlords in a relatively vulnerable position. On the other hand a rise in rents will place landlords in a position of advantage. It is therefore important to look at the effects of rent control not just on the supply of new housing but also on the stock of "old" housing available as accommodation—particularly if the landlord's cost of upkeep is more than the controlled rent.

For these reasons, therefore, changes in rent do not quickly and directly bring about variations in the supply and demand of house-room. Nevertheless in the very long run, as we shall see, the consequences of interfering with the rent mechanism can be profound and far-reaching. With this in mind let us consider the decision which was taken during the First World War to impose maximum rents for certain categories of private dwellings.

Housing policies between the wars

Up to 1910, 99 per cent of dwellings were privately built, some being for owner-occupation, but many for renting tenants. This building was the result of private demands being expressed through a free economic market. During the First World War a high level of earnings and employment, and a shortage of labour for building, led to rapidly rising house prices. In 1915 the government passed a Rent Act which provided protection against high rents both for renting tenants and for owner-occupiers paying interest on house loans.

Was this intervention in the market for housing justifiable on economic grounds? The answer is undoubtedly "yes" because, under the wartime conditions, a sharp increase in rents would not have led to any inflow of resources into house-building, and would merely have constituted a windfall gain to private landlords and unnecessary hardship to tenants.

When the First World War finished, and the market mechanism for housing came back to life, the government was therefore faced with a choice of policy. It must either remove its maximum rent controls and restore the market mechanism; or, if it wished to continue rent restriction, it must assume responsibility for increasing the supply of dwellings so as to match the artificially stimulated demand for them. It chose the latter course, mainly for political reasons. By the Second World War, rent restriction had been to some extent relaxed. Even so, the scope of rent restriction in 1939 was still considerable: of 13 million dwellings in Great Britain, three million were owner-occupied, and 1·5 million built and maintained by local councils; of the remaining 8·5 million dwellings, four million were still subject to rent restriction.

In order to increase the supply of dwellings the government decided on a policy of subsidised house-building, and in 1919 introduced a scheme which called upon local councils to construct new working-class houses and let them at varying rents according to the means of the tenant in question; any resulting losses would be covered by a state subsidy. The councils, finding the subsidy attractive, quickly went ahead with their house-building, but the central government, fearful of the likely cost of the subsidy, abandoned the scheme in 1921. What is interesting about the scheme is not its impact, which had ceased by 1923, but the fact that it allowed a selective subsidy of the tenant, rather than a "blind" general subsidy on various grades of council houses. Later schemes were largely unselective.

By the 1930's, after a decade of post-war private and council house-building, the housing problem seemed less acute, and subsidies were greatly reduced. From now on the free market mechanism of supply and demand was restored to a major role in attracting resources into house-building, though there was still some rent restriction. With interest and mortgage rates very low, and rising real incomes for those in employment, the late 1930's were to witness a substantial construction boom, with over one million private houses being built. This made it possible for the state's policy on housing to be re-directed towards slum clearance and the re-housing of large families. In 1939, when the slum clearance and de-crowding programme was well under way, the local councils built a total of over 100 000 houses.

Thus between the wars the need to subsidise new housing was essentially dictated by the policy of imposing rent restriction on behalf of various private and council tenants. What is not perhaps so clear is that the need for a policy of slum-clearance also partly stemmed from rent controls. By 1939, when the majority of older pre-1914 houses were still rent controlled, it was difficult for many private landlords to maintain the state of repair of their properties. While it is true therefore, that low rents in conjunction with state subsidies stimulated an inflow of resources into new building (nearly four million dwellings, including council houses, were built in England and Wales between the wars), low rents had exactly the opposite effect in the case of resources needed for the maintenance of older houses. Indeed, if controlled rents had been pushed to a sufficiently low level, a situation might theoretically have arisen where older properties were turning into slums faster than new dwellings were being built. Clearly, rent restrictions can be a dangerous, two-edged weapon!

The housing problem after 1945

The Second World War set back housing substantially and it was necessary to reintroduce extensive rent controls to protect tenants against possible exploitation by landlords. In addition, new dwellings let for the first time, were to be pegged at their initial rent. These rent restrictions remained in force until 1954, when the Housing Repairs and Rents Act allowed rent increases up to twice the rateable value of the dwelling, provided the extra amount went to meet maintenance costs. As we saw earlier rent control is justifiable during any period when the availability of resources is severely restricted so that the market mechanism is in effect in abeyance. This was certainly the case in Britain during the War, when a large proportion of the nation's resources was being deflected into the war effort.

In 1945 there was an acute scarcity of housing and the government's post-war housing policy was to rely heavily on subsidies both for private and for council houses. It was subsidised council housing, including the "new town" overspill schemes, which provided four-fifths of new dwellings in the years of recovery. Private house-building was restricted by a licensing system.

In 1951 the Conservative government entered office committed to a building programme of 300 000 dwellings per year. This was soon achieved and surpassed, partly with the help of increased council house subsidies. Increasingly however it was the private building sector, now freed from licensing and responding through the freer market mechanism to the demand for housing, which provided the bulk of new housing in England and Wales. In Scotland, though, the subsidised council house has continued to dominate the market.

By 1957 the time had come to relax rent restriction, and the new Rent Act removed rent control from all new private lettings and all dwellings in England and Wales with a rateable value of more than £30 (in London £40). In addition controlled dwellings might have their rents increased up to a certain ceiling, depending on the landlord–tenant share of responsibility for maintenance. To protect tenants, four weeks' minimum notice was now to be required for a landlord or tenant to terminate a tenancy. The 1957 Act was an important step towards a freer housing market, and it made possible the repair of some of the economic damage to housing which a long period of rent restriction inflicts. Let us now examine this damage in some detail.

The economic damage of rent restriction

First, as we have seen, rent restriction, like any other maximum price control, stimulates an excess of demand over supply, and therefore tends to cause a market shortage. It is true that this excess demand has been partly absorbed by new council house-building subsidised by the state. Even so, such a programme takes a long time to execute and, in the meantime, scarce council houses will have to be allocated by rationing and queues so that in some cases families most in need of housing may be the last to get it. Worse still, excess demand will spill over into the uncontrolled sector of housing, where very poor tenants in, say, furnished accommodation, may be paying grossly inflated rents, and would-be owner-occupiers facing steeply rising house prices. It was this kind of background in the big cities which led to the exploitation and bullying of tenants by ruthless landlords, culminating in the 1960's in the infamous Rachman scandal.

Secondly, rent control leads to a deterioration of property. For example, in 1950 many private landlords were receiving 1920 rents, even though repair costs had trebled since 1939. Some landlords in this kind of position continue to maintain their houses; others choose, or are forced, to neglect their properties, which slowly deteriorate into slums. In fact it is often impossible to sell older properties which yield the owner little or no net income. Sometimes however a private landlord can find a legal means of selling to a fictitious owner who, when the property degenerates into health risk, cannot be found; this forces the local authority to assume responsibility for repair or for slum clearance. It is easy to imagine the plight of the tenant in a case of this kind. After 1957 rent restriction was relaxed but many landlords of older properties continued to subsidise their tenants.

Thirdly, rent controls lead to an inefficient use of the various categories of dwellings. For example, a single old age pensioner who is the only tenant in a large rent-controlled house is discouraged from moving to a smaller private house or flat, because those available will probably charge higher free market rents, or to a council house, which might mean joining a large queue. This in turn restricts the housing prospects of, say, a young family with children looking for bigger accommodation. Again, the owner of a very large house is deterred from converting it into flats because they might attract "reviewed" rents and turn him into a "subsidising" landlord. Under a free market mechanism on the other hand it would pay owners of large houses to sub-divide them into flats, and families to move into the right size of dwelling.

Fourthly, rent restriction reduces the mobility of labour. If a worker in a "controlled" dwelling moves he is unlikely to find a similar "subsidised" dwelling, for most landlords when they obtain vacant possession either sell their property to an owner-occupier, or furnish it and convert it so that it escapes the full scope of rent restrictions. So the worker in question may well have to turn down a better-paid and more productive job, because of the prospect of paying a "high" market rent. Equally a council house tenant may be reluctant to change jobs if it means joining a lengthy council house queue in his new area of work—and having to rent dearer private accommodation in the meantime.

This fourth effect of rent control is very relevant in Britain where there is a need for economic flexibility if the older industries are to contract and new ones expand. To digress slightly, this need for structural reform is an important part of the economic case for joining the expanding and highly competitive E.E.C. market in which, it is significant, free mobility of labour is a key provision. Housing policy cannot be judged in a vacuum—it must be related to the overall working of the economy.

Lastly, the council house system, which has followed logically from private rent control, is itself open to major criticisms. One is that it provides no real way of matching the tastes and needs of tenants and the types of dwellings being built. For example, some (though certainly not all) tenants find life in tall blocks of flats extremely disagreeable; this applies particularly to mothers with young children having no convenient playing

c

space. Yet some councils continue to press on with prestige high rise developments, regardless of the tensions and social problems which are being generated. In the market for new private houses a house-building firm erecting flats in an area where the demand was for houses with gardens would soon go out of business.

The system for allocating council houses is also open to criticisms. One of these is the abuse of residential qualifications. In 1969 only 17 per cent of the 1500 housing authorities allowed local newcomers unrestricted access to housing lists. A government committee recommended that there should be a legal obligation on local authorities to accept anybody on their lists and to allocate dwellings to applicants according to need. It was also found that some councils were content merely to build a reasonable number of council houses, but were not prepared to look after the interests of *all* local tenants. For example, some private tenants can best be helped with a house loan, or even just advice. There are also vulnerable groups such as large families and unmarried mothers who get unfair treatment through prejudice. In the context of racial tensions, the dangers of bias need no emphasising.

The 1969 housing proposals

During the 1960's successive governments aimed at a high rate of new house-building, and the period saw a rising rate of construction both of private and state housing. It was at this time that the Labour government introduced the 1969 Housing Bill which aimed at repairing the damage which decades of rent restriction had caused to private rented properties. Firstly it aimed at stepping up slum clearance by providing for local authorities to pay the full market price when purchasing from owner-occupiers of condemned houses; and to pay a better price to landlords of well-kept but sub-standard houses. Also, landlords who improved their properties would be allowed rent increases to cover the cost. Moreover, the bill attacked the anomaly of landlords having to subsidise sitting tenants paying frozen rents: landlords improving these properties were allowed to increase their rent to the higher "fair rent" category created in 1965. Tenants, however, would be safeguarded through the new provisions being phased, and by legal rights of appeal against "unfair" rent increases.

Secondly, the Bill attacked the problem of large, old, under-occupied properties. Housing authorities were to be subsidised by the Treasury according to the number of flats created in each conversion of houses over two storeys high. As the number of elderly retired people increases with the changing age structure of the population, this would meet an important social need.

Thirdly it was proposed that local authorities be allowed to increase the improvement grants for private property. In this connection it was envisaged that local authorities would become responsible for the improvement of whole dwelling areas, and not just individual houses.

Thus the policy tacitly admitted that many years of rent control had been a main cause of the private slum problem. But although it was a step in the right direction, namely a freer housing market, it still left one important problem unsolved: how can poorer tenants best be helped to face the sharp financial shock of having to pay near-market rents?

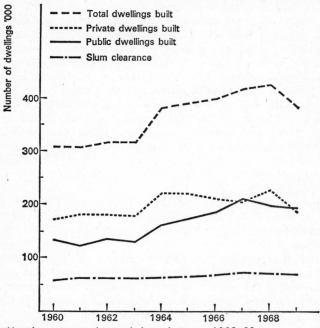

Fig 5.3 Housing construction and slum clearance 1960–69

Housing in the 1970's

The policy announced in November 1970 and incorporated in the 1971 Housing Finance Bill,[1] was an attempt to move towards free market pricing for all housing, whether state or private. It contained three important provisions. First, housing subsidies, instead of being paid to local councils to build low-rent houses, would in future be paid mainly in the form of rent allowances on a means test basis to tenants, *both in council and private accommodation*. Secondly, the "fair-rent" principle of the 1965 Act would be extended to include not only tenants in council houses but also those private tenants who had hitherto been paying "frozen" rents. Thirdly, special subsidies for land purchase and building would be given to authorities with the worst problems of slums and overcrowding.

[1] Enacted 1972.

The first proposal was a sweeping change in Britain's housing policy in that it would eventually replace subsidies on council houses by subsidies to poorer tenants: a measure both socially just and economically sound. Even so, these new subsidies would not go to some of the most needy tenants of all, namely those in furnished accommodation in the big cities.

The "fair rent" proposal (to be introduced in stages), was more a case of sound politics than sound economics. Fair rents are to be defined, by the rent officers and rent assessment panels who administer them, so as to cover landlords' costs, *but not to reflect any scarcity value in the area where the dwelling is situated.* Effectively this removes any commercial incentive for investment in building new flats and houses for private renting in the very areas where they are most needed. Worse still, private landlords will go on facing the serious fiscal burden of receiving no tax allowances at all to offset depreciation of their property. As a result there is unlikely to be any revival of the private rented sector. (Also the new subsidy system may well mean some cut-back in council building. So an increasing weight of the housing programme is bound to fall on private building for owner-occupiers in the years ahead.) In the end therefore the government may well have to grasp the political nettle and allow "fair rents" to be replaced by "market rents", even if this requires higher, or more selective, tenant subsidies.

The third proposal is economically sound: to end the sharply rising trend of indiscriminate building subsidies to all local authorities and instead to concentrate help on those areas with real problems of slums and overcrowding.

There are some over-all criticisms which can be directed at this policy. One is that it will not apply in Scotland, where a strong tradition of rent control and subsidised council housing is bound up with an acute housing problem. This too is a political nettle which will sooner or later have to be grasped.

The other criticism concerns the tax relief which private house buyers receive against the interest which they have to pay on their house loans from building societies. In effect this is a straight housing subsidy from the Treasury, and the higher the income of the borrower, and thus his marginal tax rate, the more this tax allowance is worth. In 1970 these tax subsidies to house owners amounted to about £200 million, compared with £350 million for all other housing subsidies. However, there is little likelihood of any government ending this tax subsidy. It is possible that some "affluent" council tenants may be pushed into the market for private-ownership houses and release council housing resources for poorer tenants.

The new approach was, then, an important step in the direction of an economically viable housing policy. From the point of view of the families, some of them immigrants, who have been living for years in city slums, it seemed the best bet so far for a fairer deal. However we must remember that the new policy, even if it is applied efficiently, will take a very long time to affect the way in which we maintain, improve and develop our stock of housing. In the meantime thousands of private tenants will have to go on existing in very poor housing conditions.

Houses to rent or houses to buy

By 1970 over one-half of Britain's dwellings were owner-occupied. With rising real incomes for most people, and a freer housing market, this trend is likely to continue. In the long run therefore the continued improvement in the quantity and quality of the stock of housing will depend on the profitability of new private house-building, as compared with the prospects for other forms of construction, such as offices and factories. It will depend too on the ability of the construction industry to compete for resources with other sectors of the economy such as consumer durables or services. The housing situation cannot therefore be assessed in a vacuum but must be related to the economy as a whole.

There are, in this wider context, two factors which greatly affect future housing prospects. First, the more efficient the construction industry is, the more effectively it can attract resources to satisfy the demand for housing. The picture here is still none too encouraging, for the building industry continues to consist mainly of large numbers of small firms using old-fashioned, labour-intensive methods. As skilled labour becomes scarcer and dearer, research and development is being undertaken by some firms into more efficient, capital-intensive techniques, in which many of the house parts are mass-produced in factories, after which they are assembled and erected on the spot. So far these new methods have mainly been used in high-level blocks of flats, and the collapse of Ronan Point, a system-built council tower block, in London in 1968 underlined unsuspected engineering risks. In "traditional" houses however the new methods have made little headway, on account of conservatism both on the part of house buyers and builders. If really fast and efficient construction methods, such as are used very successfully in, for example, North America and Scandinavia, are to become widespread, it may well be necessary for demand to be organised, possibly by private housing associations, so that builders and suppliers of components receive large contracts and continuous orders.

Another problem in areas like the South-East where demand has been booming has been the shortage of land for private house-building. This shortage derives partly from the post-war Town and Country Planning Acts which i) stressed the need for green belts around large towns in order to prevent built-up areas from encroaching into and destroying the countryside, and ii) entrusted to local authorities the planning of the acquisition, release and development of land for house-building, subject to central government control. The scarcity of building land created in

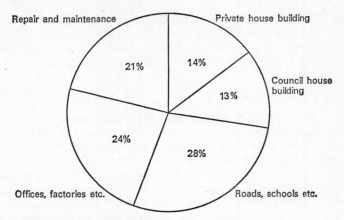

Fig 5.4 Britain's construction industry by sectors 1970

this way has been aggravated by the hoarding of unused land both by private owners and some local authorities in the expectation of capital gains arising out of soaring prices for land. In May 1972 the Housing Minister decided to speed up the release of land for housing by allowing local authorities an £80 million loan sanction to buy land over the ensuing two years so that they could put in services such as sewage disposal plants and sell the land to builders for immediate development. An expanded land release programme of this kind, it was hoped, would in turn, by moderating the land shortage and the escalation of land prices,

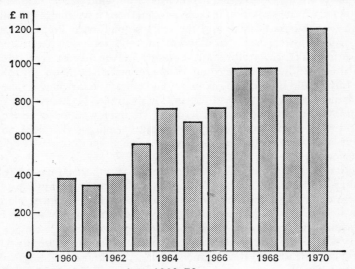

Fig 5.5 Loans for house purchase 1960–70

induce private land owners to "unwind" their speculative positions and release land on a large scale.

Secondly, there is the demand for new and secondhand private houses (the one market, of course, supporting the other) which is mainly financed in the form of mortgage house-loans. House buyers obtain these from building societies which in turn get their funds from savings deposits which the general public places with them. The societies make their living on the difference between the lower rate of interest they pay depositors, and the higher interest they charge to borrowers. Like the commercial banks they must be careful to have a safe liquidity reserve so as to be able to pay cash to depositors on demand. In the 1960's and early 1970's Britain experienced persistent inflation and interest rates continually tended to rise. This had a serious effect on the private demand for houses as the building societies had to keep raising the interest rate which they must offer the depositors and charge to house-buyers. In these circumstances, the societies partly "ration" the demand for house loans i) by rejecting less "secure" applicants and ii) by reducing the proportion of the house price against which they are prepared to lend money.

The present conventions on which building societies base their house financing are probably over-cautious. If these were relaxed the effective demand for housing could be increased. Four possible reforms have been proposed. First, the societies should consider lending to a wider range of buyers, and for classes of higher-risk properties (at present only one-sixth of mortgages are for pre-1919 houses). Secondly, mortgages covering the whole of the house price, and perhaps even including furniture, could be introduced for applicants with adequate income but insufficient savings. Thirdly the societies could allow longer repayment periods for mortgages, possibly tying particular loans to particular properties. Fourthly, and in order to accommodate these three other reforms, the societies could lower their liquidity ratios which in most cases are probably unnecessarily high.

It is true that more easily available mortgages might lead in the short run to inflated house prices, as in 1971 when house prices went up by 15 per cent. In the longer run, however, higher profits stimulate an inflow of resources into building: in fact the number of new private houses started in 1971 showed an increase of 25 per cent compared with 1970, whereas council housing was down by 11 per cent.

Thus there is scope for development on both the demand and supply side of the market, to assist it in attracting the resources needed to overcome the housing shortage. As yet there is a very long way to go. The D.E.A. Economic Progress Report of January 1968 estimated that there remained "at least two million houses which are unfit for human habitation and perhaps half a million not worth repair or improvement". An enlightened housing policy on the part of the local authorities will thus be essential for many years to come if one of Britain's most serious social problems is to be solved.

The restrictions on rents in recent decades have created the belief that owning a house is more desirable than renting one but it is of necessity more expensive and puts difficulties in the way of moving from a job in one place to a job somewhere else. Young people may be wiser to rent accommodation until they are fairly sure of where they are going to settle. The same applies to people who can expect to move around in their jobs although, of course, they may like buying and selling houses and be in the financial position so to do. There are others who would sooner spend their earnings on other things than home ownership and there are no economic grounds for denying them this choice. We must take care that the status symbol thinking of a particular section of society does not deny to others that choice which would yield them the highest levels of satisfaction. A freer market is an important safeguard of this freedom of choice.

QUESTIONS

Why has Britain's housing shortage lasted for so long after the Second World War?

Is there a sound economic argument for controlling the rents of houseroom?

Why have recent British governments avoided using market mechanisms for determining the supply and demand for house-room?

"Subsidising houses leads to social injustice: it is the people who live in them who should be subsidised." Comment.

Why has the stock of privately owned rented houses declined in recent decades? Should this trend be reversed and, if so, how?

Discuss the view that municipally owned housing should only be provided when the private sector fails to respond to normal market forces.

"Economic rents are unfair." Is this true?

REFERENCES AND FURTHER READING
W. Hagenbuch: *Social Economics* (Nisbet and Cambridge, 1958)
W. B. Reddaway: *Housing Problems* (*Three Banks Review*, September 1954)
H. W. Richardson and J. Vipond: *Housing in the 1970's* (*Lloyds Bank Review*, April 1970)

6 Inland transport

The opportunity costs of any transport service are those things which could have been produced with the factors involved. Consequently the economic objective of any country's transport policy must be to ensure that the benefits obtained from each service exceed or, at least, equal those which could be obtained from alternative uses of the resources concerned. However, the measuring of costs and benefits presents us with considerable difficulty in the matter of transport because social considerations are very important. These social factors cannot be easily quantified and there is, therefore, a constant danger of either according them more weight than they merit or of ignoring them altogether. Cost-benefit analysis has developed to the point at which it can be of real assistance in coping with this problem. This form of analysis seeks to quantify all costs and benefits both direct and ancillary, commercial and social, so that a comparison can be made between the costs to the community and the value to the community of any given service. When the construction of the Victoria line of the London Underground was being considered cost-benefit analysis brought into the deliberations such matters as the time which would be saved by passengers, the savings to passenger and commercial vehicles by the reduction of road congestion and even increased passenger comfort. In constructing urban motorways the addition of the social costs of surface tracks to the money costs of acquiring the land might add up to more than the costs of building them underground. When we turn our attention to existing services in contrast to new construction jobs it is more difficult to be objective and one is tempted to give more than due weight to the effects of disturbing existing patterns. Thus branch railway lines and village bus services gain added importance from their very existence; their removal looms as catastrophic in the local setting and any suggested substitutes appear immeasurably inferior. Nevertheless, an analysis of such services in cost-benefit terms provides the most reasonable approach available to us for reaching decisions compatible with the realities of opportunity costs and consumer choice.

Costs and choice

There are two basic questions of choice which have to be answered in relation to the transport industry: i) how extensive a transport system in general do we want? and ii) how much of each particular transport service do we want? We can view each of these problems of choice through production possibility curves. In Fig. 6.1, if a community produces OB of other things it must do without transport. If it moves to W on its production possibility curve it gains OM units of transport at the cost of TB of other things. Let AN equal OM and it can be seen that an equal gain in transport from point V as from point B has a higher opportunity cost of OS of all other things (OS > TB). This deduction derives from the diminishing marginal substitutibility of factors as production moves from one commodity to another and also from the diminishing marginal returns of

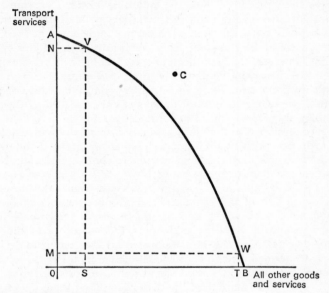

Fig 6.1 Opportunity costs of transport services

combining more units of one factor with other factors which cannot increase in the same proportion. The community's choice must be somewhere along AB unless it is within the curve and, therefore, using its resources inefficiently. It might like to be at C, any point outside the curve, but this choice is not open to it until it has pushed the frontier outwards throughout its length by means of raising its ability to produce goods through, for example, increased investment. The more transport the community wants, the more of other things it must give up unless it increases its total production capacity.

Usually, the demand for transport is not considered in its totality. People want better railway services together with the retention of branch lines, the maintenance of existing bus services especially in rural areas, more motorways and properly constructed trunk roads, and vast schemes to reduce urban congestion. This list adds up to "more transport". A further problem involved here is that investment in the transport infrastructure has a high capital-output ratio, i.e. a lot of investment is needed to yield proportionately little extra output. Therefore, if a community is striving to get to C in Fig. 6.1 its best choice may lie nearer to B than A in the present, devoting more of its resources to growth investment and less to transport so that it may more quickly push out its frontier to include C.

Although this total view of transport must remain in the background of our thinking we can now turn to consider the more immediate problem of how much of the resources presently directed into transport should go to any particular service. It is not really practical to divorce the total from the particular problem in everyday conversation but it is important that we should emphasise that there is a deep difference between deciding to go without other things in order to have more transport and deciding into which forms of transport to direct any given available resources.

Alternative forms of transport

The great debate since the 1920's has been between road and rail and to-day there is an equal debate between public and private transport. In each case we can construct production possibility curves as in Fig 6.2 (a) and (b). In (a) the community can choose to have a lot of rail and little road transport, vice versa, or any mixture along AB. Similarly the choice of the combination of public and private transport can be anywhere along AB in (b). In both cases, any combination of the variables

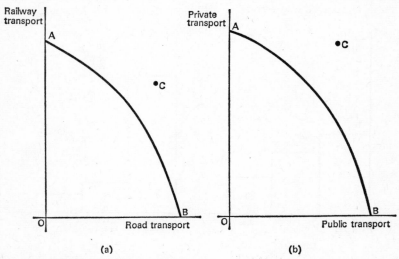

Fig 6.2 Alternative transport systems

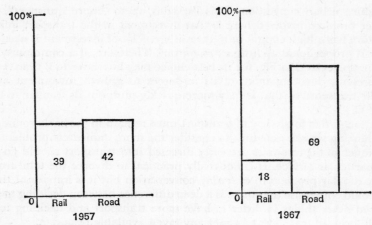

Fig 6.3 U.K. Freight traffic: Percentage of ton miles

beyond AB, e.g. at C. In the short run this would necessitate the diversion of other resources into transport from the production of other goods, i.e. a movement along AB towards A in Fig 6.1.

Broad decisions of this type are the ingredients of any true transport policy and the economic validity of any such policy depends upon its being based on the measurement of the social and private costs and benefits involved. This problem of measurement is a thorny one as there are so many factors involved that clear guide lines only emerge if we accept some simplified indicator. This point can be illustrated by a consideration of transport trends in Britain in recent years. Figs 6.3 and 6.4

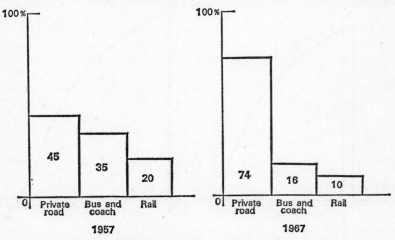

Fig 6.4 U.K. Passenger traffic: Percentage of inland passenger miles

indicate the relative changes in importance in the various sectors of the
industry and the figures must not be interpreted as absolute changes in
the amounts carried.

Nevertheless it is significant that the railways were responsible for
fewer ton miles of freight and that both rail and "buses and coaches"
suffered a drop in passenger traffic at a time when the whole transport
industry was expanding quite rapidly.

Traditionally the carriage of heavy, bulky traffic has been carried mostly
by rail but improved roads and larger lorries has eroded this position, as
has also the decline in the coal traffic. In Britain where most hauls are
relatively short, carriage by road is often more convenient and less costly
because it minimises the time-consuming processes of loading and un-
loading. Even long distance heavy traffic has been switching to the roads
and we must beware of assuming that there is some "natural" advantage in
the carriage of minerals, coal and suchlike by rail—such traffic often
means a line being used intensively in one direction only and most of the
reverse traffic being "empties". Although the introduction of highspeed
freightliners, the integration of road and rail freight services under the
National Freight Corporation and the use of "quantity licensing" to
restrict the growth of the carriage of bulky cargoes by road, may reverse
these trends it must not be assumed that this will necessarily be a more
economic use of resources. That can only be decided by a careful comparison of opportunity costs.

Whatever transpires in long-haul bulk traffic it would seem that such
short-haul small quantity traffic as remains on the rail will be lost to
roads—probably to the advantage of the railways—and that this fastest
growing sector in freight will further ensure the rapid expansion of road
transport. The main change that might take place here is a reversal of the
trend for firms to carry their goods in their own vehicles. This was, in part,
the artificial result of the licensing system which existed between 1933
and 1968. Now that the restrictions on the use of vans under 30 cwt. have
been removed it would be reasonable to expect to see the processes of specialisation and rationalisation result in the growth of distinct carrying firms.

The rapid rise in private motoring which has dominated the passenger
side of the transport industry has been and will continue to be an integral
part of increasing individual affluence. In many respects personal transport provides a convenience which public transport, as conceived at
present, cannot hope to match. The more a family owning a car uses it
the greater the number of miles over which its capital cost can be spread,
i.e. the lower the total cost per passenger mile of running the vehicle.
Moreover, for any one journey it is only *necessary* for the car-owner to
cover the variable costs involved (petrol and oil) whereas the price for any
journey on public transport will include something towards the over-
heads of the bus company. The convenience and cost considerations
of private motoring have led to its increase when growing traffic con-

gestion might have been expected to result rather in an increased use
of buses. There is a cumulative effect of a decline in bus services: their use
becomes increasingly inconvenient and a decline in their use leads to
further curtailments of services and so on. In this process there is no reason
to suppose that the end result is an efficient use of resources. This, as has
been underlined already, can only be achieved if people make their choices
about transport in the light of charges that reflect all the costs involved.

An industry or a social service?

Before it is possible to work out a framework of charges for various transport services one has to decide whether to treat them as branches of an
industry or as parts of a social service. If our aim is industrial efficiency
in the satisfying of wants, the price mechanism can be given the main job
of deciding which services shall expand and which decline. Cost-benefit
concepts can be incorporated in pricing policy. If the cost of services
exceeds the price potential users can afford the State can either i) subsidise the services which it wants kept open or ii) subsidise the people it
wants to be able to use them.

Sometimes, however, it is argued that transport is a social service and
should not be subjected to commercial criteria; it is roughly on a par with
health and education.

As many users of public passenger transport are those who do not own
cars and as a large proportion of this section of the population can be taken
to be relatively poor (and also because a large proportion of the poor are
"the old") the case for subsidising transport services appears strong. Is it
sensible to try to help the weak by maintaining uneconomic services on a
basis which makes them available to everyone at less than cost? If we
are thinking, for instance, of the poorer families in a rural area would it
not be cheaper, more economical in terms of the allocation of resources
and more convenient for the families concerned if they received direct
subsidies which would enable them to hire taxis when required rather than
to subsidise a very infrequent bus service? The problem of poverty does
not yield to the general subsidy approach; the subsidy has to be small if it
benefits everyone and, therefore, less is available for the poor than if they
receive specific help. They also suffer from the slower growth rate of the
community which precludes increasing aid for them as fast as might be.

It isn't possible to make a good economic case for subsidising freight
traffic. If firms are so badly located that their products cannot stand the
full costs of moving them to their markets then there is a clear case for
closing those firms and ending the waste of resources which they represent.
The problem of resulting localised unemployment, it can be argued, is
much better dealt with by re-training and, if necessary, helping people to
move to new areas than by bolstering up occupations which are almost
certain to sink in the relative income scale.

One peculiar aspect of subsidising which is encountered in transport is the cross-subsidisation of unremunerative services by the profitable ones. Thus the main-route bus passengers and coach passengers subsidise those using rural and some urban services. The main line railway routes tend to subsidise the branch lines. This again is usually justified by reference to the concept of "a public service". This ignores the considerable twisting of the industry as a result of users being unable to make rational decisions. If the rail fare from Southampton to Glasgow is higher than it need be because passengers have to subsidise branch line travellers the scales may be tipped in favour of making the more tedious coach journey or using one's car. The person who lives in a village and travels to work and back by bus may decide that it's just worthwhile as long as the fare is as low as it is, but would move into town if faced with an economic charge for his journey. It can never be over-emphasised that any distortion of market forces, however well-intentioned, can often lead to wastage, a lower standard of living and a lower competence to deal with the problems which provoked the original interference.

Let us now accept that transport is a public service but remove the emotive implications of this term. All service industries serve their public and each should charge according to its costs so that the public can decide how much of each service it is prepared to substitute for other things, i.e. so that decisions are made in the light of opportunity costs.

Not all unremunerative services provide for the poor. In many cases they are wanted irregularly by transport users in general. Many people want bus and train services to exist in case their private and normal arrangements break down. It is very comforting to feel that if ever one's car or lorry breaks down or if ever it just seems more convenient to use public transport on a particular occasion that it is possible to do so. This self interest probably explains why so many people protest at the closure of services which so few people use. There can be no economic objection to the maintenance of such services if the use of them is charged according to the costs of providing them; but that is not what the public want. They want the impossible, *viz.* a *cheap* alternative form of transport. It has been suggested[1] that this problem might be dealt with by piecemeal increases in charges over a period of time as evidence indicates that the public would accept this whereas they would create a storm over any single act of rationalising charges. It is necessary to stress that the objectives of such a policy would be the discontinuation of those services for which people were not prepared to pay adequately and in this way to release resources for alternative uses. Professor Sargent suggests that if transport users insist on the provision of these unremunerative services at less than cost then those services should be subsidised on a passenger mile or ton mile basis so that the operators would be able to compete in an otherwise free market. There would be scope for consumer choice where it is now

[1] J. R. Sargent, *British Transport Policy* (Oxford), Ch. V.

restricted and transport users would be aware of the real costs of maintaining the unremunerative services. The burden of financing a subsidy would only be placed on the general public when the government, local or central, ordered the continuation of a service on social or strategic grounds. Where it is the general convenience of transport users and not the achievement of some governmental policy objective which is at stake then the cost of any subsidy should be spread across the whole transport industry on a ton or passenger mile basis. People would then have a motive for checking their wants against the costs of meeting them and thus choice could rest on a more rational basis.

Professor Walters suggests[1] that evidence indicates that subsidies have an adverse effect on managerial and general efficiency because of the feeling that "the State will always foot the bill; and the acid test and spur of efficiency—the ability to sell at a profit against competitors—is lost". He concludes his article by saying "If pressed to generalise, however, I would argue that solutions other than subsidies should always be pursued first. A subsidy is a last resort." If we reflect that the desire for a comfortable life is probably a more usual human trait than a compulsion to efficiency we can see that Professor Walter's conclusion is in sympathy with economists' distrust of monopoly: remove the outside compelling force of competition and wastage of resources is almost certain to result.

Can the price mechanism co-ordinate transport?

"Depending on the price mechanism" is not a euphemism for "resorting to a free-for-all". If it seems unlikely that any committee or government department or supreme co-ordinating authority would be able to devise a transport structure tailored to the ever-changing cost and demand conditions of a developing economy, a reasonable approach would be to devise a freely operating market system through which to attain our objectives. The forces of demand can reflect the choices of transport users in response to prices reflecting the opportunity costs of those choices. The price mechanism can adjust itself rapidly to changing cost and changing demand conditions. So far, it will be noted, the word "can" has been used repeatedly. The price mechanism cannot work efficiently in securing an optimum allocation of resources if its operation is warped by recurrent political interference. From now on it will be assumed that this proviso is understood and that our job is to see in what sort of framework a rational transport network might result from reliance on the price mechanism.

Professor J. R. Sargent[2] suggests that the charges for each transport service should reflect its direct costs, i.e. the saving of resources that would be effected if that service were discontinued. Transport users would then be able to choose in their own interest in the light of true opportunity cost ratios. There are many indirect costs of any transport system but,

[1] *Lloyds Bank Review*, January 1967.   [2] J. R. Sargent: *op. cit.*

whether we think of rail or road, these cannot be apportioned to each particular service. As regards rail there are the costs of track depreciation and maintenance, and of the signalling, loading, marshalling and station services. For road transport there are the costs of roads, policing, traffic signals and so on. These could be charged collectively on a ton mile and passenger mile basis. For rail transport this would be a fairly easy addition to the direct charges of any service but for road services it could not be achieved with the same precision. However, Professor Sargent suggests that road users could be charged these indirect costs by taxing petrol and diesel oil (and, of course, any new fuel that comes on to the market). In this way, it is suggested, all transport users, private and public, would be faced with charges which would cover both the direct and the indirect costs of the various services but they would be able to make rational decisions according to opportunity cost concepts because the overall costs would reflect the ratios of the direct costs involved.[1]

The ideas already discussed for subsidising uneconomic services could be integrated with this price mechanism system quite easily. Where the beneficiaries were transport users in general this would be taken as an extra indirect cost and charged uniformly to all services on a ton mile and passenger mile basis. Where some local community benefited it would provide the subsidy for the relevant service and only where the nation as a whole was held to benefit would a subsidy come from the central government.

There are other ways[2] than these of establishing a transport network based on a price mechanism which takes into account cost-benefit ideas. The point to note is that competition can be used as an ally in ensuring that resources are used in an optimum manner.

Opportunity costs and choice in towns

Urban road congestion is an increasingly pressing problem. Some bright ideas have been put forward for dealing with it but, so far, only makeshift palliatives have been administered. Complicated one-way street systems, parking meter zones and central car parks do not prevent an ever increasing blockage of un-zoned roads by kerbside parking thus causing an ever slower crawl along the roads. Our towns are growing and are likely to grow. The number of cars and lorries on the roads is growing and is likely to grow. What can be done to prevent chaos? Once again we are face to face with the problem of the extent to which we can back the foresight of experts and seek to impose a ready made solution or try to use market forces to direct us towards solutions; for it may be that what is best for one town is not best for another.

[1] J. R. Sargent, *op. cit.*, p. 120.
[2] See discussion of two-part tariff, pages 101–106.

In 1963 the Buchanan Report caught the imagination of the public and for some months it was a general topic of conversation. Professor Buchanan advocated the remoulding of the traffic flow of cities. Each approximate square mile of city would be considered as an environmental area into which only local traffic would be admitted. Through traffic would pass around these areas on distributor roads of varying degrees of importance according to whether they were feeding into adjacent areas or leading away to other parts of the country. This way of coming to terms with increasing traffic would require heavy capital expenditure for the re-structuring of urban roads but it does accept the fact of the increasing number of vehicles and is designed to preserve or revive the quality of urban life. No real action followed the report partly because the parlous economic condition of Britain precluded vast capital expenditure of the order that would be required: it was estimated in 1963 that the implementation of Buchanan ideas would cost for London £6,450 millions, for Leeds £188 millions and for Newbury £4½ millions.[1] There was also the doubt as to whether the final product would match up to requirements. Even a strong, thriving economy must pause before devoting such a massive share of its resources to dealing with a single, though major, problem.

In 1964 Dr. Smeed's report on "the technical feasibility of various methods for improving the pricing system relating to the use of roads, and relevant economic considerations" was published. The Smeed Committee concluded that it would be possible to operate a scheme whereby vehicles were charged according to the length of time they spent in any urban area. This would have no connection with parking but would be based on each vehicle covering the costs of its contribution to congestion, i.e. paying for the costs its presence imposed on other vehicles. To this could be added the costs imposed on the general community in terms of delays, noise and pollution. Thus the "congestion taxes" as they have been called would be calculated very much on a cost-benefit basis. The charges would be adjusted so that any road network could be filled to its Optimal Economic Capacity which is that at which marginal road users enjoy net benefits equal to the costs which their presence imposes on other users. When the costs imposed on others has been calculated, on a time basis, the road user is left free to judge whether it is worth his while to use the road as planned. Such a system would avoid all the bureaucratic complications involved in other proposals about banning inessential traffic or private motorists. Who can tell what is inessential to whom? or whether a private motorist considers his journey of great importance or not? The Smeed approach would leave individuals free to weigh for themselves the anticipated satisfaction of any car journey through a town against the price they would have to pay to cover the costs to others of that journey.

The use of congestion taxes could be linked to guiding road investment decisions. As routes tended to confer greater benefits on their users they

[1] *The Statist*, November 29th, 1963, and February 21st, 1964.

would be used more, congestion and consequent charges would increase, thus indicating that a satisfactory return could be obtained from expanding that route. This would certainly aid the linking of new road construction to the developing requirements of traffic and ensure that schemes were not separated from their costs to the community.

It has already been mentioned that congestion charges must not be confused with the costs of parking vehicles. This problem is also best solved by linking charges to direct costs and the costs imposed on others. One thing is certain and that is that the idea of the free occupation of road-space as a parking plot is a costly anachronism. Kerbside parking not only adds to the congestion on the road but also imposes costs on the general public in the form of loss of amenity. Vehicles cannot stop to let passengers alight without holding up the mainstream of traffic; there is the annoyance of having "strange" vehicles parked outside one's premises; there are the added difficulties of street cleaning and there is the hazard to pedestrians seeking to cross the road. All these costs should rightly be covered by vehicles wherever they are permitted to park on the road— and one must add to the direct costs of installing and operating meters the social costs of their unsightliness and their interference with free movement along the pavement. As the amount of traffic using urban roads increases the costs to the community of kerbside parking rise to the point at which it has to be discontinued altogether. When this happens we have to consider the costs of using land for parking and there can be no economic justification for charging vehicles less than the cost of providing such facilities.

Conclusion

Whether we are considering how much transport to have in total, how much of an accepted amount of resources to devote to one form of transport or another, or how much of different types of transport to have in towns we are faced with the same basic set of economic problems:

  i) the availability of resources
 ii) the measuring of costs and benefits
iii) the necessity of making a choice
 iv) deciding on a mechanism to implement that choice.

QUESTIONS

"The market mechanism is no use as a guide to the provision of transport facilities." Comment.

In what way can cost-benefit analysis help in deciding i) whether to close a railway line and ii) what route a new motorway should adopt?

"Fifty miles of new motorway cost £50 millions. The same length of canal can be renovated for £3 millions." What are the economic implications of this statement?

Would a newly built railway network for Britain be very different from the one inherited from the past?

Should all unprofitable railway lines be closed?

Discuss some of the ways in which urban traffic congestion could be relieved.

"Rural bus services cannot pay and, therefore, they should be subsidised by the local authorities." Is this sound economic argument?

Is a national transport network more than a pipe dream?

"Britain completed her railway network just as new forms of transport began to make railways obsolete. Her new road network may repeat the experience." Discuss.

Find out i) the provisions of the 1968 Transport Act and any later legislation ii) the current transport policies of the political parties iii) recent thinking of economists (Bank Reviews, the *Economist*). Discuss these in the light of opportunity costs and the optimum use of resources.

Consider a local transport problem, e.g. the closure of a branch railway line or rural bus service, or the building of a trunk road or urban motorway. Make lists of all the costs and benefits involved. What alternatives exist? Compare your findings with the expression of public opinion in local newspapers.

REFERENCES AND FURTHER READING

P. Donaldson: *Guide to the British Economy* (Ch. 5) (Penguin, 1971)

Edited by D. Munby: *Transport* (Penguin, 1968)

G. Roth: *The Problem of Traffic in Towns* (*Westminster Bank Review*, November 1965)

A. A. Walters: *Subsidies for Transport?* (*Lloyds Bank Review*, January 1967)

The Economist: December 4th, 1971

7 The economics of farming

Agriculture is the name given to a number of industries whose common link is their heavy dependence on the fertility of soil as a factor of production. The word "agriculture" really means "the cultivation of the fields", i.e. what we would nowadays call "arable farming" but, of course, it is also used to cover pastoral and, more latterly, factory farming. In fact an industry is best thought of as a collection of firms classified according to their product, their processes or their raw materials and therefore it is more rational to think of the beef industry, the wheat industry, the potato industry, etc., than to use the one all-embracing term "agriculture". However, it would be fruitless to flout common usage but we must be careful not to follow it into the everyday oversimplified approach to the economics of farming.

We must also take care to avoid accepting at their face value the many claims that are put forward for the special treatment of agriculture. Our starting point must be an impartial analysis of this group of industries so that any measures which may emerge for securing their efficient development will be as consistent with the facts as is possible. We shall assume that we are dealing with privately owned agriculture and that the objective of farmers like any other businessmen, is to make as much profit as possible out of their enterprises, *ceteris paribus*, i.e. other objectives such as pride in good farming are taken to remain the same. This does not mean that our analysis of the economic problems of agriculture would not apply to state-owned farms but that it becomes impossible to generalise about measures which deal with such problems when a variety of entirely political criteria may apply to the industry.

The economic problems encountered in agriculture can be quite usefully classified as i) those arising out of marketing its products and ii) those arising out of the organisation of production, but we must be ready to find a great deal of overlapping between these categories. In the first place we shall find the tendency for the prices of farm products, in common with most primary goods, to fluctuate considerably through time. In the second category come the sluggishness of production changes in response to price movements and the extreme immobility of factors. Our next concern will be to consider measures to deal with these problems and then to compare these with government policy in recent decades, particularly British government policy.

Fluctuating prices

In the theory of value we find it explained that the extent to which a change in demand or supply affects the price of a product depends upon the elasticities of those market forces. It is, therefore, to the theory of value that we must turn to see what light can be thrown on this besetting problem of agriculture.

The flow of any agriculture product on to the market at any given price per unit is unlikely to be very susceptible to changes in that price because output must be planned a long time in advance; it can rarely be

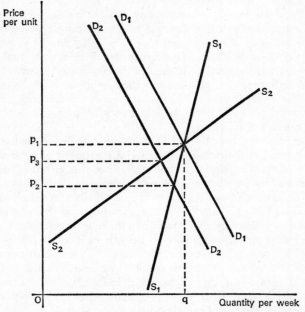

Fig 7.1 Effect of a decrease in demand on price when elasticities of supply differ

brought forward and often it can only be delayed at the expense of disturbing the work needed for the next phase of production. Moreover storage of perishables is likely to be expensive and, from the point of view of taking a surplus off the market, is quite likely to create a problem of disposal in the subsequent period. The likelihood of difficulty in disposing of stored surpluses can be underlined by reflecting that individual farmers must keep to the production schedules determined by the nature of their existing farms or possibly face a complete cessation of income. A farm cannot be stopped and started like a factory and the changing of its product is not just a question of re-tooling—it may mean a complete change in buildings, machines and skills employed. Most farmers, operating on a relatively small scale and with limited resources, would find it difficult enough to change the nature of their output in times of prosperity and they would find it almost impossible in those times of low prices for their existing product when such change would be beneficial. Moreover, it might well be difficult to find other products not adversely affected by a fall in price because it is often the case that the prices of agricultural products move up and down together under the general influence of the weather, changes in supply brought about by techniques of production or distribution, and changes in demand resulting from income changes.

Let us underline these points by considering the lot of a small dairy farmer whom we can allow to keep a few hens and pigs. Now let the demand for milk fall from D_1D_1 to D_2D_2 (Fig 7.1). Our farmer must continue milking his cattle or they will go dry; he might slaughter any suitable animals for beef but unless they are of the right age they will not be readily marketable and if other farmers are in the same plight their joint action will glut the market for beef cattle; in any case, such policies will reduce his future capacity to produce milk. Some of his farm's milk output might be fed to his pigs—but that is not going to be of much help. He is certainly not in a position just to throw away his milk and he will, therefore, market it for at least as long as he can recover his variable costs and earn something towards his fixed costs. Therefore the supply of milk on to the market from this farm and, since it is taken to be typical, in aggregate from all farms, is likely to be relatively inelastic as indicated by S_1S_1.

The fall in demand from D_1D_1 to D_2D_2 around price Op_1 per unit causes the price to fall to Op_2 which is a greater fall in price than would have occurred with a relatively elastic supply S_2S_2 when the fall would have been to Op_3.

In a converse direction it can be seen that, for the same sort of reasons, farmers will be practically unable to increase supplies when there is an increase in the demand for their products. They can only market what is available, augmented a little by drawing on any stocks of their product and, in some cases, by bringing forward the marketing date of current output— but this will be at the expense of later supplies. Thus changes in demand are likely to cause considerable fluctuations in the prices of farm produce.

The price elasticity of demand for agricultural goods will tend to be low except where a number of such goods are substitutes for one another so that a fall in the price of one will lead to consumers using it in place of the others, e.g. beef, pork, mutton. Apart from the case of substitutes a given fall or rise in the price of an agricultural commodity is not likely to cause as proportionately great an inverse change in the demand for it. This arises out of the fact that any community will want a certain quantity per week of any particular foodstuff to maintain its current way of life: a little less will create a sense of hardship, a little more will prove a surfeit. In the former case relative scarcity will force prices up, in the latter case relative plenty will drive them down. This is a reflection of the rapidly diminishing rate of substitution of foodstuffs for other goods: as more of any foodstuff comes on to the market people will be less anxious to substitute the extra quantities of it for other things and, therefore, they will only buy more if the price of the foodstuff is greatly reduced. Conversely, a small decrease in the supply of a foodstuff will tend to drive up its price considerably because people will strive very hard to resist a reduction in their consumption of it.

Under the combined conditions of relative inelasticity of both supply and demand we would expect to find any change in either of those forces causing a more than proportionate change in price of the relevant commodity and, therefore, in the incomes of its producers. This expectation has been borne out in the experience of farmers over the years and lies at the root of the establishment of international commodity schemes, national marketing schemes and price support schemes.

Production cycles

Although the elasticity of supply of agricultural goods is necessarily low the large price fluctuations noted above cause farmers to over-react to market conditions. Given very low prices for a commodity they have often made long-period decisions to reduce their output of the commodity in question. This involves switching to some other line of production—a process taking a number of years so that the reduction of output is likely to become effective long after market prices have recovered. Prices now soar and the reverse process is set in motion.

These cycles arise, then, out of the time lag between market price being established and output reacting to it. In Fig 7.2 a) SS was the intended supply so that Oq_1 units would be supplied at Op_1 to suit the market conditions ruling at the beginning of the cycle. However, bad weather or some pest is taken to reduce SS to S_1S_1 so that those units which are marketed fetch a price of Op_2. Fig 7.2 b) indicates that in reaction to this year's price of Op_2 plans are set afoot to increase supply to S_2S_2 and when that is achieved price per unit falls to Op_3. Turning to Fig 7.2 c) it is noted that price Op_3 causes farmers to plan a reduction in output which, on maturing, pushes price up to Op_4 which, in turn, can be expected to produce another increase in supply in the subsequent period. This output/ price oscillation may equally start with an unexpected shift in demand. Any unexpected change in supply or demand is certain to result in the price of a product being higher or lower than suppliers anticipated, and to initiate a cycle.

This process is sometimes analysed in terms of "the Cobweb Theorem". In Fig 7.3 it is assumed that present output is Oq units which fetch a

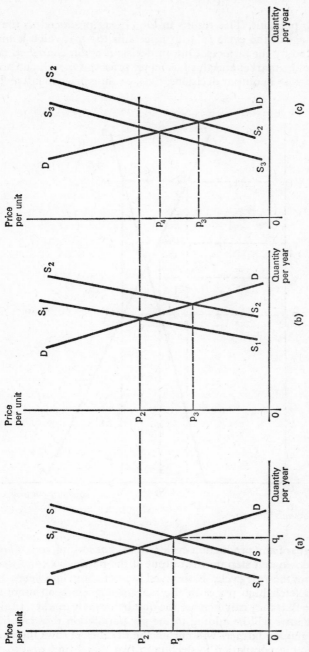

Fig 7.2 Price fluctuations and the production cycle

price of Op per unit. This results in Oq_1 being produced so that in the following stage of the cycle $(t + 1)$ price falls to Op_1 which is much less than required by the farmers. Output decisions again change so that Oq_2 comes on to the market and this pushes up price to Op_2 which encourages another increase in output decisions, Oq_3, causing price to fall to Op_3 and so on.

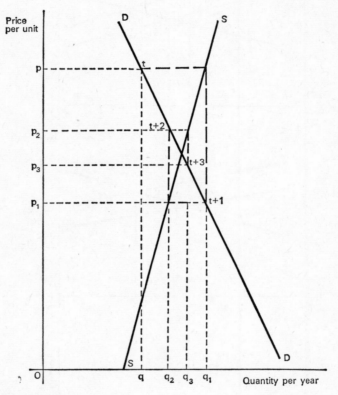

Fig 7.3 Cobweb theorem

The length of any production cycle will vary according to the time needed to run down and step up the output of the particular commodity concerned. Thus the "pig cycle" is observed to be of about four years duration. When pigs fetch high prices in the market farmers keep more sows for breeding so that they can increase the numbers sent to market. In about two years these sows will be adding to the pig population thus causing prices to fall whereupon farmers will curtail the number of sows they keep thus causing the pig population to decline in two years' time and so on. This cycle is largely due to the fact that each farmer produces so little in relation to the total supply of pigs that he cannot by his own action influence prices and is therefore, if anything, over-sensitive to low or high prices. It is the combined effects on supply of many farmers' production decisions which, in conjunction with relatively inelastic demand conditions, cause big shifts in prices.

Similar cycles have been observed in the case of poultry, potatoes and vegetables. In these cases output can be changed much more quickly and therefore low prices one year lead to reduced output in the next. The resultant high prices lead to expansion of output within one year and prices tend to fall again. Thus there is a two year cycle in these products.

Sheep and cattle production have much longer cycles because more time is needed to convert from arable to pasture and vice versa, to change the equipment of farms, and to build up or run down flocks and herds. It has been suggested that the period of adjustment to very low or very high prices might be from three to four years for sheep production and from eight to nine years for cattle production.[1]

The long-run sensitivity of farmers to low and high prices must not be overstressed. Small farmers are rarely able to adjust themselves to new patterns of production. They tend to be very traditional in their methods and outlook and to have insufficient resources to reorganise their farms in response to market conditions. Farmers are essentially "production managers" and yet one would not expect to find many who were qualified to study and understand likely future trends in prices and costs. Consequently, they are more than likely to treat abnormal prices as temporary phenomena and certainly, on the basis of experience, they are likely to consider them poor indications of what is to come. Furthermore, many commodities produced on any one farm are complementary, e.g. root crops, silage, hay, and milk or beef—and it is difficult to adjust the output of any one of these to price conditions without upsetting the output of all of them. Finally, as we noted earlier, the actual output of farms is subject to variation by the hazards of weather and this diminishes the value of adaptation to present prices.

How can we reconcile these reasons for farmers' production inertia with observed production cycles? With the great number of farms in existence (and in all countries this industry still lags in the adoption of large-scale production), there only needs to be a small proportion of farmers ready to change at any one time to cause a cycle effect. Any such effect will have a disproportionate effect on prices because of the relative inelasticity of demand for the product. Thus quite a modest change in supply has a significant impact on the market and on farm incomes.

[1] Thomas, *An Introduction to Agricultural Economics* (Nelson, 1949), p. 210.

Income elasticity of demand

Any society's income elasticity of demand for a commodity "m", around its current income level can be indicated thus:

$$\text{Income elasticity of demand for "m"} = \frac{\text{proportionate change in weekly demand for "m"}}{\text{marginal proportionate change in social income per week}}$$

As the standard of living rises in other than the poorest countries, people spend proportionately less of their incomes on food. A family with a weekly income of £100 doesn't spend ten times as much on food as one managing on £10 per week and some of the extra it does spend on food is on expensive highly processed varieties instead of on simple foods. In short, a wealthy family probably eats very little more than a poor one in quantity and it is quantity which affects farmers most.

The rising incomes of a mature society are associated with the development of new techniques of production and transport. Faster transport, refrigeration, deep freezing and improved packaging all open the market for food to sources of supply hitherto barred by the combination of distance and the perishability of the product. New farming techniques increase the output per man-hour from all farms adopting them. These forces tend to result in supply increasing faster than demand even when we allow for increases in population in addition to increases in incomes. Thus the marginal revenue productivity of any given unit of production (a farm in this case) tends to fall and the only way in which a farmer can maintain his relative income is to increase the size of his farm. At this stage in our analysis we come face to face with the hard core of the problem *viz* the extreme inertia or immobility of farmers.

Table 1   Average sizes of farms (1971)

	(hectares)
Italy	7
France	18
Denmark	20
U.K.	32
U.S.A.	122

The majority of farms even in countries like Britain, France and Germany are very small and are run on a family basis and as such are more a way of life than economic propositions in the modern world. A family will operate a farm in return for a very small income for a mixture of reasons:

it may be their own farm by inheritance or it will have taken them many years to save up its purchase price or enough for tenant's capital. There will be little or nothing else to which the family can put its talents, partly because of the high average age of farmers,[1] partly because of their tendency to lack education,[2] and partly because no other way of life is thinkable for them. In economic terminology, farmers have very low transfer costs; to them the net advantages of farming include weighty non-economic returns and they will continue in their existing line of production even when its monetary rewards are very poor.

British agricultural policy

The objectives of state policy for agriculture in Britain have been to raise farm incomes, to stabilise food prices at relatively low levels and to save imports. A fourth objective has been introduced against massive conservatism, *viz* the rationalisation of the structure of farming. The means used to attain these objectives have been i) a wide variety of subsidies and grants, ii) import controls, iii) marketing schemes, iv) regulations pertaining to the supply of capital.

Subsidies envisaged as a way of keeping down the domestic price of food are an anachronism in days when cheap imports are available and domestic production is itself artificially restricted. In Britain subsidies are, therefore, producer subsidies whose aim is to enable farmers to obtain higher incomes than the output from their farms would earn in a free market. Fig. 7.4 a) indicates that the *world* price of commodity "x" is Op_1 per unit and that we could therefore obtain it at that price. In Fig 7.4 c) the price of "x" which would give *domestic* farmers an "adequate" return is Op_3 per unit. Restrictions on imports, tariffs and quotas, raise the domestic price of imported "x" to Op_2 in Fig. 7.4 b), and producer subsidies and grants increase the domestic supply from S_1S_1 to S_2S_2 Fig 7.4c), thus reconciling the price of home produced and imported "x" at Op_2 per unit.

Prior to entry into the E.E.C. Britain encouraged farmers to increase supply by direct supports which, in the 1960's, amounted to some £100 millions per annum. The list of these supports reads as follows:

> fertilisers subsidy
> lime subsidy
> ploughing grants
> field drainage grants
> water supply grants
> grants for farm improvements
> marginal production assistance

---

[1] Martin, *Economics and Agriculture*, p. 91.   [2] Martin, *op. cit.*, p. 88.

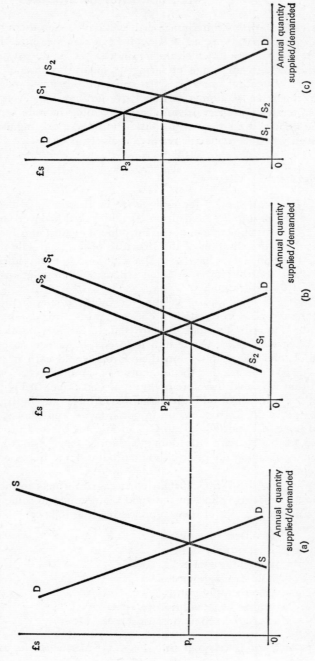

Fig 7.4 a) International market price of commodity 'x'
b) The imposition of import controls raises domestic price of imports of 'x'
c) Subsidies lower the price of domestically produced 'x'

> grants to small farmers
> bonus payments for attested herds
> cattle subsidy
> hill cattle subsidy
> silo subsidy
> exemption from local rates.

In addition, deficiency payments were specifically designed to keep up farmers incomes whenever the market prices of their products fell below those guaranteed by the Annual Farm Price Review. In the 1960's these deficiency payments were in the order of £150 millions per annum and went mainly to producers of eggs, cereals, sheep, pigs and milk, and much smaller amounts went to cattle, wool and potatoes.

The use of subsidies to safeguard farmers' incomes has certain obvious disadvantages: i) the cost to the State is unpredictable, depending on the course of free market prices both at home and in the world as a whole; ii) an annual review puts the whole matter on a political basis which perpetuates uncertainty for the farmers and militates against reorganisation on a large-scale, low-cost basis. In an attempt to deal with the first of these disadvantages and give some security to farmers the 1957 Agricultural Act provided that the total value of guarantees was not to be reduced by more than $2\frac{1}{2}$ per cent per year. This total value to be arrived at by multiplying the appropriate quantities of output in the current year by the current guaranteed prices and adding the value of the production grants. This meant that farmers would not be completely insulated against fluctuations in their incomes caused by variations in their outputs. The Act also allowed for the gradual reduction of subsidies but it stipulated that gross farming income was not, in consequence, to fall by more than $2\frac{1}{2}$ per cent in any one year, and that for individual commodities the maximum reduction in subsidy was not to exceed 4 per cent in any one year or 9 per cent in any three consecutive years.

Very little has been done to foster re-organisation of the industry. The 1964 Farm Price Review exercised an indirect pressure on regrouping into larger units through measures designed in fact to further limit the cost to the Exchequer of the support programme. The purport of these measures was that any increase in output beyond standard quantities of cereal would result in a fall in domestic farmers' total receipts since any increase in sales would be shared with overseas suppliers. The increase in competition involved gave extra emphasis to efficiency and, therefore, to regrouping into larger units. The 1965 Small Farm (Business Management) Scheme made provisions for outside help being made available to improve small farm administration but, clearly, could not contribute to the major cause of inefficiency, *viz* the unit being too small.

Import controls whilst basic to the limiting of the state commitment to subsidising agriculture have usually been discussed in terms of benefiting the balance of payments. This is certainly not a straightforward question of a direct benefit to the extent that output goes up as a consideration of the following points will show:

a)   increased agricultural output which is the result of deflecting more resources into agriculture as opposed to the more efficient use of existing resources, will diminish the availability of resources for other industries including those concerned with exporting;
b)   the reduction of purchases of agricultural goods from abroad will to some extent lower the purchasing power of the suppliers in the countries concerned and this could result in a diminution of their purchases of our exports;
c)   increased agricultural output may only be possible if there is an increased importation of feedstuffs and fertilisers;
d)   if the policy results in prices for agricultural products being higher than if they are imported this will have some effect on the costs of producing other goods and therefore on their prices and this could adversely affect exports.

One estimate in 1965[1] was that an increase of £125 million of agricultural output would make a comparatively small net contribution to the balance of payments of between £19 million and £36 million. Although the authors of this estimate considered this to be a worthwile balance of payments contribution they were doubtful whether "greater intensity is desirable except in so far as raising productivity succeeds in keeping costs under control, or unless food imports become permanently dearer". In 1969 the Ministry of Agriculture, Fisheries and Food announced a programme for expanding the output of grain, beef, and milk, pork and bacon through increased productivity. The produce of farms was to rise by some £400 m. (at 1969 prices) per annum by the year 1972/3 and, in that year, yield an expected net import saving of £160 million. This higher expectation by the government of the import saving effect was probably attributable to the assumption of increased productivity, i.e. increased output per manhour and per acre. It would seem doubtful whether this is likely (as opposed to technically feasible) in view of farmers' resistance to amalgamations and other structural reorganisation which would enable them to spread their increasing overheads over larger outputs.

When the inability to compete stems from economic inefficiency it is in everyone's interest to rectify this matter rather than to perpetuate it by hindering imports. In Britain, as we have seen, the main protection against cheap imports has taken the form of subsidies. Tariffs have been used mainly to protect horticulture and import quotas have been used mainly as weapons in the battle to safeguard reserves of foreign exchange rather than as means of protecting farmers.

Marketing schemes, dating back to 1931, have been introduced to regulate output in order to stabilise prices at levels acceptable to farmers without

[1] L. Moore and G. M. Peters in *Westminster Bank Review*, August 1965.

putting an intolerable strain on the Exchequer. Marketing schemes exist or have existed for eggs, hops, milk, pigs, potatoes and wool. These monopoly organisations stem from the Agricultural Marketing Acts of 1931 and 1933. At first farmers did not look favourably on the compulsory powers without which the Marketing Board for each product would have been ineffective and the 1933 Act smoothed this situation by empowering the restriction of imports of relevant products: an odd affair since few of the products concerned were subject to the competition of imports!

The Milk Marketing Board will serve to illustrate the tight cartel structure which has come to characterise the industry. All milk producers have to be registered with the Board, all milk has to be sold through the Board and all payments between farmers and distributors and between farmers and factories are made through the Board. Each farmer is paid at liquid and manufacturing prices in the same ratio as the total supply sold to the liquid and manufacturing markets. Although the scheme is operated on a regional basis there is an inter-regional compensation fund, which effectively, transfers money from farmers whose supplies mainly reach the fresh milk market to those who sell their product at very low industrial prices, thus preventing a flooding of the fresh milk market.

The various Marketing Boards were supposed to improve distribution and marketing, as their name implies, but their achievements in this field have not been on a significant scale. In fact in 1947 the Lucas Committee on the distribution and prices of agriculture products and the Williams Committee on milk distribution both, inter alia, suggested that produce monopolies were not the best way to improve marketing. However the farmers rallied to the support of the old-style boards which again became a feature of British Agriculture after their wartime suspension.

The provision of capital for farmers presents two sets of problems. In the first place, since the industry is largely based on family units there is no viable market for long-term capital. Nevertheless modernisation of even small farms is often beyond the means of family finance and this was recognised in the rather hopeful, generous 1972 Price Review award of an extra £72 millions per year which, it was hoped, would help the farmers, among other things, to put themselves in a competitive position so that the cost to the balance of payments of entering the E.E.C. might be reduced both by cutting imports of some products and expanding exports of others, particularly cattle products. However, an adequate capital market will only develop when sufficient large farms exist to make use of it.

The most active market for farmers' capital is, consequently, the short-term one. Farmers obtain a great deal of *trade credit* from their suppliers of seed, fertilisers and machinery. Sometimes advances are available for specific purposes through the Marketing Boards e.g. the Milk Marketing Board sells some dairy equipment and deducts its cost from the farmer's monthly milk cheque in instalments over 6 months.[1] Loans at 5 per cent interest are

[1] A. Martin, *Economics and Agriculture*, p. 135.

D

available for approved purposes through the Country Agricultural Committees. The Commercial Banks have special schemes for loans to farmers. The production cycle in farming, i.e. the long time between first incurring production costs and reaping any rewards, may necessitate a fairly specialised short-term capital market but it does not warrant any privilege of lower than market interest rates. This latter privilege is often dlaimed on the grounds of the alleged inability of the small family farm to pay market rates. This is just another example of the outlook which considers aid justified rather than reorganisation. If farmers do enjoy privileged rates then it means that the community's capital is deflected into agriculture from more profitable uses i.e. there is a misallocation of resources.

The Radcliffe Committee (1959) did not consider that there was any gap in the provision of short-term capital which needed filling by the government nor did it think that there was any justification for privileged rates of interest for farmers. The Committee's positive recommendations were that, on the one hand, farmers could be persuaded to understand more about and make more use of the credit facilities open to them and, on the other hand, that the banks could do more to offer farmers specific-term loans rather than overdraft facilities where this was suitable.

The Common Market

Entry into the E.E.C. will involve Britain abandoning her present support structure and adopting the continental one—an adaptation which was tentatively set in motion when minimum import prices for cereals were introduced in 1964. In the Common Market the basic assumption is that users should pay a price which will yield a "reasonable" income to farmers. (This compares with the traditional British policy of making up the price to that level by deficiency payments). In the E.E.C. the market is "managed" in order to achieve the results which have been attained in Britain by subsidies. Target prices are set for each main commodity and variable levies are charged on imports to raise their prices to the target price. For some commodities a supply price 5–10 per cent below the target price is fixed and any produce can be sold to the E.E.C. Agricultural Fund at that price. This support or intervention price has so far been considerably higher than the guaranteed price in Britain as regards soft wheat, barley, rye, beef and butter and, in general, it would seem as though British farmers would enjoy higher incomes under the European system.

The import levies collected in Britain would, on the basis of 1969 prices, amount to some £250–£300 million per annum and as these would have to be paid into the E.E.C. Agricultural Fund they do, at first sight, indicate a sizeable balance of payments problem. In fact this "guesstimate" does not take into account any variation between the British *regional target price* and the *basic target price* for the community as a whole which might be negotiated. Nor does it allow for the re-negotiation of world commodity schemes with higher support prices which would, of course, reduce the E.E.C. import levies by bringing the international and the European prices closer together. Finally the net balance of payments effect would be influenced by any increase in the exchange of farm produce between Britain and Europe.

The main danger of the E.E.C. system is the political pressure to set unrealistic target and intervention prices which would leave the Fund with accumulating surpluses, as it did in the case of butter during 1968 and 1969. Although the E.E.C. system is in itself just as harmful as the British in protecting the misallocation of resources it does contain a built-in provision for encouraging change. The Fund (the European Agricultural Guidance and Guarantee Fund) besides supporting certain prices also finances structural reforms in agriculture. The pressure of mounting surpluses when price supports are used could possibly act as a persistent incentive to fostering reform. British agriculture is already, on the average, more efficient than agriculture in most parts of the E.E.C. and should be able to make the transition without undue difficulty. Whatever the system of support the economic argument remains unchanged: the aim must be to increase efficiency and thus serve best both the consumers' interest in as cheap a product as possible and the farmers' interest in an income comparable with that obtainable for the same input of effort and skill in manufacturing industries.

The face of change

The economic argument against the prevailing patterns of support is that they lead to a wastage of scarce resources of both capital and labour. The agricultural labour force is shrinking faster than recruitment of young workers and this is partly because the starting wages of young workers in agriculture compare closely with those obtainable in manufacturing industries.[1] However, in the absence of a formal wages structure for the industry, the time soon comes when age for age the agricultural worker is considerably worse off than his manufacturing counterpart. He then joins the drift into largely unskilled work elsewhere, having missed the opportunity for training in other types of work. It is, of course, the sons of agricultural workers who are penalised by this process: why uproot oneself and leave one's family and rural neighbourhood if it doesn't immediately pay so to do?

A multiplicity of small farms means both too many managers and too much basic capital (buildings and machinery) in relation to the overall output of the industry. Given the high rate of technical improvement in farming, ever larger units and higher grade management are needed to take advantage of their unit-cost-lowering potential.

[1] M. C. Whitby, *Labour Mobility and Training in Agriculture* (*Westminster Bank Review*, August 1967).

The Mansholt Plans

It is interesting in this context to consider the trends in agricultural policy in the E.E.C. where the problem of adjustment is more acute than it has been in the U.K.

Table 2   The Agricultural Sector 1971

	Percentage of working population engaged in agriculture	Agricultural output as percentage of G.N.P.
Eire	28·4	19·7
Italy	21·5	11·0
France	15·0	6·0
Norway	14·7	6·5
Denmark	11·9	8·9
Luxembourg	11·6	6·2
Germany	9·6	3·6
Netherlands	7·5	7·0
Belgium	5·2	5·3
United Kingdom	2·9	3·0
U.S.A.	4·8	3·0

In Britain in 1970 agricultural employment represented about 3 per cent of the total workforce, in the Common Market the figure was 14 per cent, having fallen from 28 per cent in 1950 and 21 per cent in 1960. By 1980 the likely figures are 2·5 per cent for Britain and 6 per cent for "the Six". This trend is coming about largely under the influence of market forces: as manufacturing expands people leave agriculture to find better-paid work in the factories in the towns. This process does not take place tidily and without hardship and the European Commission is working to put agriculture in a sound economic basis which will yield adequate incomes for farmers by 1980 or thereabouts. The leading figure in this development planning has been Dr Sicco Mansholt. The first Mansholt Plan was rather too definitive and, therefore, brittle and met with little response. His second, produced in 1970, was much more flexible, depending more on credit facilities than direct payments to achieve its ends, and opening up the whole range of agricultural questions to continuing negotiation. The basic idea is to bring into being "farms which are in a position so as to achieve rational production", i.e. farms which can stand on their own feet without governmental support. The whole programme would be worked out within the framework of the Community's regional policy. The viable farms are seen as being on average much larger than at present: 200–300 acres for grains and root crops; 40–60 cows for dairy farming; 150–200 cattle for beef production; 100 000 chickens for poultry farmers; 10 000 laying hens for eggs production. The whole programme involves i) providing local manufacturing employment for displaced farmers and agricultural workers, ii) encouraging farmers to amalgamate into farming companies owned jointly by their constituent families, and iii) turning over some 12½ million acres of land from agriculture to forestry or recreation. There is no doubt that such a policy would be most helpful in dealing with the problems of agriculture in Britain and would remove the persistent tax burden of supporting the industry. For Europe as a whole there is need to escape from the embarrassing surpluses of dairy products produced by the existing policies both in the E.E.C. and in the U.K. However, the implementation of Mansholt's ideas is not assured. The point to be made is that official thinking on agriculture in the Common Market is, if anything, in advance of that in Britain and holds out considerable hope of establishing a sound industry, thus relieving the general public from the burden of supporting it.

Opportunity costs

Throughout the discussion of the economic aspects of agriculture or any other industry one is bound to come up against the recurring theme of

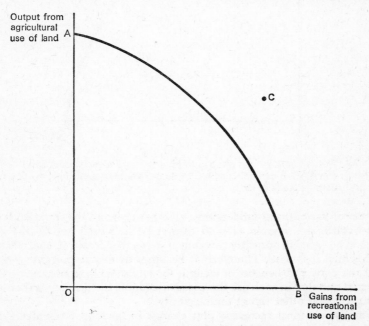

Fig 7.5 The community can choose to be anywhere along production possibility curve AB. It can only reach C by giving up some other use of land.

efficiency. This arises out of the fact that the use of any factors of production in farming denies them to the output of other things. In particular the use of land for farming denies its use for recreation, urban development and forestry. For each of these alternatives we could construct a production possibility curve AB, Fig 7.5, and because the amount of available land is fixed a community cannot push the curve outwards unless it forgoes one or both of the other alternatives. In Fig. 7.6 we set

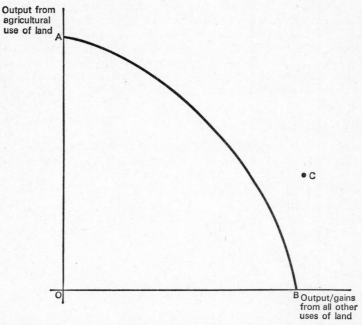

Fig 7.6 The community can choose to be anywhere along production possibility curve AB. It can only reach C by an increase in the efficiency with which it uses its stock of land.

the use of agricultural land against all other uses and the situation is even more stark, the amount of land cannot be increased and so the curve cannot be pushed outwards without a general increase in the efficiency with which it is used. Therefore, it becomes doubly important to ensure that the costs and benefits of using it for any other purpose are carefully assessed and that in each use there is no avoidable inefficiency as this means going without other things unnecessarily.

Finally, we must recognise that change in farming probably involves greater personal hardship than in most other industries because there are no similar occupations to which displaced farmers can transfer. This makes it imperative, from a social viewpoint, that an adequate proportion of the community's first fruits from change should be used to ensure that families which are adversly affected are recompensed, as fully as possible, by the provision of resettlement grants and pensions. In the end we shall surely arrive at large farms, it is better that the process be rational and humane than that it be a long-drawn-out, harrowing process such as has characterised agriculture in earlier periods of change.

QUESTIONS

What measures have British governments taken in recent decades to increase the prosperity of farming?

Compare the agricultural policies of a) the U.K. and b) the E.E.C. in the period 1957–71.

Give a critical account of British agricultural policy over the past fifty years.

Why did Britain's agricultural output expand in the years after 1945?

"The family farm is a thing of the past." Discuss.

Why did Britain develop a system of subsidising agricultural output?

Why do strongly fluctuating prices plague farmers?

Is it true to say that with less support for small farms Britain could produce more food?

Discuss the view that a thriving agriculture could and should stand on its own feet.

FURTHER READING

P. Self and H. Storing: *The State and the Farmer* (G. Allen and Unwin, 1962)
G. McCrone: *The Economics of Subsidising Agriculture* (G. Allen and Unwin, 1962)
Anne Martin: *Economics and Agriculture* (Routledge and Kegan Paul, 1958)
D. Metcalf: *The Economics of Agriculture* (Penguin, 1969)
D. Eltringham: *Agriculture* (Ginn, 1970)

8 The nationalised industries

Although examples of public corporations can be found before 1939—the Central Electricity Board was set up in 1926 and the B.B.C. in 1927—the most important period for the nationalisation of key industries in Britain came after the Second World War. During the first post-war Labour Government (1945–50), coal, electricity, transport, gas, and iron and steel were nationalised; three public corporations for air transport were set up; the capital of the Bank of England and of Cable & Wireless Ltd. was transferred to government nominees; and other public corporations were established, for example for cotton buying. Despite changes in detail— iron and steel was denationalised in 1953, and renationalised in 1967; long-distance road transport was also denationalised in 1953—the general pattern established during that period has persisted despite several changes of government.

Organisation of the nationalised industries

The organisation of the nationalised industries varies considerably from one public corporation to another. Coal has a monolithic structure—the National Coal Board took over all coal mines in 1947, and works through divisions, areas, groups and units. Electricity, on the other hand, is organised into a Central Electricity Generating Board, which is responsible for output, and Area Electricity Boards which are responsible for the distribution and sale of electricity.

Gas is different again; Area Gas Boards are responsible both for production and distribution. Since 1965, however, the Gas Council has been a trading body as well as a co-ordinating council, and this first function is likely to grow in importance with the development of natural gas.

Transport has undergone many reorganisations since nationalisation, but the essential change has been towards greater autonomy of the separate authorities. In the case of civil aviation there are two independent nationalised airlines.

Arguments for and against nationalisation

From the point of view of applied economics, there are many reasons put forward as to why a particular industry should or should not be nationalised.

1   A nationalised corporation is necessary to provide a product or service which would not otherwise be provided. The maximisation of profit would hardly lead private enterprise, for example, to link remote Cornish farms to the national electricity grid; nor to provide air services for the Scottish highlands and islands. Nevertheless, such services are held to be essential in the public interest. Thus a public body should provide them in the absence of private provision.

2   There comes a point when competition is wasteful, as in the case, for example, of rail transport between cities or a postal service to the public. The economies of scale are so great, or the amount of capital needed so large in such cases that duplication of their provision would be unnecessarily wasteful. A monopoly, however, in private hands might be too powerful or dangerous. Hence a monopoly under public control is taken to be the answer.

3   The reasons why a private monopoly might be dangerous include the temptation to restrict output and raise prices, the lack of accountability to the public at large, and the power which such an organisation could wield.

4   It may be impossible to raise the large amounts of capital involved from private sources. The coal, electricity and railway industries have all been involved in huge capital development programmes in recent years. Atomic energy production involves very large amounts of capital. Such capital is either not available from the private sector or carries too low a return to attract such investors. If the investment is essential (and most of it is in the nation's basic industries) it is only a public corporation that can finance it.

5   On the other hand, the nationalised corporation is accountable to no one. The private firm is restricted by market forces, by the need to make a profit, by the pattern of consumer demand. The public corporation has no such restrictions. It is not accountable to the public, who have to purchase its wares on a "take it or leave it" basis. It is not answerable to share-holders, for it has none. It is rarely answerable to politicians, who have no expertise capable of challenging that of the corporation. It may be answerable, in a vague way, to Parliament and to the appropriate Minister, but day-to-day running is specifically excluded from such supervision. In fact, the discipline of the market place is taken away and there is little to put in its place.

6   Such lack of accountability does not promote efficiency. If the private firm is inefficient, its competitors will succeed where it fails and it is likely to go out of business. But the nationalised industry cannot go out of business. It will be supported by the government and if necessary by a government subsidy. For the same reasons, public corporations are more likely to waste resources or money, since there is no market penalty for so doing.

7   Finally, the monopoly nature of the public corporation means that

there is no consumer choice. If a customer is dissatisfied with the telephone service he cannot switch to another firm. If he falls out with his Area Gas Board there is not another one round the corner. Of course, this fact arises wherever there is monopoly, private or public. There can be competition between industries, for example coal and gas, or between private and public provision, for example one's own motor car and railway travel. But basically, the consumer has no remedy. He can only choose to accept the service or do without it.

The general principles of operation of the nationalised industries

Initially, the nationalised industries were expected to follow the general commercial principle that revenues shall not be less than sufficient to meet outgoings which are properly chargeable to the revenue account, taking one year with another. These outgoings were intended to include interest, depreciation, and the provision of reserves. Unfortunately, this admirable commercial principle—that the nationalised industries should not lose money—has been blurred by a number of conflicting ideas.

For example, the nationalised industries should serve the "national interest". The electricity industry, for example, is required to extend electricity supply to rural areas as far as possible. It is also required to promote the welfare, health and safety of employees. In so far as this principle conflicts with the commercial principle it is not clear which is to be paramount.

Then we have the "social service" principle. This requires public corporations to provide uneconomic services because of public need. A prime example is the provision of unprofitable railway lines. Although many branch lines and stations have been closed as a result of the Beeching proposals, others, scheduled for closure on economic grounds, have been kept open in the interests of particular community needs. As a result, the losses incurred on such services must make more difficult the task of "breaking even" overall. Similar arguments apply to the inland telegram service, which is most uneconomic but which is maintained for social reasons, and to the domestic B.E.A. services to the Scottish highlands and islands which were mentioned on the previous page.

Further examples of principles which conflict with the commercial principle are:

a)   government pressures to aid wage restraint; ideally the corporations should be allowed to pay what they feel they can afford commercially, raising their charges accordingly as is the case in private industry.

b)   government control over capital expenditure, which may prevent badly needed renovation and development and so frustrate the realisation of a surplus: and, on the other hand, more favourable treatment by the government, for example, the protection of the domestic coal industry by the imposition of a tariff on oil imports.

Of course, one of the purposes of nationalisation is to realise certain social ideals rather than simply to make a profit. What is essential, however, is that the commercial principle, of breaking even, should be clearly distinguished from any other considerations, such as the public interest. It is then necessary to identify any non-economic factors, to allow for them and cost them separately and, preferably, to cover them by a separate public subsidy. If, for example, British Rail is required to keep open a particular branch line because the government feels that it serves a vital social need, then it is essential that the operating loss on that line should be identified, calculated and shown separately. Since such a loss hinders British Rail in its attempts to break even, it should ideally be covered by a public subsidy. In fact, the Transport Act of 1968 provided for just such a subsidy, to cover the cost of unremunerative but "necessary" passenger services.

Similar arguments apply to the pricing policies of public corporations. If, in the interests of a national policy, e.g. in order to combat inflation, an industry is refused a price increase which it considers necessary on commercial grounds, then the loss resulting from such a decision should be costed and shown separately. We shall then be able to see more clearly how the Board would have performed in a freer commercial atmosphere.

The pricing policy of the nationalised industries

In the early days of nationalised industries it was widely argued that the public corporations should deliberately keep their prices low in the interests of the public. They should be regarded, not as commercial undertakings providing a commodity or service at an economic price, but as organisations providing a public service at subsidised rates. While this principle is often adopted in the public sector, for example in education or national insurance, it is not generally applicable to the nationalised industries, although, as we have already seen, governments do tend to influence such bodies to keep their prices artificially low. If we accept the premises that, in general, prices charged by the public corporations should be economic, i.e. that they should cover costs with a reasonable margin for reserves, then it is worth examining in detail the principles on which public corporation pricing should be based.

The three main features of most nationalised industries are:

1   *A very high ratio of fixed to variable costs*
The provision of railway track, sidings, depots, stations and terminal buildings is very expensive in relation to the operating costs of running a train. The erection of power stations, the provision of cables, grids and wires is high in relation to the running costs of providing electricity. The

installation of telephone exchanges, cables, wires is costly when compared with the costs of running the telephone service. This common characteristic requires rather special pricing procedures.

2   A high degree of monopoly power

All nationalised industries are either complete monopolies in their sphere or are in control of a substantial section of the industry. The Coal Board monopolises the production of coal in the U.K. (but not its distribution). British Rail controls all rail travel (but not all internal travel). The B.B.C. is in sole control of internal broadcasting, at least at the time of writing,[1] and shares the television service with another public corporation, the Independent Television Authority. These examples are typical, and indicate that we cannot allow such bodies to charge monopoly prices. They also mean that there is no competitive market price to serve as a basis for comparison.

3   The requirement to promote the public interest

We have already considered this point in some detail, and have seen that the main effect is to keep prices lower than they would otherwise be, or to compel the public corporations to provide uneconomic services.

White Papers

Present thinking on the pricing policy of the nationalised industries is reflected in two White Papers. The first, Command 1337, *The Financial and Economic Obligations of the Nationalised Industries* (April, 1961), indicated that public corporations must have freedom to make upward price adjustments, especially when prices were artificially low. This was a step forward from immediate post-war thinking, but even so the realisation of the principle was still hampered by Ministerial influence.

The second White Paper, Command 3437, *Nationalised Industries: a Review of Economic and Financial Objectives* (November, 1967), went very much further. It argued that the nationalised industries should adopt pricing policies relevant to their economic circumstances. The commercial principle, that revenue should cover costs in full, was sound but not in itself enough. Prices in the public sector, as in the private sector, should attract resources to places where they could make the most effective contribution to meeting the demands of users. It was therefore essential that pricing policies should have reference to the costs of providing particular goods and services. Otherwise there was the risk of "undesirable cross-subsidisation". The consumer should pay the true cost of a service wherever this could be identified, or resources would be misallocated. By way of illustration: if it were found that the postal

[1] July, 1972.

service was running at a loss while the telephone service was making a handsome profit, the White Paper suggestion would mean, not that the telephone profit went to subsidise the postal service, but that either postal charges were raised to a more economic level so that users were paying the true cost or the service was reorganised in order to make it pay its way. Similarly, if the cost of providing commuter services was very high because of congestion or for other reasons, while the provision of off-peak travel was very cheap, the charges to commuters should be raised and perhaps those for off-peak journeys lowered considerably to redress the balance and to cost each separate service more realistically.

Although the general principle was to be a pricing policy related to costs, the White Paper admitted the existence of exceptions. There might be good commercial reasons for charging prices which differed from costs, perhaps to attract new customers. It may be impracticable in some cases to cost operations separately. This is particularly the case where over-heads cannot easily be distributed over a large number of diverse operations. On the other hand, cross-subsidisation may be justified in particular cases by statutory requirements or by some wider economic or social considerations. A further possibility was the existence of spare capacity for relatively long periods of time or at certain times, places, or seasons. Examples are the provision of electricity in off-peak periods, particularly during the night, or the existence of spare railway capacity during the non-rush hour periods. Such under-utilisation of capacity could be met by offering low price incentives to consumers to move to off-peak periods. Provided that such prices covered the variable costs incurred, they were justified on economic grounds. A related point concerns the very high proportion of fixed costs which is typical of many nationalised industries. The problem here is to spread such fixed costs over as wide an output as possible. One solution is the two-part tariff: the first x units at a high price, the subsequent units at a much lower rate; another, very similar, way out would be to make a fixed charge and add a variable charge (the procedure, for example, in the telephone service and increasingly with the gas and electricity boards). Such devices ensure a contribution, sometimes a large contribution, towards fixed costs, and further revenue to offset variable costs.

Basic principles

Bearing in mind all the above points the basic pricing principle should be that prices are reasonably related to costs at the margin. In the classic monopoly situation, the profit maximisation position occurs when marginal revenue is equal to marginal cost. In this situation, a monopolist can fix his price according to demand. A public corporation will ideally also fix output at the point where MR = MC but would fix price at a level somewhat lower than the monopolist would. Within an industry, if prices or charges

are related to the different marginal costs in different sectors of the industry, the more efficient use of resources will be encouraged. In the short
run, marginal costs are concerned only with variable costs; capacity is
taken as fixed. So that, for a short period, spare capacity can be utilised
by very low charges, since the marginal cost of (for example) an extra
passenger on a half-empty train is very low. Similarly, excess demand can
be penalised by very high charges, since the marginal cost of (for example)
extra electricity consumption at peak periods may be considerable. This,
however, deals with only the short period. In the long run, all costs
become variable. Provision must be made for the replacement of capital,
maintenance and interest on the capital invested. Consequently, long-run
marginal costs will be higher than in the spare capacity case above, but
lower than in the excess demand case. A long-run pricing policy must
therefore be aimed at continuing to supply services and products; prices
and charges will be related to long-term marginal costs where separate
costing is practical. There may be divergences from long-run costs for a
period because of transition problems but the relationship of charges to
long-run marginal costs is the ideal at which the public corporation
should aim.

As in any large scale, capital intensive industry, a public corporation
may be faced suddenly with new technological developments which
greatly reduce long-run marginal costs. The problem here is to make the
change gradual, not sudden. Pricing policy should be adapted to the
replacement of major assets over a period, not necessarily immediately.
This may, indeed, reflect the practical limits imposed on the rate of
modernisation by the availability of resources and so on.

Other difficulties in carrying out the marginal cost pricing principle
are, first, the lumpy nature of marginal costs. This means that the
determination of the extra cost attributable to one more unit of
output or service is very difficult or impossible. It is more logical, for
example, to talk about the marginal cost of an extra train (or, perhaps,
an extra coach on a train) rather than the marginal cost of carrying an
extra passenger. The solution here is to "average out" extra costs, which
may be inexact but which is at least practicable. Second, it may be difficult
to allocate costs to specific services or activities. Many fixed costs, as we
have already seen, appear to be indivisible, and any allocation to particular services must be arbitrary. Finally, any pricing policy must be modified
in the light of government policy for the public sector as a whole. Marginal
costs may be ascertained, prices may be provisionally fixed in the light
of such marginal costs, but a particular twist in government policy may
consider such prices too high and they may therefore have to be modified.

Conclusion

The conclusion of the 1967 White Paper was that managements should be
given the maximum discretion in adjusting their price structure to meet

Table 1

Passenger Transport in Great Britain

Estimated Passenger Mileage '000 millions

	1960	1961	1962	1963	1964	1965	1966	1967	1968	1969	1970
Total	158·6	167·6	173·0	180·2	196·3	206·7	216·0	227·3	236·0	242·5	253·7
Air	0·5	0·6	0·7	0·8	0·9	1·0	1·1	1·2	1·2	1·2	1·2
Rail	24·8	24·1	22·8	22·4	23·0	21·8	21·5	21·2	20·8	21·6	22·2
Road-PSV	43·9	43·1	42·4	41·5	40·3	39·2	37·5	37·0	36·3	35·7	34·1
Private Transport	89·4	99·8	107·1	115·5	132·1	144·7	155·9	167·9	177·7	184·0	196·2

Source: *Department of the Environment.*

Table 2

Goods Transport in Great Britain

Ton Miles ('000 millions)

	1960	1961	1962	1963	1964	1965	1966	1967	1968	1969	1970
Total	61·1	63·9	64·6	66·0	72·2	73·7	76·1	75·5	79·5	81·8	83·3
Road	30·1	32·3	33·6	35·1	40·2	42·1	44·8	45·6	48·3	49·3	50·8
Rail	18·7	17·6	16·1	15·4	16·1	15·4	14·8	13·6	14·7	15·3	16·4
Coastal shipping	11·9	13·5	14·3	14·9	15·1	15·3	15·5	15·2	15·0	14·8	14·2

Source: *Department of the Environment.*

Table 3   The Coal Industry. Production and Labour Force, Great Britain

	1963/4	1964/5	1965/6	1966/7	1967/8	1968/9	1969/70	1970/1
Total Saleable Mined Coal (million tons)	187·56	184·10	174·42	164·77	162·74	153·08	140·03	133·35
Total Wage Earners (thousands)	517·0	491·0	455·7	419·4	391·9	336·3	305·1	287·2
Output Per Man-Shift (cwt.)	33·4	34·8	36·1	36·6	39·0	42·5	43·4	44·2

Source: *Department of Trade and Industry.*

competition and to take advantage of commercial opportunities, within the framework of the general principles which it laid down. However, since price stability in this sector is of major importance to the economy, all major price increases proposed in the nationalised sector would be referred to the Prices and Incomes Board. The demise of this Board with the return of a Conservative government removes this sanction, but price increases are still subject to the over-riding authority of the appropriate Minister.[1]

[1] We have deliberately concentrated in this chapter on Pricing Policy as an illustration of the application of economic principles to the nationalised industries. The 1967 White Paper also proposed a test rate of discount (first 8 per cent, later raised to 10 per cent) to which projects submitted to the Government for approval should match up.

QUESTIONS

What is meant by "a nationalised industry"? Give a critical account of the development of any one nationalised industry.

What economic arguments are there for nationalising an industry?

What economic problems are associated with nationalisation? What light has British experience thrown on these problems?

Why have the nationalised industries in Britain often failed to make any profit?

What do you understand by the "social service principle" as applied to nationalised industries?

Is it true that problems of monopoly could be solved by nationalisation?

What is the "public interest"? Do you consider that a nationalised industry can serve the public interest better than a number of competitive private firms?

Should public transport in London be provided free?

Is marginal cost pricing the right policy for a nationalised industry?

REFERENCES AND FURTHER READING

Clegg and Chester: *The Future of Nationalisation* (Blackwell, 1953)
G. L. Reid & K. Allen: *Nationalised Industries* (Penguin, 1970)
F. R. Perrott: *Industry in the Public Sector* (Ginn, 1971)
P. Donaldson: *Guide to the British Economy* (Penguin, 1971)
White Papers: *Cmnd. 1337. The Financial & Economic Obligations of Nationalised Industries*, 1961
Cmnd. 3437. The Nationalised Industries; a review of Economic & Financial Objectives, 1967
Reports of the Select Committee on Nationalised Industries.
W. A. Robson: *Nationalised Industry and Public Ownership* (Allen & Unwin, 1960)
A. H. Hanson: *Nationalisation. A Book of Readings* (Allen & Unwin, 1963)
Ed. R. Turvey: *Public Enterprise* (Penguin Modern Economies, 1968)

9 Monopoly policy in Britain

The two faces of monopoly

A monopoly exists when a firm, or group of firms acting together, can exercise a dominant influence over the output and price of a product and therefore the level of profit earned. A monopoly may also exist in the supply of a factor of production as, for example, in the case of some trade unions which control the amount of labour available to a firm or industry; or in the *demand* for a good or service—this is sometimes termed a "monopsony".

When monopoly power resides in one firm we may speak of a *single firm monopoly* (sometimes called a "combine" or "trust"). Single firm monopoly sometimes involves a concentration of ownership which may be complete and obvious. Very often, however, it is hidden from view because a number of firms which have amalgamated continue to operate under their own names. Sometimes a company is set up with a controlling shareholding in a number of ostensibly "competing" firms. Another form of monopoly which is hard to detect is one that operates through inter-locking directorships, where a handful of men control most, or all, of an industry. When a group of independent firms collaborate to pursue monopolistic policies we use the term *cartel*. An important feature of cartels is the restrictive practices which they adopt to enforce their policies; these devices act partly as a "cement" which keeps the cartel intact against the various internal and external stresses which could undermine it.

The aim of monopoly policy

The essence of monopoly policy is to eliminate the disadvantages while retaining the advantages which may stem from the monopoly situation.

The main case against monopoly is that it tends to lead to a misallocation of the community's resources. In Fig 9.1 a monopoly in long-period equilibrium is depicted as operating at an output OQ_1 which a) is produced at less than minimum average costs and, therefore, at less than its most efficient output, OQ_2 b) yields it greater than normal profit i.e. profit in excess of that required to persuade it to continue in that line of business, and c) sells at a higher price per unit OP_3 than would be the case if it were operating at its most efficient output and earning only normal profit when price would be OP_1.

The inefficient use of resources which tends to result from the existence of monopoly is, in effect, a warping of the economy in the favour of producers and to the disadvantage of consumers whose interest lies in being able to choose between goods whose prices reflect their opportunity costs.

This contrasts with a firm working under conditions of perfect competition which would be in long-run equilibrium when its output is such

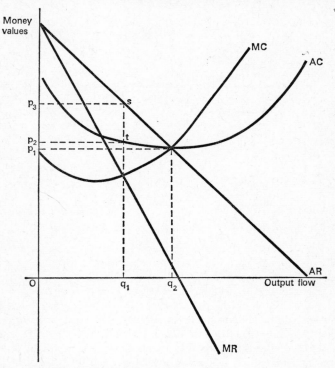

Fig 9.1 Long-period equilibrium of a monopoly

that its average costs are minimum and it is earning normal profit. This situation is demonstrated in Fig 9.2 in which i) the coincidence of the average and marginal revenue curves establishes the condition of perfect competition that price to the individual firm is fixed and, ii) the tangency of average revenue and average cost curves indicates that at output OQ the firm is making normal profit.

Since in the long-run average cost is at a minimum each firm will be making the most effective use of its factors of production. Moreover as marginal cost is equal to market price, each firm's resources are being put to the best use from the point of view of consumers, in the sense that the price they are prepared to pay for the marginal unit of production is equal to the (marginal) cost of producing it. Thus the opportunity cost of an extra unit of output is then equal to the value of it to the consumer. In this way, therefore, the community's resources would under perfect competition tend to be used in the most efficient manner.

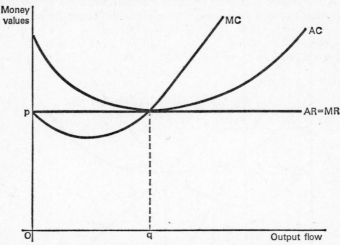

Fig 9.2 Long-period equilibrium of a firm in perfect competition

A monopolist's power to bend the market to his own advantage depends primarily on the inelasticity of market demand for his product: the greater this inelasticity the greater scope for the restriction of output, the raising of price per unit and, therefore, the earning of super-normal profit.

The tendency towards high-cost, high-price output restriction will for similar reasons also tend to occur under imperfect competition (where a number of "competing" firms in an industry all have weak "monopolies" in their own brands) and oligopoly (where a few very large firms "compete" in producing expensively advertised branded products).

The case for monopoly

However, it would be wrong to conclude that a monopoly is necessarily harmful. Mergers of firms may enable a resulting monopoly to take advantage of economies of large-scale production denied to smaller competing firms. The economies of scale, which need not be examined in detail here, are: technical; financial; marketing; risk-bearing; and managerial. When a firm becomes very large, however, managerial "diseconomies" occur. There tends, therefore, in any given industry, to be an intermediate "optimum" size of firm where the average cost structure is at a minimum. Thus the average cost curve of a large monopolist may be lower at maximum profit output than the minimum average costs of smaller competitive units. This is a possibility that must be considered when formulating policy but it must not blind us to the ever-present danger that the absence of the stimulus of competition may encourage the acceptance of a comfortable, inefficient high-cost structure even though the opportunities of economies of scale are present.

The other possible advantage of a monopoly situation is that it may favour the innovation of new production techniques. This view, which is associated with the name of J. A. Schumpeter, holds that what is really fundamental to the consumer's interest is not mainly the level of monopoly profit *but the level of monopoly costs*; and that the competition "in a given industry" which is described in theory textbooks only protects consumers against excessive prices *at a given level of costs*. According to Schumpeter what is crucial is not competition within the same industry *but between different industries*: competition which arises from new products and new techniques changing the whole cost structure of industry.

It is argued that the profits which a monopoly makes are an important source of finance for research and innovation; for only really large and secure firms, outside the threat of direct competition and thus with assured markets and prospective profits, are likely to risk the resources needed for developing new techniques and products. There is a continual cut-and-thrust between such firms, and, therefore, monopoly in any one field is seldom immune for long from attack from other firms in other fields.

Of course there are qualifications which could be made to this approach; in particular there is a good deal of evidence that many key innovations have come from research and development carried out by smaller firms. Even so there is little doubt that in an age of increasing technological complexity and widening international markets, Schumpeter's view carries considerable validity and is (or should be) relevant to monopoly policy.

The sources of monopoly power: barriers to entry

Monopolies depend for their existence on barriers to entry into their industries, for without these barriers a monopoly's super-normal profits would sooner or later attract new competing firms and erode its position and its excess profit. First there are *"natural" entry barriers*.

i)   a monopoly may maintain (or achieve) its position through the low costs of large-scale production which enable it to undercut, and perhaps take over, the smaller new entrant. This is likely when the plant in a given industry is specialised and expensive. "Octopoid" services like gas supply and postal services may well end up with a monopoly position, for duplication of their service by a competitor would be costly and unprofitable. This is why they have usually in the U.K. been taken into state ownership;

ii)   a monopoly position may rest on the control of some localised raw material;

iii)   a monopoly may derive from a restricted local market in which there is insufficient business to support a rival firm. This could be due to transport costs or tariff protection, for example.

There are also *deliberately erected barriers* intended to exclude competition:

i)   there are legal monopolies. These include the public utilities already mentioned as well as private firms holding a patent for a limited period of time;

ii)   a monopoly may deter competition by gaining control over retailers and insisting on a system of tied outlets, thus denying new firms a foothold in the industry;

iii)   a monopoly may set up a fighting company to market a brand at or below cost prices for as long as is necessary to break the will and profits of a smaller competitor;

iv)   it may deny the use of essential equipment to competitors.

Restrictive agreements of cartels

In addition, cartels have their own monopoly weapon in the form of restrictive agreements:

1   Unwritten "gentlemen's agreements" between firms regarding minimum prices, areas of sale and so on. These may take the form of price leadership: one firm's price is accepted by all the others as the cartel's minimum price.

2   Some cartels use formal agreements between member firms, in the form of complicated documents on prices, freight rates and so on. Also prices may be supported by output quotas sold, possibly, through a common agency.

3   Cartels may face problems of internal discipline; for while each member wishes the others to restrict output and respect price agreements, it will be tempted (especially if there is unused capacity in the industry) to undercut on price so as to sell a larger output. For this reason some cartels set up "courts" to impose fines, boycotts and other penalties on recalcitrant members who over-produce, cut prices, offer customer rebates and so on.

4   Some cartels use "pooled tenders", where members collaborate in secret to quote lowest prices in rotation for contracts; this also has the effect of undercutting and excluding outsiders.

5   Resale Price Maintenance (R.P.M.) may in its "collective" form act as a cartel-type restrictive agreement. R.P.M. is a system in which manu-

facturers enforce a minimum selling price on retail outlets selling their brands.

The 1948 Monopolies Commission

The first modern monopolies policy in Britain was introduced in the post-war period at a time when the new full employment and reconstruction policy demanded a production flow unhindered by restraints and distortions of monopoly influence.

In 1948 the *Monopolies and Restrictive Practices (Inquiry and Control) Act* made provision for a Monopolies Commission to investigate monopolies. This body, consisting of up to ten full members, was to be responsible to the Board of Trade in its work, and so an "administrative" rather than a "legal" approach on monopolies was chosen. Having been referred by the Board of Trade to an industry it was to investigate monopolistic tendencies and recommend the removal of practices considered to be against the public interest. But it was for the Board of Trade to decide what action (if any) to take on the Commission's recommendations.

For its definition of monopoly the Act took market control as its criterion: there was taken to be a *prima facie* case for investigation when in a given industry a single firm controlled one-third of total output, or where cartel agreements were seen to be operating. Bearing in mind the looseness of the term "industry" it is evident that the Act's scope theoretically covered a large part of (private) industry.

The working of the Monopolies Commission in the years after 1948 revealed important weaknesses. First, it was too slow. Only twenty monopolies, mainly cartels, were investigated between 1948 and 1956. The main reason for this was the small membership and resources of the Commission; even after the 1953 Act which enlarged it, the Commission was limited to a maximum membership of 25.

Secondly, the Commission had no "teeth": it had to rely on the Board of Trade to implement its findings. The Board was usually prepared to receive promises from firms that they would modify their practices which, being confident of no likely follow-up action, they freely gave. In one case where there was a follow-up (imported timber in 1958) it was found that the cartel had done little to implement its earlier assurance.

Thirdly, the scope of the policy was too limited for there were large sectors of the economy where the "search-light" of the Commission was not allowed to penetrate: public utilities, state cartels, the supply of services, and trade unions' restrictive practices. (The 1965 Act brought services into the Commission's ambit).

Fourthly, the Board of Trade was criticised for selecting trivial cases, such as light bulbs, linoleum and rubber footwear. The choice has been defended on the grounds that it built up experience on as wide a range of cases as possible.

Single firm monopoly policy

As far as single firm monopolies are concerned the Commission in its early years up to 1956, mainly investigated the restrictive agreements operated by them, rather than the structural damage due to monopoly dominance itself. A good instance was the 1955 investigation into the supply of industrial gases, which was dominated by one firm, British Oxygen. The Commission found that this firm had not been content to rely on its superior large-scale efficiency, but was deliberately suppressing potential competitors and earning excessive profit by its control of gas-making machinery, by take-over bids, by fighting subsidiaries, and through exclusive dealing. The Commission recommended that the Board of Trade should supervise British Oxygen's activities in order to prevent further abuses. But, significantly, it did not go as far as to recommend making the *structure* of the industry more competitive by unscrambling the dominant combine. Nor did it propose any other way of injecting competition.

In 1966 the Commission completed an investigation into the supply of colour film in Britain. It found that Kodak was supplying 70 per cent of the market and using its dominance to make excessive profit, for although Kodak's colour film business was only one-sixth of its business, it yielded one-third of its total profit. The high price of Kodak's colour film was also allowing retailers a profit margin of about 30 per cent on sales and processing. The Monopolies Commission proposed, *inter alia*, that the import tariff on colour film should be abolished so that continental firms which had already got a foothold in the British market, could expand their sales here and through their competition erode Kodak's monopoly. But the Board of Trade instead persuaded Kodak to reduce its retail price by $12\frac{1}{2}$ per cent with the object of reducing Kodak's excessive profit. This decision caused some surprise for the effect of it may have been to strengthen, rather than weaken, Kodak's monopoly. Inevitably Kodak's price cut was followed by its competitors, such as Ilford, but these were operating on a smaller scale of sales and had relatively high unit costs. They thus received a much greater setback to their profitability and expansion prospects than did Kodak. So probably the colour film market became less competitive and more monopolistic following the Board of Trade's policy! In the Kodak case then, the Board of Trade could be argued to have attacked the symptoms of monopoly (high profit) rather than the root cause; and in attacking Kodak's profits it weakened a magnet which had gradually been attracting new competition.

The problem of oligopoly

Let us consider another investigation by the Monopolies Commission—into household detergents in 1966, in which two "competing monopolies" (i.e. oligopolies), Anglo-Dutch Unilever and Proctor and Gamble of the

United States, dominated the market. In this type of situation each firm, fearful of provoking a damaging retaliation from the other if it cut prices, tends to "compete" by spending heavily on brand advertising so as to retain or expand its share of the market. The Commission recommended a substantial reduction on the two detergent firms' advertising, in order to allow lower prices. Unfortunately this attacked symptoms only and did not make for, or allow, lower prices through increased competition. On the contrary, as long as the oligopolistic market structure continued, the two firms would tend simply to use other, less effective forms of marketing than direct advertising and these would, if anything, tend to increase final costs and prices. After long negotiations the two firms agreed to market alternative "low-advertised" (but high quality) powders at a low price; but these lines were not much in demand by consumers. Evidently the connection between advertising, costs and prices in an oligopoly situation is complicated and until it is fully analysed the scope for monopolies policy in this direction will remain limited.

The problem of mergers

In many of its investigations into single firm monopolies the Monopolies Commission had been faced with the dilemma of dealing with a firm which through its size is relatively efficient and which, therefore, earns its super-normal profit not necessarily through operating restrictive agreements but primarily on account of its monopoly status. This dilemma was made more acute by a wave of mergers, some voluntary, others through aggressive take-over bids, in Britain in the 1960's. Some of these were probably an escape route out of the jaws of the Restrictive Practices Court and towards a new monopoly or oligopoly form; but others were a genuine attempt to achieve through size the economics of large-scale production.

The *1965 Monopolies and Mergers Act* gave the Board of Trade powers to delay and, on the advice of the investigating Monopolies Commission, to prohibit or dissolve a merger if it is found to create or strengthen a monopoly against the public interest. (The Commission was also given power to investigate monopoly structures and restrictive practices in the supply of services.) To perform these extra functions the Commission was enlarged to its 1953 maximum strength of 25 members. Its approach was to compare the efficiency benefits (if any) of the merger with the effects of the reduction in competition (if any). For example in rejecting the proposed merger between United Drapery Stores and Montague Burton, the multiple tailors, the Commission argued that the merger was unlikely to improve efficiency, but was likely to reduce competition and keep up prices. On the other hand, in five of the six other enquiries carried out by January 1968 the Commission found in favour of the proposed mergers.

One criticism of the 1965 Act was that the delay pending investigation leads to uncertainty for the parties to the merger. Another was that there is uncertainty in the minds of businessmen as to the principles on which the Board of Trade selects proposed mergers for investigation, which might deter some worthwhile mergers. No doubt as the policy develops this drawback should lose weight.

Summing up on single-firm monopolies

The experience of the Commission since 1948 shows that the single-firm type of monopoly is particularly difficult to deal with. It is possible to attack a cartel by banning its restrictive agreements; but it is not generally feasible to "ban" a single-firm monopoly by unscrambling it into smaller separate firms. Again, as we shall see, it is possible, with a "gateway/tail-piece" procedure, to attempt to assess the damage inflicted by a cartel; but it is much harder to determine whether a particular single-firm monopoly is operating a price/output policy which is on balance against the consumer's interest. These difficulties arise because in the case of a single-firm mono-poly there is really no alternative market structure which can be considered: changing the structure of an industry would disturb its efficiency. It is thus extremely difficult for the Commission in the case of a single-firm monopoly to prove that a modified market structure would be in the public interest.

Britsh policy on single-firm monopolies has reflected these difficulties by adopting a cautious, case-by-case approach which treats each case on its merit (or demerits). This contrasts interestingly with American policy which has always been to maintain competition by attacking all forms of monopoly through its anti-trust laws. Such a policy is more feasible in the huge United States home market, which has "room" for many large efficient competing firms, than in the much smaller British market.

The pricing policy of state-owned monopolies

There is a range of public utilities, such as gas and electricity supply, which fall into the category of "natural monopolies" since competition through duplication would be costly and unprofitable. In Britain most of these industries are operated as state-owned firms, which are to charge prices consistent not with maximum, super-normal profit but with the interest of the consumer, that is normal profit. If anything, the criticism of most of these "monopolies" would be that in order to deal with their competitors they have set their prices *too low* so that they have earned insufficient profit, and in some cases needed artificial support from the state. Thus the coal board has not only been subsidised out of the general public taxes but has also received protection against imported coal and oil fuel. Overall, the effect of this type of policy has been to prevent the release of resources to other, expanding sectors of the economy. In the case of British Rail the pricing policy has even caused a serious misallocation of resources within the railways themselves, as well as between different forms of transport. Some state firms, for example gas and electricity, even spend substantial sums on competitive advertising similar to that of the private oligopolies.

Moving on to the question of cost, there is little evidence that state firms have operated in the consumer's interest. The reasons for this is that, in the last resort, they have been indemnified against loss by the state. Under private ownership firms which go on making a loss must lower their costs or go out of business, but state firms have been denied this stimulus to efficiency, in some cases with disastrous consequences. Some state firms have been kept "competitive" by an inefficient use of massive investment at a rate of return which would have been too low to pay off under private ownership.

One possible answer might be to find some viable method of selling these firms back into private ownership where, incidentally, they would have the advantage in bad years of being able to shed losses by cutting shareholders' dividends, and where they would be subject to the scrutiny of monopoly policy. On the other hand the present structure of state ownership could perhaps be efficient, provided that state firms are made to compete on equal terms with private firms in the open market for their investment resources and other factors of production. A third possible approach would be to follow the Italian pattern of allowing utility-type "monopolies" to remain nominally in private ownership but to submit them to direct control through state ownership of part of their share capital. The question of how the state takes potential monopolies into public ownership or control is therefore a complex one, and needs to be related carefully to every aspect of monopoly policy.

The problem of cartels

The Monopolies Commission investigated and criticised in its first eight years of operation, a number of cartel activities. However, the main policy on restrictive practices dates from 1956, when the *Restrictive Trade Practices Act* was passed. Part Three of this Act dealt with the continuing role of the Monopolies Commission vis-à-vis single firm monopolies. Part Two, which covered resale price maintenance, we shall look at later. Part One dealt with restrictive practices. Its central feature was the setting up of a new monopolies body called the *Restrictive Practices Court*. The Court consists of five High Court judges, assisted by ten laymen including economists. It is provisionally assumed by the Court that any restrictive agreement brought before it is against the public interest: restrictive agreements are thus "guilty unless proved innocent". The Act lays down that all firms using restrictive agreements must register them with the "Registrar", who examines them and selects cases for presentation to the court. To this extent therefore he acts in effect as a prosecutor. The procedure followed is that of an ordinary court of law, based on cross examination of expert witnesses. In the case of cartels then, Britain's policy is based on a hostile, legal approach aimed at maintaining competition, although it does not go as far as in the United States, where *all* restrictive agreements are illegal.

The seven gateways

The Act gives the judges in the Court various economic criteria for testing any possible benefits of cartel agreements—the so-called "gateways". It is for the cartel operating the agreement to prove that it yields one or more of these benefits. They are that an agreement:

1   protects the safety of the consuming public;
2   makes other specific and substantial benefits available to the public;
3   is a defence to counteract a restrictive practice operated by some other monopoly;
4   is a defence to counteract market dominance by some other monopoly;
5   prevents serious and persistent local unemployment in an area dependent on that trade;
6   substantially assists export earnings;
7   supports some other restrictive agreement which the Court has already accepted as beneficial to the consuming public.
8   In the *1968 Restrictive Practices Act* an eighth gateway was added: that the agreement does not materially restrict or discourage competition.

However even if the Court does accept that there are one or more benefits of this type it is still required to balance these against the general damage the agreement is assumed to inflict by restricting competition; this is the so-called "tailpiece" of the Court's judgement. For example in the 1959 case of the Yarn Spinners' cartel, the Court, although it accepted that without the price agreement there would be significant local unemployment, nevertheless concluded that the general damage outweighed this benefit and, therefore, that it was contrary to the public interest and must cease.

On the other hand some restrictive agreements were approved by the Court. One of these was the system of price-fixing for glazed and floor tiles which, the judges accepted, allowed firms to standardise their products and reduce their costs. In the permanent magnets case the members of a cartel successfully defended their price agreement as a support for the exchange of individual research activities, the pooling of patents, and the running of a central research laboratory: price competition, it was argued, would weaken technical co-operation. A third case was that of the import cartel for sulphuric acid; the Court accepted that this was a necessary defence against the dominance of the American export cartel, Sulexco.

None the less, of the 2300 agreements which were on the register by 1960 nearly one-half were abandoned or modified by the cartels operating them, and by June 1963 the proportion had risen to two-thirds. This high rate of success was achieved by a kind of "domino effect". Only eleven cases had actually been contested in the full Court by 1960, but ten of these had been outlawed, and this had set up a chain reaction as other cartels using similar agreements changed or abandoned them.

How effective has the Court been?

On the whole the Restrictive Practices Court has been fairly effective against cartel agreements and has shown the value of a "legal", open court approach in which the law is demonstrably hostile to most restrictive practices. One weakness however was that many firms realised that they had nothing to lose (legally) by not registering, and this placed the onus of enforcement on the Registrar. Secondly, the 1956 definition of a restrictive practice was not wide enough to include most open agreements on price, etc. even though these can in fact be used to restrict competition. However the 1968 Act tightened up on these two weaknesses by imposing a time limit for registration, and penalties for non-registration; and by making information agreements registrable. Thirdly, a cartel can continue to operate a registered agreement for perhaps several years, and then finally abandon it only when the Court is about to initiate proceedings. There is therefore a possible case, since most agreements are harmful and few beneficial, for legally banning *all* restrictive agreements.

There was also a tendency for cartels to evade the hostile attitude of the Court by merging their member firms into a single firm monopoly, which would be subject to the weaker control of the Monopolies Commission. (In 1965 the Monopolies and Mergers Act was passed partly to frustrate such mergers).

Although the Restrictive Practices Court has had considerable impact in the field of private industry, we must not forget that in the last resort the degree of free competition in a given industry reflects its businessmen's attitudes to competition at least as much as the market structure brought about by government policy. If firms are fearful of open competition, and if they instinctively collaborate when under pressure, the influence of policy will be slow to operate. However, many businessmen seem to be sensitive to public opinion and the impact of the 1956 Act, leading in one case in 1968 to an Old Bailey criminal prosecution of two electrical firms, provided a healthy stimulus towards more competitive attitudes in industry.

Part Two of the 1956 Act: Resale Price Maintenance

The 1956 Act classified R.P.M. into two categories: *individual R.P.M.* under which one manufacturer alone enforces a set of minimum prices on the shops or other retail outlets distributing his product; and *collective R.P.M.* in which a group of manufacturers, acting as a cartel, enforce minimum resale prices on their retailers.

In Britain resale price maintenance developed before the First World War when many small retailers, wanting some defence against competition from the new and more efficient multiple stores, succeeded in persuading various manufacturers to enforce minimum retail prices. (As time went by many manufacturers themselves came to see that minimum retail prices could be used as a device for restricting competition between themselves—as well as between retailers.)

The 1956 Act made collectively enforced R.P.M. illegal. On the other hand individual R.P.M. agreements, between a single manufacturer and his sales outlets, were allowed and indeed given the added force of legally enforceable contracts; under the 1956 Act manufacturers could, and did, take price-cutting retailers to a law-court.

Thus the 1956 policy while hostile to cartel-type collective R.P.M. was not in principle against minimum retail price agreements. Indeed it probably reflected the fact that a number of advantages were often claimed for R.P.M.:

i)   a minimum common retail price gives manufacturers an incentive to maintain high quality products;
ii)   the retailer, having an ample margin, can provide customers services (credit, free delivery, etc.);
iii)   the abolition of R.P.M. would inconvenience the consumer by driving many retailers out of business. (The "advantages" were in due course to be embodied in the "gateways" of the 1964 Resale Prices Act).

It is clear, however, that this type of defence is spurious because the so-called advantages are all obtained at the expense of the customer, without his consent, in the form of higher prices. It is better to let the customers choose for themselves: better "services" or lower prices? Since the 1964 Act they have mainly chosen the latter.

A fundamental drawback of R.P.M. is that it protects high cost retailers from direct price competition from low cost retailers, and so hampers the transfer of consumers' business from the one to the other. It therefore leads to the employment of excessive resources in retailing.

The uneasy ambivalence of the 1956 policy in R.P.M. was later resolved in the 1964 Resale Prices Act, which took place against a rapidly changing retail background.

The post-war revolution in British retailing

This has taken the form of the growth of large retailers such as supermarkets, discount stores and mail order firms which eliminate costly "services" and which rely on exploiting the economics of bulk buying and selling. This makes it possible for them to operate on small margins and pass their lower costs to the public in the form of lower prices, unless they are frustrated by legally enforceable R.P.M. In the case of the supermarkets the self-service layout has proved attractive and efficient. So the large retailers have been providing an ever-increasing share of the manufacturers' business. In the late 1950's retail warfare broke out, and by 1964 more than 200 injunctions had been obtained under the 1956 Act against the price-cutters. For example in 1962 Kayser Bondor successfully took Tesco to court to prevent that firm from selling its women's stockings and underwear at cut-prices.

It was against this background that the *1964 Resale Prices Act* was passed. The main effect was to place individual R.P.M. in the same sort of category as other restrictive agreements. Firms wishing to continue using R.P.M. have to register with the Registrar of Restrictive Practices, who is empowered to refer cases to the Court. Firms are allowed to continue using R.P.M. until the Court has pronounced on their application. There are five gateways under which exemption may be applied for:

1) that the quality of goods and their variety would be substantially reduced by the abolition of R.P.M.;
2) that the number of retail outlets selling the goods would be substantially cut;
3) that retail prices would be increased in the long run;
4) that goods would be sold under conditions dangerous to health;
5) that after-sales services would cease or be substantially reduced.

There is also a tailpiece: the Court has to be satisfied that any benefits proved under the gateways will outweigh the detriment due to restricting competition. In cases where the Court bans R.P.M. a manufacturer may not withhold supplies from cut-price retailers, with the exception of a retailer using a product as a "loss-leader".

The first case heard by the Court, in the summer of 1967, was R.P.M. in the sale of sweets and chocolates (though even before then firms in the furniture industry, sensing the shape of things to come, had abandoned minimum prices). The confectionery manufacturers argued that the opportunities for price cutting were slight and that without R.P.M. the consumer public would suffer from a reduced variety of goods and number of shops, but the Court ruled R.P.M. in confectionery illegal. In the next few years the Court was to reach the same verdict in case after case: the general effect of minimum prices in restricting retail competition outweighed any incidental benefits. The effect of ending maintained prices has varied from product to product. In some fields little or no price-competition developed, for example cosmetics and office equipment. In others, such as wines and spirits, cigarettes and paint, price-cutting was widespread and fierce. In fact in the course of one year (1968) the supermarkets increased their share of cigarette sales from $3\frac{1}{2}$ per cent to 10 per cent!

As in the case of other restrictive agreements, much depends on the attitudes of businessmen towards price competition. A good example of this arises in connection with manufacturers' "recommended" prices, which in some goods began to replace R.P.M. as a minimum price instrument accepted by retailers. Also, there was evidence that some manufacturers were denying supplies to aggressive price-cutting retailers.

The effects of competition on the small retailer

The 1966 Census of Production showed the number of shops was falling, and this trend has continued. Partly this was due to the Selective Employment Tax, but the ending of R.P.M. has probably played its part. A good many small shops have survived, however, by improving their efficiency in response to competition. One vehicle for this has been voluntary retailer chains (e.g. Spar) which have made available bulk buying to small retailers in food, wallpaper, paint etc. Even so, a good many small retailers, reluctant to shed any independence, have kept out of such chains. Another development has been the growth of "self-service" cash-and-carry wholesale warehouses for grocers, chemists and others; in these the small retailer can buy cheaply by avoiding the costs of delivery, sales representatives, credit and paper work. Some small retailers, again, have exploited their ability to give the customer good personal service and flexible shopping hours. The same applies to mobile "shops". Probably a balance will be reached in which a good many smaller, flexible, specialist retailers will, by exploiting their advantages continue to survive against the multiple stores, the discount stores, the mail order houses, and the supermarkets.

In conclusion

Monopoly policy should not only prevent or eradicate the direct damage done by the exercise of monopoly power; ideally it should be able to analyse (possibly along Schumpeter-type lines) the general impact of a lack of competition on economic growth: the effects on profit levels, research, investment, and other factors affecting the costs of existing and new products. Unfortunately the Commission and the Court have seldom adopted, or perhaps felt competent to adopt, this macro-economic approach. Also there is some doubt whether for legal framework a monopoly policy is really suitable, as it might prove difficult for high court judges to handle complex economic analysis.

As far as the scope of U.K. monopoly policy is concerned the most serious weakness is that large sectors of the economy are still outside its ambit, for although the 1965 Act brought professions and other services into monopoly policy, it still does not cover state-owned industries; official cartels (such as the agricultural marketing boards); or the trade unions.

In the end the solution to the monopoly rests on the development of competitive business attitudes, and the policy since 1948 has probably helped to bring about a more conducive climate in this respect. Also, we can in any case expect the British economy (especially when we enter E.E.C.) to be subject to increasingly competitive pressures, including those areas which have long been artificially protected (e.g. coal and agriculture). Perhaps, then, we should agree with the old saying, "The tariff is the mother of monopoly" and conclude by adding "and free trade the father of competition".

QUESTIONS
What are the economic arguments for state control of monopolies?

Are measures designed to restrict competition ever in the public interest?

What are the arguments for and against mergers?

How effective has British anti-monopoly legislation been?

What do you understand by "restrictive practices"? How does the Restrictive Practices Court function?

Should all price agreements between firms be condemned?

Why has Resale Price Maintenance been held to be against the public interest?

What are the main principles on which restrictive practices legislation in the U.K. is based?

What are "take-over bids"? Should the government seek to prevent them?

Discuss the economic advantages and disadvantages of single-firm monopolies compared with cartels.

What are the sources of monopoly power?

REFERENCES AND FURTHER READING
G. C. Allen: *Monopoly and Restrictive Practices* (Allen and Unwin, 1968)

D. Lee, V. Anthony and A. Skuse: *Monopoly* (Heinemann, 1968)

G. C. Allen: *The Structure of British Industry* (Longmans, 1970)

G. Cyriax and R. Schaffer: *Monopoly and Competition* (Longmans and I.E.A., 1970)

P. Noble: *Markets and the Entrepreneur* (Longmans and I.E.A., 1970)

R. B. Stevens and B. S. Yamey: *The Restrictive Practices Court* (Weidenfeld and Nicolson, 1965)

10 Regional policy

New industries rarely grow up in the areas in which old established industries have been concentrated. This feature of economic development has frequently led to the decay of the older industrial centres, sometimes causing great hardship to those engaged in the declining industries. As long as manufacturing was conducted on a domestic basis, or factories were relatively small and any one industry accounted for a relatively small proportion of the working population in any area, the hardship inflicted by that industry's decline or change of location could be accepted as just one more of life's trials. In a highly industrialised society, however where the decline of a localised industry puts a large percentage of a locality's labour force out of work the problem attracts public attention and provokes governmental action.

Twentieth century Britain has experienced the decline of nineteenth-century industries centred on the coal-fields. They concentrated in those areas because of the large amount of coal required to fire their furnaces for the generation of steam power or for heat. Some of these industries declined because of the emergence of new products or of successful competitors elsewhere and some declined because new locational factors made new areas more attractive. Whatever the reasons, areas like South Wales, Flintshire in North Wales, much of Lancashire, West Cumberland, Tyneside and Central Scotland felt the clammy hand of decay on their shoulders. Throughout the old industrial areas, whether or not they were in actual decline, the inheritance of streets of close-packed rows of small, terraced houses without gardens lining drab streets and clustering round dingy, dominating mills and, all too often, set in a wilderness of slag heaps created an air of decay. Inhabitants of these areas and commentators might recite the ritualistic "where there's muck there's brass" but this could only be a cheerful "face saver" when new, wealthier areas were springing up built to twentieth century standards in other parts of the country. These new areas were not by any means remarkable for their beauty or orderliness, there was no wide scale attempt to plan new development until the second half of the century, but they had a remarkably fresh appearance by comparison with the older areas.

Even towards the last quarter of the twentieth century there is little being done to tackle this basic problem of refurbishing the older industrial areas. Attention remains riveted primarily on dealing with the structural unemployment found in some of them. Vast amounts of money have been

spent in trying to revitalise the industrial structure of the affected areas
and many Acts of Parliament dealing with them have been passed, but
they still remain in need of help.

Policy guidelines

It is a commonplace in trades union and other circles that "work should
be taken to the workers and not the workers made to go to the work".
The reasoning behind this is that labour is very immobile and that moving
to new regions is a hardship which, it is thought, society should prevent
by directing new industrial ventures to the places of heavier than average
unemployment.

In fact labour seems to be quite mobile between regions.[1] The geographical mobility of workpeople is not a one-way migration and so we
must beware of interpreting the net movement out of some of the older
industrial areas as being just a matter of the unemployed going in search
of work. Occupational mobility is also higher than is often credited,[2] and
thus the considerable movement of people between jobs and places
suggests that a policy of helping workers to migrate to regions where there
is labour scarcity would, in fact, be justifiable on humanitarian as well as
economic grounds. Oddly enough it is the latter which are suspect.

When people leave an area their purchasing power moves out with
them and so net emigration means a net loss of purchasing power. The
demand for labour to supply local wants is likely to fall, thus accentuating
the problems of localised unemployment. On the other hand, the receiving
areas will enjoy a rise in local purchasing power and the demand for
labour is likely to rise. Thus the discrepancy between the low and the
high levels of unemployment in different regions may be perpetuated and
even increased. An additional factor suggesting the likelihood of this
continued gulf is the increase in investment in housing and general infrastructure stimulated by immigration and the obvious lack of the need for
such additions to social capital that will characterise declining regions.
In the former case there will be an upward multiplier effect on incomes
thus perpetuating the high demand for labour.

This analysis may make us feel that the accepted policy of directing
work to the workers is right even though its usual justifications do not
hold good.

The maintenance of a wide geographical dispersion of population is
usually accepted as desirable, partly to avoid the growing congestion of a
few great conurbations and partly to maintain some active population in
the rest of the country. How far these matters are economic it is difficult
to judge. Congestion does bring added costs to transport. Dense population

[1] Lionel Needleman in *Lloyds Bank Review*, January 1965, and A. P. Thirwall in
Westminster Bank Review, November 1966.
[2] idem.

does put up housing costs. Similarly, a lack of enough people makes the provision of some services uneconomic. On these grounds it can be reasoned that the direction of work to declining areas saves costs both in those areas and in the new, expanding areas. Of course, it might be better to develop new growth centres near to the declining areas rather than to try to breathe fresh life into the old areas themselves. The latter and traditional course may be doomed to failure from the start however much is spent on it.

Policy concerning the location of industry can be influenced by the assumption that firms know what is best for themselves. This involves an assumption that their sole objective is to maximise profits and therefore, by implication, to make the best use of the community's relatively scarce resources. It would seem, in fact, that firms rarely make a careful study of locational factors.[1] Left to their own devices they meet any necessity for building new premises by looking around their own neighbourhood and opt for the first reasonable site they can find. This results from coming fairly quickly on the need for extra plant and, therefore, having little time for, as well as little or no expertise in, location costing. Moreover the greater the distance between the existing site and the new site the more difficult is the task of co-operation, administration and, perhaps, integration. Thus firms cannot act rationally, in the economic sense, in these matters and there are also non-economic considerations which weigh heavily in their decision making. The attachment of key personnel to the existing area: the actual or fancied benefits of the association of the firm with the name of the locality; a dislike of moving to relatively unknown districts; a fear that away from the known environment all sorts of new problems will arise. All of which again underlines the necessity of reminding ourselves that we are studying the activities of human beings not economic automatons. We talk of enterprise but it is quite natural that firms should have no more enterprise than any other human institutions. We may deduce that if we wish to see an efficient industrial framework we may have to do a lot of work to show firms the facts in connection with locational costs and exercise considerable pressure to make them behave in the way which is traditionally attributed to them!

Regionalism

A final piece of current conventional wisdom that we might inspect is the opinion that regional problems are best dealt with by the regions concerned rather than by the central government. Whether or not this philosophy is sound in social and political matters, there must be great scepticism about its relevance to economic affairs. When we look around the world at large we are bound to notice that the poorer countries of the

[1] B. J. Loasby in *Lloyds Bank Review*, January, 1967.

world are in desperate need of outside help in order to get on to an adequate growth path and thus attain an acceptable standard of living. Only too often the countries from which aid flows complain that some of it is wasted on prestige objects and usually the recipients struggle under the feeling that the aid given is too meagre to enable them to cope with their problems. Why should we expect a different state of affairs to exist between regions within a country? Can we expect the central government to provide funds, a good deal of which will be siphoned from wealthy areas, for the poorer regions to use at their own discretion? If this did happen would not the poorer regions always feel inadequately aided and yet be looked upon as potential if not actual wastrels by the rest of the community? Each region would feel that its duty lay in promoting growth within its own boundaries whereas it might sometimes be the case that the most sensible thing was to de-industrialise it and disperse the bulk of its population. In a free society the latter policy would be ruled out by any regional authority; local pride would frown on such a notion. There would be a greater danger of balkanisation and a consequent misallocation of resources. One line of approach might be along that of the T.V.A.,[1] i.e. the setting up of semi-autonomous regional authorities operating on a fairly clearly fixed budget and centrally approved line of attack. Alternatively, a Colombo Plan approach might work: the regional authorities discussing their plans and working out the possible degrees of mutual co-operation and the amount of "outside" help needed.

Whichever way we look at it the matter is more complicated than it seems at first sight. The counsel of perfection is probably to determine the principal growth points in the country for the immediate future and to encourage the movement both of firms and people to those areas. This would involve positive inducements to move such as creating attractive economic, social and cultural infrastructures as well as offering financial, re-training and housing aids. It would also be necessary to have penalties for staying in or setting up in congested areas and positive plans for re-shaping the older industrial areas. However, rather than develop this line of thought in any detail it will be rewarding to consider how regional policy has evolved in the U.K.

Beginnings of policy in U.K.

In the U.K. a high disparity in the regional levels of unemployed emerged in the 1920's with the decline of the older industries and the first reaction of the State was to help people to move to the more prosperous areas of the country. People willing to move were offered financial help by the Ministry of Labour, some provision was made for re-training to help mobility and further assistance was given by the *Industrial Transference Board* set up in

[1] Tennessee Valley Authority in the U.S.A.

1928. In the following year the *De-Rating Act* sought to eliminate the disparity in local rates between the declining and the growth areas of the country: it being held that the higher rates in the former, necessitated by providing both for the unemployed and for the usual services from a diminishing amount of occupied property, were contributing to the failure of new industry to establish itself in them. De-rating was probably irrelevant because rates constitute such a small part of a firm's costs. The encouragement of labour to move out of the areas, if effective, would have had a cumulatively depressing effect through the multiplier effect of withdrawn incomes.

In 1934 the *Special Areas (Development and Improvement) Act* introduced a new approach which was to influence all subsequent action *viz*, the encouragement of firms to move into the depressed areas. Four *special areas* were designated: South Wales, West Cumberland, Central Scotland and the North-East Coast of England, and within these financial assistance was made available for economic and social improvements and for retraining the unemployed. In 1936 a second Act provided for the establishment of government trading estates on which factories would be built to be rented out and for financial inducements such as low interest loans, subsidised rents and rate and tax reliefs to be offered to firms setting up in the areas.

Development Areas

This line of thought was crystallised in the 1940 *Barlow Report* on the Distribution of Industrial Population. The concentration of two fifths of the population in seven large conurbations, castigated as "sprawling agglomerations of humanity", was judged to be economically, socially and strategically undesirable. Hence it was suggested that the further industrial development of these conurbations, particularly London, should be restricted and that a reasonable balance of industrial development between regions and the diversification of industry within each region should be encouraged. The path had been chosen and the return of peace witnessed a spate of Acts designed to implement the choice.

In 1945 the *Distribution of Industry Act* re-named the previously designated areas as Development Areas: these were somewhat wider in exent and included the large towns of the region; financial aid was extended to include firms already established in the areas. An important instrument of control was added in the form of Industrial Development Certificates by the *Town and Country Planning Act* of 1947. Before any new premises of over 5000 square feet could be built an I.D.C.[1] had to be obtained from the Board of Trade which usually made one more readily available to firms willing to build in a Development Area. The *Distribution of Industry Act 1950* increased the amount of financial aid available for loans and

---

[1] Industrial Development Certificate.

grants, for assisting with the cost of moving plant and machinery, and for moving and resettling key workers. This renewed pressure followed a decline in the proportion of new factory building going to the Development Areas after 1948.

The rather simple pattern which had dominated thinking in these matters was disturbed in the 1950's by the discernment of pockets of higher-than-average unemployment in places outside the Development Areas. There was also a first official realisation that non-industrial activity might be as useful as industrial activity in creating jobs—there could be brass without muck! The *1958 Distribution of Industry (Industrial Finance) Act* accordingly extended aid to any firm, industrial or non-industrial, which might raise the level of employment in any place where unemployment was or was deemed likely to become particularly high.

Development Districts

This new trend took over completely in 1960 when the *Local Employment Act* abolished the Development Areas which, in the intervening years since their inception had increased to nine in number: South Lancashire, North East Lancashire, Merseyside, Wrexham, and North-East Scotland having been added to the original four. By this Act any area of high or potentially high unemployment could be designated a Development District and become eligible for the now traditional forms of aid. Some of the Districts were much larger than the old Development Areas and many were much smaller. In 1963 another Local Employment Act increased aid to include a 10 per cent grant towards the cost of non-movable plant and machinery and a 25 per cent grant towards the cost of buildings for firms in the Development Districts. The Budget of the same year enabled firms in the Districts to set aside depreciation allowances for their capital as deductions against revenue when estimating their tax liabilities at whatever rates they chose instead of being limited by the Inland Revenue to stated percentages.

This piecemeal approach resulted in a proliferation of Development Districts to over 160 in number which was clearly out of keeping with the overall idea of attacking large concentrations of heavier-than-average unemployment resulting from declining industries. On the other hand it widened the scope of aid to include non-growth areas such as the South Western peninsula of England, Pembrokeshire and parts of North Wales and the Highlands of Scotland and the Orkney and Shetland Isles. This rather odd combination of a wider view of structural unemployment but a narrower definition of the size of a District was not likely to persist for long and minds were turning to "new" concepts during the early 1960's: Regional policy was born.

Regional policy

The *1964 Industrial Training Act* gave renewed blessing to the idea of increasing labour mobility through re-training. This aspect of policy has never received the amount of attention that it might have done because of the general bias against expecting workers to change jobs or habitat. Gradually it may be coming to be realised that a fairly high mobility of labour, particularly occupational mobility, is not only helpful in stimulating economic activity in an area but also in securing greater security and a higher standard of living for the individuals concerned.

The Regional flag was nailed to the mast in 1964 when Regional Planning Areas were established but two years were to elapse before there was any effective change of course.

In the meantime a new importance was given to those physical controls which had erstwhile been thought of as pulling industry towards areas of high unemployment. There had long been a school of thought that the deterrent effect of the measures on building in the high-growth areas was inadequate. In 1965 the *Control of Office Development (Designation of Areas) Order* put restrictions on the development of office buildings within forty miles of London and within the vicinity of Birmingham. This picked up the earlier idea that office building in unemployment areas could be as beneficial as, and perhaps better than industrial building in providing jobs. In the same year the *Town and Country Planning (I.D.C.) Exemption Order* brought the exemption limit for obtaining an I.D.C. down to 1000 square feet for much of South-Eastern England and the Midlands. Here again we see the application of pressure to push new investment to less congested areas.

Before a wider, regional outlook could become effective it was necessary to reverse the balkanisation implicit in Development Districts and return to the concept of Development Areas. The 1966 *Industrial Development Act* abolished the Districts and created five large Development Areas. These covered most of Scotland, a large part of Wales, Cornwall and North Devon, Merseyside and the Northern Planning Region together with the Furness Peninsula. The usual mixture of grants was applied: i) investment grants at 40 per cent compared with 20 per cent in the rest of the country; ii) building grants at 25 per cent; iii) grants for plant and machinery; iv) grants for training workers; v) grants for key workers; vi) grants to local authorities for up to 85 per cent of the cost of improvements in their services. Government Training Centres to increase the occupational mobility of labour in the areas and the use of I.D.C's to encourage firms to site new premises in the Areas: these completed the bag of the "powerful range of incentives to economic expansion and modernisation".[1]

[1] Broadsheet on Britain D.E.A. No. 16. 1968.

Economic planning regions

The completion of the picture lies in the tying up of this fairly traditional approach with regionalism which had been born in 1964. Within the framework of a new concept of national planning the country had been divided into ten Economic Planning Regions: Scotland (Edinburgh), Northern (Newcastle), Yorkshire and Humberside (Leeds), North-West (Manchester), East Midland (Nottingham), West Midland (Birmingham), Wales and Monmouth (Cardiff), South-West (Bristol), East Anglia (Norwich), South-East (London). The bracketed towns were designated as regional capitals.

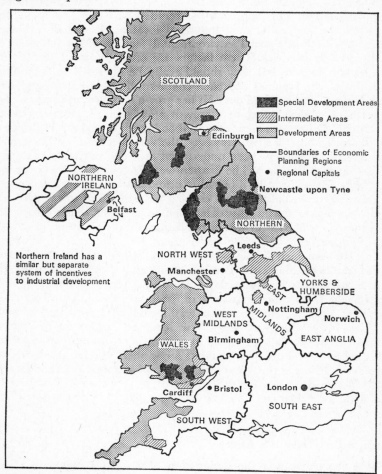

Fig 10.1 Economic planning regions and Development Areas

Each Economic Planning Region has a Regional Economic Council consisting of men and women selected for their wide range of interests and their special knowledge of their region. These Councils work in co-operation with Economic Planning Boards which consist of senior civil servants from government departments concerned with regional planning. The Boards co-ordinate the work of government departments and the Councils and advise the government on the regional impact of national policies. The first task faced by any Council is to prepare a study of its region; to find out what has been happening and what could be possible for the future. Most of these studies have provided a great deal of interesting information on the basis of which regional strategies have been formulated. This approach has resulted in a more comprehensive approach to the problems of industrial location. Regional bodies give more weight to the social environmental factors which influence the siting of new factories. These factors are often discussed *in contrast to* economic influences but they should really be discussed in conjunction with them. The regional approach enables full attention to be given to each region's problem and out of it has grown a fuller appreciation of the importance of developing new growth areas such as Humberside and Severnside. Other such areas may well be Wearside and the Portsmouth–Southampton coastal strip. However, the very fact that the Humberside and Severnside surveys were undertaken centrally underlines the possibility that each Region will be so attentive to its local pressure groups that detailed study will not be directed to brand new concepts. The tendency to concentrate on bolstering up existing industries and towns may work against increasing the mobility of labour as required for a faster growth rate.

It may have been with this in mind but more likely in order to avoid loss of authority by the central government, that the initiation of regional policy has remained in the latter's hands. Special aid to Development Areas has been increased. Between 1966 and their abolition in 1970 investment grants for industrial machinery and plant were higher for firms in the Development Areas than for those outside them. In 1967 the Regional Employment Premium was introduced, applying to manufacturers in Development Areas. This scheme provided for payments to firms of thirty shillings per week in respect of each man employed on a full-time basis and of lower amounts for women, children and part-time employees. Firms in the Areas also qualified for training grants of various kinds designed to lessen the problems of occupational immobility. Financial assistance continued to be given for public works intended to regenerate the Areas.

Special Development Areas

A new departure was the designation of Special Development Areas which are largely parts of the coalfields where the closing of uneconomic pits would cause particularly severe structural unemployment. In these areas larger grants are available towards building factories and operating costs and there is even provision for firms to occupy Board of Trade factories rent free for periods of up to five years.

Intermediate Areas

The report of the *Hunt Committeee* in 1969 focused attention on a third type of area in need of assistance, *viz.* Intermediate Areas. These can be thought of as "on the way to becoming Development Areas", i.e. they are marked by slow growth, declining employment opportunities, low average earnings, heavy reliance on industries with declining labour requirements, stagnant infrastructures inadequate for modern industry and generally run down environments. The Hunt Committee indicated that the decay of these areas was being accentuated by the aid being given to Development Areas because this diverted to these latter such new industrial development as would have taken place in these Intermediate or "grey" areas. The areas which were deemed by the government to fit into this new grouping were:

1   the Yorkshire coalfield area;
2   parts of the Notts/Derby coalfield;
3   North Humberside;
4   the main industrial areas of N.E. Lancashire;
5   areas to the S.E. and N.E. of the South Wales coalfield;
6   Leith;
7   an area around Plymouth.

The measures which emerged for these areas were, as one might expect, a modified version of those applicable to the Development Areas. The deliniation of the boundaries and the nature of the assistance were announced after consultation with the Regional Economic Planning Councils in an obvious attempt to tinge national policy with a flavour of regionalism.

Industrial Development Certificates were made available in the Intermediate Areas on the same basis as in development areas. Building grants to firms and grants to local authorities for derelict land clearance, assistance under the *Key Workers Scheme* and under the *Resettlement Transfer* and the *Nucleus Labour Force* schemes were extended to these new areas. The Key Workers Scheme assists employees transferred by their employers to jobs in factories in the designated areas with the costs of moving, buying and selling houses, lodging and other incidental expenses. The Resettlement Transfer Scheme helps the unemployed and those about to become unemployed through redundancy to move to permanent new work elsewhere until new work can be found in their present district. In these cases there is also assistance for return fares for interviews for jobs. The Nucleus

Labour Force Scheme aids the unemployed recruited in areas of heavy unemployment who are required to go for training to their employers' factories in other areas.

Finally, in the Intermediate Areas, new and expanding firms can obtain grants towards training new employees, aid with the renting of temporary accommodation for training purposes, and with the cost of training supervisory staff.

The E.E.C.

From its inception the E.E.C. has been concerned to promote the harmonious development of its regions. If anything, the disparities between growing and declining regions were greater in E.E.C. countries than in the U.K. and the job of spreading the benefits of growth was, therefore, both more difficult and more urgent.

In 1965 the Common Market Commission recommended giving priority to re-training the workers, improving the infrastructure and offering financial inducements to firms to establish factories in the declining regions. Thus a very similar approach to that of the U.K. was adopted. In 1969 the Commission added its recommendations that there should be i) a development plan for each region, ii) a permanent organisation for reviewing the situation and implementing policy, and iii) the provision of extra finance for regional development. There are four main community sources of direct aid for the regions: a) the European Investment Bank which finances investment projects; b) the European Agricultural Fund which makes grants for structural improvements in farming; c) the European Coal and Steel Community which makes loans to new industries moving into declining areas; and d) the European Social Fund and E.C.S.C. readaptation grants for the retraining and re-settlement of workpeople.

The right approach?

In the U.K., the early 1970's saw embryonic moves towards greater reliance on market forces to weed out inefficient firms and create a more satisfactory growth rate. However, the regional planning approach was not abandoned and the question of how much to depend on planning and how much on market forces to achieve the desired ends remains unanswered. Nor does economic analysis suggest that either approach is clearly, exclusively right. In these circumstances the key virtues would seem to be continued observation and analysis and a flexibility of outlook which, unclogged by ideologies, will enable new ideas to be tried out.

To suggest that the mixture seems about right is not to say that we know all the answers. Study over the past forty years has made us aware of the great complexity and ever-changing nature of the problem. Let us review some of its faces:

1   The decline of a region tends to be cumulative: should we fight against this as at present or would it be better to work with it and try to create new growth points? There is no apparent reason why industries in the future should be located in the same places as different industries in the past.

2   Some industries are said to be "foot-loose" in that transport costs are only a small part of their total costs and there seems to be no strong, obvious reasons why they should not be directed to areas of heavy structural unemployment—or to new growth points. Here the government may intervene best by disseminating information about new locations and the experiences of firms which have moved to them, by providing an easily understood aid service for such moves so that firms can reach decisions in the full realisation of their opportunities.

3   The occupational and geographical mobility of labour can be increased through more comprehensive re-training, job and house-finding schemes so that the closing of firms in localities to which it is impossible to move new ones ceases to assume the proportions of a major catastrophe in the lives of the people dependent on them.

4   The encouragement of other than manufacturing concerns to move to locations outside the congested conurbations is necessary if we are to avoid a division of the population into those who live and work in office-towns and those who live and work in factory-towns. This is particularly important since offices are both manpower intensive and heavy users of highly educated manpower.

5   The conventional wisdom behind our present policies is that the dispersion of industry and population is both socially and economically beneficial. This must be challenged before it is accepted. Large conurbations are economical in the use of land and provide the economic basis for many social activities. The concentration of living- and work-places in a relatively few areas enables the preservation of open country for recreation.

Wider horizons

Finally, let us realise that the problem we have been looking at is one which affects the whole world. As comparative cost conditions change so does the location of industry. The growth of one area may depend upon the unfettered development of an industry which has been the staple industry of another country. The world economy is as subject to change as a national one. The South East of England grows under the pull of the expanding industrial region of northern Europe. A Channel Tunnel will strengthen this force. These are not matters which regions can settle, they are not even within the full competence of national governments and success in dealing with them satisfactorily will depend increasingly on the emergence of international collaboration.

QUESTIONS

What have been the principal changes in industrial location in the U.K. over the past fifty years?

Why are some industries highly localised whilst others are dispersed throughout the country?

Discuss the economic case for state control of the location of industry.

What effect might a channel tunnel have on the location of industry in Britain?

Discuss the impact of motorways on industrial location.

What light has British experience thrown on the factors influencing the siting of new factories?

What do you understand by "the drift to the South" in the U.K.?

Comment on the view that work should be taken to the workers as opposed to workers being expected to move to where there is work.

Trace the development of British government policy towards areas of industrial decline.

"The problem of development areas is not so much one of arresting decline as one of promoting growth." Comment.

READING REFERENCES

D. Lee: *Regional Planning and Location of Industry* (Heinemann, 1969)

M. Wright: *Industrial Location and Regional Policy* (Longmans and I.E.A., 1968)

P. Sargent Florence: *Atlas of Economic Structure and Policy*, Vol. II. (Pergamon, 1970)

G. Herbert: *The Management of the Economy* (Ginn, 1971)

H. W. Richardson: *Elements of Regional Economics* (Penguin, 1971)

11 Government expenditure and taxation

The Budget we refer to in this chapter is the U.K Government's Budget. It shows the projected pattern of government spending for the following year and how it is proposed to finance such spending. The Budget is normally presented to the House of Commons early in April, and Budget Day is the opportunity for a wide-ranging review of the country's economic position by the Chancellor of the Exchequer. Under the general heading of "Public Finance" it is now customary to include, as well as central government spending, local authorities' spending, which has been rising very rapidly in recent years, and the nationalised industries' expenditure. But in this chapter we shall concentrate on central government spending and revenue and how these are used to control the economy.

Government spending

The figure of government spending has risen very rapidly in recent years. In the financial year 1913/14 it was a mere £175 millions; by 1965/66 the figure was £8484 millions; and the figure for 1968/69 was £10 848 millions. The figures represent current expenditure in money terms. For comparative purposes we can express them as a percentage of the gross national product. In these terms, 1913/14 expenditure represents about 12 per cent of the gross national product. For 1938/39 the percentage is 18 per cent; whereas for 1965/66 and 1968/69 the percentages were 26 per cent and 28 per cent respectively. This rise in this percentage figure brings out clearly the increasing importance of the government's role in the economy, which we shall discuss shortly. There are, however, other factors which help to explain the rising figure of government expenditure.

a) *Rising population*

As a country's population increases, public expenditure is bound to rise. There are more children to educate, more babies to care for, more old people to draw pensions. The population of the U.K. in 1913/14 was 42 millions; by 1968/69 it had risen to 55 millions. It would therefore be more meaningful to express government spending per head of the population, but even in these terms it has increased very rapidly in the twentieth century.

The age distribution of the population is also important. A larger proportion of young people means greater expenditure on child welfare and education. A growing percentage of old people will entail larger spending on pensions, on care for the aged, and on health. Before World War I the proportion of people over 65 in the U.K. population was 5 per cent; in 1968 it was 12·5 per cent.

b) *Changing value of money*

If prices rise, all government spending on goods and services will tend to rise. A similar argument applies to rising incomes. Much government expenditure is on salaries and wages, for example civil servants, the armed forces, and health service workers. A rise in these incomes will in itself necessitate greater government spending. Prices in 1968 were between five and six times the level in 1913. It would therefore be more useful to allow for these price changes before comparing government spending in two different years. Even after this has been done, government spending per head of the population at constant prices is still many times greater now than it was before the First World War.

c) *The changing role of government*

We next consider the increasing part which the government plays in the economy. During the nineteenth century the general aim was to keep both government expenditure and revenue as low as possible. The government's main concern was with defence, law and order. During the nineteenth century there was a considerable expansion of services under the heading of security and regulation, dealing, for example, with "noxious trades" or with conditions in factories.

The real expansion of government activities came in the twentieth century, however. It began with the Liberal Administration of 1906–14, which introduced the rudiments of insurance for sickness and unemployment and the first old age pensions. These services developed between the wars, and the provision of council houses on a substantial scale added to the scope of government spending. After 1945 the process accelerated; a comprehensive health service and an insurance scheme were supplemented by a system of family allowances. A rapid development of education took place. Economic expenditure also became important, on such items as aid to agriculture and assistance to the development areas. Although governments of different political parties may change the emphasis in government spending, all parties in the U.K. now accept the "mixed economy", in which private enterprise is associated with a good measure of government control and regulation of economic and social affairs.

Functional finance

One of the main reasons why the role of government has changed so much in recent years is the change in view concerning the nature of government activity. Until perhaps the outbreak of the Second World War the Budget was essentially an accounting device. It had to balance.

Expenditure and Income must be equal. And in the event, if income lagged behind expenditure, then expenditure had to be cut. The new doctrine was enshrined in the 1944 White Paper on Employment Policy, and since that time the notion of "Functional Finance"—the use of the budget for economic control and for economic change—has become increasingly important. We now talk of "budgetary policy"—the use of the budget, not simply to balance the books, but to pursue definite economic aims.

One overall aim of budgetary policy is to control the level of aggregate demand in the economy. The total expenditure in an economy is the sum of consumption spending, investment, government spending and export spending. This may be reduced by withdrawals in the form of savings, tax payments and import spending. If we isolate the two items, government spending and tax payments we can see that if government spending (G) is counterbalanced by its tax revenue (T) there will be no net effect on aggregate demand. A balanced budget is therefore effectively neutral with regard to aggregate demand. If, however, G is greater than T—a budget deficit—the net effect will be an increase in aggregate demand. If, on the other hand, T is greater than G—a budget surplus—aggregate demand will be reduced. (We ignore for our present purposes such complications as the different effects of government spending on goods and services rather than on transfer payments.)

Now let us suppose that the level of total demand in a closed economy is not sufficient to maintain full employment. This situation calls for an increase in aggregate demand, and one method of achieving this end is to budget for a deficit. Government spending (G) will be greater than tax revenue (T), and this excess will be financed, not by borrowing from the public—this would have the effect of increasing savings (S) and so adding to total withdrawals from the circular flow—but by borrowing from the banking system. The greater aggregate demand will raise the level of money national income and also create more employment. A diagrammatic representation of this process is shown in Fig 11.1,[1] where OY_1 is the equilibrium level of national income in the absence of budgetary considerations. When these are taken into account and there is a budget deficit the new equilibrium level of national income becomes OY_2. The excess of G over T is shown by the distance ab on the diagram.[2] The $C + I + (G - T)$ line intercepts the $E = Y$ line at a point which is cd (which is the same as ab) above the former $C + I$ line. Since the level of employment has a direct functional relationship with Y the increase in the latter will result in a higher level of employment.

If, however, the level of total demand in the economy is already sufficient to guarantee full employment, a different result ensues. As before, the

[1] For construction of 45° line diagrams see J. C. Powicke, *Economic Theory*, Chapter 14.
[2] Taking G − T as an injection avoids having to add G to the I line and T to the S line thus complicating the diagram unnecessarily in this context.

increase in aggregate demand will raise money national income, but the increased demand for labour which results cannot be translated into increased employment.

It is true that the existing labour force can be employed more fully, on overtime working, for example. It may be that the existing labour force can be "stretched" in various ways, for example the increased employment of part-time workers. But, in this situation, the elements of labour shortage appear—excess overtime working, a large number of unfilled vacancies—and with these elements, pressure for higher wages builds up.

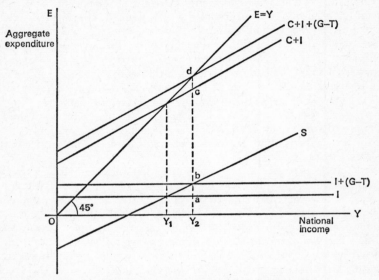

Fig 11.1 The effect of a Budget deficit on the level of employment

The increase in aggregate demand results finally in inflation, i.e. a rising level of prices and incomes with little corresponding rise in employment and output.

Let us now consider the reverse situation—where aggregate demand in the economy is too high, where cyclical unemployment is non-existent, and where there are strong inflationary pressures. The solution here is to reduce aggregate demand, to lower G in relation to T, i.e. to budget for a surplus. Such a budget surplus will lower aggregate demand and money national income. It will reduce the demand for labour and thus ease the inflationary pressures. It may lower employment to the full employment level or even create some unemployment. This process is illustrated in Fig 11.2 where a situation of $T > G$ is introduced when national income is in equilibrium at OY_1. The net effect on the $C + I$ line is to lower it to $C + I - (T - G)$ so that the latter intercepts the $E = Y$ line at national income OY_2.

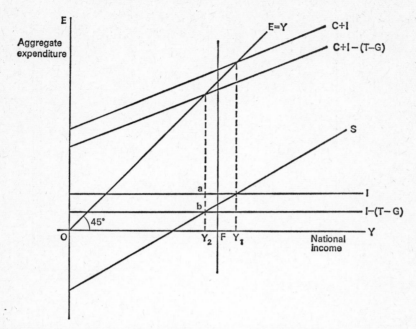

Fig 11.2 The effect of a Budget surplus on the level of employment

At this lower level of national income the excess of T over G is shown by the distance ab. The lower equilibrium level of national income implies a lower level of employment which may be even below "full employment" as indicated in the diagram by OY_2 being less than OF, which is the size of national income consistent with full employment.

The exact point at which increasing aggregate demand ceases to increase employment and instead causes inflation—or at which reduced aggregate demand ceases to ease off inflationary pressure and instead causes unemployment—is a matter for controversy. The L-shaped curve, illustrated in Fig 11.3, associated with the earlier work of J. M. Keynes, suggested that there was a point of equilibrium, at the full employment level, below which increases in aggregate demand would raise employment but above which such increases would raise the level of prices. In Fig 11.3 the equilibrium level is somewhere above the 98 per cent employment rate. Prior to this level any increase in national income causes employment to rise but does not affect prices but beyond it employment cannot increase and the whole effect of increased expenditure is to force prices up.

The curve associated with Professor Phillips, illustrated in Fig 11.4, suggested that there was a band of aggregate demand levels in which increases would raise both employment and prices. In this theory all

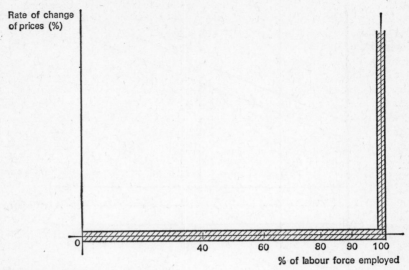

Fig 11.3 The L-Shaped curve

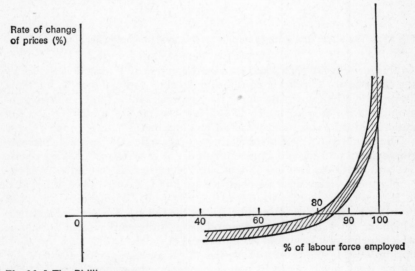

Fig 11.4 The Phillips curve

changes in national expenditure have some effect on both employment and prices. The lower the level of employment the greater the effect on employment and the less the effect on prices of any increase in expenditure. As the level of employment rises a given increase in expenditure will have greater price effects and lesser employment effects. Thus the concept of full employment becomes less definitive—there is no sudden change from less-than-full to over-full employment. It also poses the question "how far is it practicable to increase aggregate demand above the full employment level?".

In practice, the U.K. Government, since 1945, has pursued a policy of full employment. The budget occasion has been used to maintain aggregate demand at a level sufficiently high to ensure full employment. Other governments have pursued the same end. There can be no doubt of the success of budgetary policies in maintaining a level of aggregate demand sufficiently high to maintain full employment. Some critics would argue that the success has been the result rather of good fortune than of deliberate planning; that increased demand, particularly from higher incomes and vastly greater consumption, would have raised employment levels in any case. Ignoring this complication, however, it is more generally accepted that budgetary policy has been conspicuously unsuccessful in reducing inflationary pressures.

The budget surplus, attained in a large number of years between 1945 and 1970, may have reduced the level of employment but it failed to keep price levels stable. Among the possible explanations advanced is that rising incomes more than counter-balanced reductions in the circular flow as a result of the increased T; that the increases in T brought about corresponding reductions in S; that the "band" implied in the Phillips' Curve was wider than previously thought, so that increased unemployment was still accompanied by some rise in prices; or that the inflation evidenced during these years was not caused by excess demand but was of the "cost-push" variety, and so could not be treated by the reduction of aggregate demand. Whatever the explanation, it seems clear that, although a budget can be used successfully to create full employment, we cannot yet use it to combat inflation.

Taxation

Most government spending is financed by taxation. The chief sources of government revenue in the U.K. are shown in Table 1. Here we are concerned, not with the details of individual taxes, but with the broad divisions of taxation and the relative effects of different kinds of taxation.

The most useful division of taxes into types is into a) taxes on income; and b) taxes on expenditure. In the U.K. group (a) is usually extended to include taxes on capital. The major tax in this group is income tax, including surtax, but a tax of increasing importance since 1965 is corporation tax, replacing the old profits tax on company income. Capital taxes in the U.K. are still in their infancy.

Taxes on expenditure include all customs and excise duties, such as the high-yielding taxes on alcohol, petroleum and tobacco, purchase tax, and motor vehicle licence duties. This group also included Selective Employ-ment Tax. During the twentieth century the relative importance of the first group has increased. In 1900/01 for example, only 36 per cent of total government revenue was raised by taxes on income, the remainder being raised by taxes on expenditure. However, in 1969/70 the percentage raised by taxes on income had risen to 56 per cent while the corresponding percentage for taxes on expenditure had fallen to 44 per cent. The reason for this change in relative importance has been the increased use of progressive income tax. In 1969/70, for example, income tax and surtax alone accounted for 70 per cent of all group (a) taxes and 39 per cent of all government revenue.

Table 1   The chief sources of government revenue in the U.K. 1969/70

	£ million	£ million
Taxes on Income and Capital		7476
of which— Income Tax	4900	
Surtax	255	
Corporation Tax	1687	
Death Duties	365	
Capital Gains Tax	127	
Stamp Duties	120	
Taxes on Expenditure		5896
of which— Tobacco	1143	
Purchase Tax	1110	
Oil	1302	
Spirits, Beer, Wine	862	
Motor Vehicle Duties	419	
S.E.T. (net)	527	

Before we consider the effects of taxation a further subdivision of taxes is useful. We can distinguish between progressive, proportionate and re-gressive taxation. Progressive taxation takes an increasing proportion of income or capital as either increases. Examples are income tax, where the effect of granting allowances at the bottom end of the scale and of in-creasing the rate of surtax at the top end is to make the whole system progressive; and estate duties, where the rates, after a low exemption limit, rise with increasing value of the estate.

Proportional taxation takes the same proportion from all incomes or assets. Obvious examples are corporation tax, levied currently[1] at 40 per cent of all company income; and capital gains tax, at least for long term capital gains, at a rate of 30 per cent of any gain.

Regressive taxation takes a smaller proportion of income or capital as either increases. This effect, usually unintentional, is achieved by the imposition of flat rate taxes. National Insurance contributions, before the introduction of a graduated scheme, used to take the same amount from

[1] September, 1972.

all adult male incomes, irrespective of the size of those incomes. The result was regressive; a larger proportion was taken from the smaller incomes. Other examples are offered by licence fees, such as those for television or motor cars, and by Selective Employment Tax, which was lowered from £2·40 to £1·20 per adult male worker in July 1971 and is due to be abolished in April 1973.[1]

The effects of taxation

1   On incomes

The first obvious effect of increased taxation is to reduce disposable incomes. This is equally true of taxes on income, where the effect is immediate and obvious, and of taxes on expenditure, where the initial effect is to reduce consumer's income by increasing prices of some (or all) goods or to reduce businessmen's profits if they absorb the increase in tax without putting up prices.

Taxation may also lead to the redistribution of incomes. This is particularly true of progressive taxation, and one of the aims of a government levying highly progressive taxation is to reduce the inequality of incomes. Far more is taken from the rich than from the moderately well-to-do or the poor, and this brings the incomes of all more closely into line. If the policy of a highly progressive tax system is accompanied by a lower limit below which taxes are not levied, and a system of grants or subsidies to the lowest paid workers, then income is redistributed—taken from the rich and given to the poor.

Proportional taxation, while taking the same percentage of all incomes, has the effect of reducing the gaps between different levels of income. For example, the gap between a man earning £2000 and one earning £500 per annum is £1500 and this is reduced by a 10 per cent tax. As a result of such a tax, the higher income becomes £1800 and the lower £450—a gap of £1350 instead of the original gap of £1500. Regressive taxation, however, may increase the inequality between incomes.

While certain progressive taxes, for example income tax combined with surtax, aid in the redistributive process, this may not be the overall effect of a tax system. Expenditure taxes can be progressive, proportionate or regressive, depending not only on the way they are levied but also on income elasticity of demand for particular goods. A percentage tax on a good which is bought largely by the very rich, for example, will tend to be progressive and help to redistribute income, whereas a similar tax on a good the consumption of which tends to fall off as incomes rise will be highly regressive. The overall effect of expenditure taxes in the U.K. is regressive. The considerations above are magnified by the greater propensity to save as incomes rise. It is also probable that the regressive effect of expenditure

[1] See Appendix on Value Added Tax.

taxes more than counterbalances the progressive effect of income taxes, so that, on the whole, the U.K. system of taxation is regressive.

2   *On savings*

The major effect of taxation on savings is to reduce the ability to save. If savings are largely a residue, i.e. income which is not spent, then any reduction in disposable income will tend to reduce the residue which is left for saving. This is true of all income taxes. However, it may not be true of expenditure taxes. The imposition of expenditure taxes may increase the attractiveness of "not-spending" (savings) compared with spending, and consumers may increase their savings rather than pay the increased price brought about by the expenditure tax. However, such an effect is likely to be accompanied by a reduction in business incomes and therefore in savings from this sector. It is probably true that increased taxation, in whatever form, has the effect of reducing savings.

3   *On prices*

Taxes on income have no direct effect on prices. In fact, by reducing disposable incomes they have a deflationary effect and may therefore lower prices, or at least help to keep them down. Taxes on expenditure, however, will tend to raise prices. The possible effects of a unit tax on a given commodity are illustrated in Figure 11.5 (a), (b), (c). In all three graphs the supply curve S_1 and S_2 are identical and S_1 intersects the demand curve D at price Op_1.

Only where the demand is infinitely elastic (c) will there be no rise in price as a result of the tax. In other cases, the rise in price depends on the relative elasticity of demand for the particular commodity. The rise is greater in (a), where the demand-elasticity is lower than in (b). Taking all commodities, however, the effect of commodity taxes must be to raise prices. Whether or not this effect is inflationary depends on how far the initial rise in the general level of prices is perpetuated by rising incomes and a consequent impetus to further price rises.

4   *On effort*

It is sometimes argued that taxes on income act as a disincentive to effort. If the work load can be varied, for example by varying the amount of overtime worked, or by dealing with more or fewer clients in the case of professional men, then income taxation, by reducing the yield from the extra effort, increases the relative attractiveness of leisure. Workers will tend to substitute leisure for work. Similarly, retirement will become relatively more attractive than working, so that the age of retirement will be advanced where this is possible.

This argument considers only the substitution effect of income taxes. There may well be an income effect. Increased taxation will reduce the income derived from working, and in order to maintain the previous level of income, more work is necessary. This will lead to a result exactly opposite to that above. So that, in theory, the effect of income taxation could lead equally well to a reduction in effort or an increase in effort.

The argument can best be resolved by an appeal to empirical evidence. A number of investigations have been carried out to determine the effects

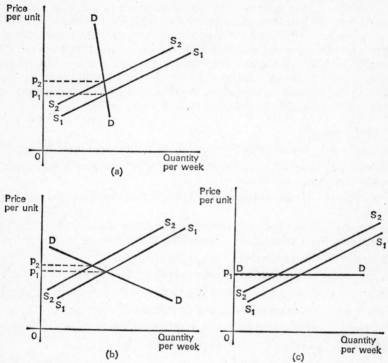

Fig 11.5 Effect of a Unit Commodity Tax

of income taxation on incentives. Without detailing them all here, we can summarise the results so far obtained by saying that:

a) Samples investigated have been so small that any conclusions must be very tentative.

b) All investigations have indicated that income taxation is not in general a disincentive to effort.

c) There may well be disincentive effects at very high levels of taxation (70 per cent or more).

d) Two undesirable results of high levels of income tax may be to hinder the mobility of executive labour and to stimulate the tax-avoidance industry.

The disincentive argument is not proven, despite its wide acceptance by the public. What is probably true, however, is that expenditure taxes will have no disincentive effects, so that if there is any doubt about the effect of particular taxes on effort, a government is likely to favour expenditure taxes rather than income taxes.

Summary

A government may well wish to decide whether taxation of income or expenditure will best serve its purposes. Assuming for the moment that both forms are equally buoyant, i.e. they rise as incomes and expenditure rise, a government going for deflation will favour income taxes rather than expenditure taxes. If the aim is to reduce inequality of incomes, income tax will again be favoured. But expenditure taxes are likely to have less effect on savings and on incentives. A government will balance one argument against the other in deciding its budgetary policy.

QUESTIONS

How may governments use fiscal policy to reduce economic inequality?

What do you understand by "fiscal measures"? How can they be used to control phases of trade cycles?

What reforms of the tax system would you recommend on economic grounds?

Discuss the balance between direct and indirect taxes in the U.K. and compare their effectiveness for controlling the economy.

When should the government budget for a surplus?

Do high rates of taxation have a disincentive effect on effort?

Discuss fiscal means of exercising day to day control over the economy.

What is a value added tax? Discuss its merits and demerits.

Why has government spending risen so rapidly in the U.K. in recent years?

How far can a budget be used to pursue the aims of
a) reducing unemployment
b) stimulating economic growth
c) combating inflation
d) maintaining a balance of payments surplus?

REFERENCES AND FURTHER READING
G. Herbert: *The Management of the Economy* (Ginn, 1971)

C. T. Sandford: *Public Expenditure and Fiscal Policy* (Longmans and I.E.A., 1971)

S. Brittan: *Steering the Economy: the Role of the Treasury* (Penguin, 1969)

C. T. Sandford: *Public Finance* (Pergamon Press, 1969)

A. R. Prest: *The U.K. Economy* (3rd edition) (Weidenfeld and Nicolson, 1970)

Annual Budget Speeches and Debates (H.M.S.O.)

A. R. Prest: *Public Finance* (Weidenfeld and Nicolson, 1967)

White Paper: *Value Added Tax*, Cmnd 4929 (H.M.S.O., 1972)

12 The money supply: a discussion

The depression years of the 1930's ushered in an era of disillusionment with monetary policy as a means of controlling the level of economic activity within a country. Fiscal or budgetary policy emerged as the panacea, J. M. Keynes had demonstrated how to defeat trade cycles, full employment could come to stay. Then, during the 1950's and 60's it became apparent that something was going wrong. Full employment seemed inseparable from inflation, inflation from balance of payments crises and a slow rate of economic growth. In Britain this trend culminated at the end of the 60's and in the early 70's in the state of affairs which came to be known as "stagflation", i.e. a mixture of stagnation and inflation. Unemployment, other than strictly structural and frictional, came to exist side by side with inflation, a situation which, up to this point, would have been considered impossible. This was not an universal experience, many countries escaped it altogether, none was as acutely affected as Britain. In this setting a new look was taken at monetary policy and a great debate developed between those who still thought monetary measures to be of minor significance and those who accorded them pride of place in the armoury of the state.

Throughout these years a third voice had been endeavouring to make itself heard in advocating an incomes policy but, although it had long been incorporated in the practices of Swedish governments, it received little attention in Britain. The essence of an incomes policy is that increases in money incomes must be closely linked to increases in productivity so that they do not exert an upward pressure on prices. If this is achieved, it can be argued, it is possible to keep an economy in a state of full employment without it bubbling over into inflation. An incomes policy must relate total incomes (aggregate monetary demand) to total output (gross national product) but it must also allow and, even, encourage flexibility in the income structure of society so that differentials in earnings can direct labour out of those uses in which it is least efficient in satisfying wants and into those in which it is most efficient.

Such a policy must not be confused with the "wage freezes", "pay pauses", etc., which have been used from time to time as temporary anti-inflation measures. These merely attempt to hold incomes down indiscriminately until a particular crisis has passed. The short reign of the Prices and Incomes Board (1965–71) had some of the appearance of an incomes policy but it operated very much on an ad hoc basis, i.e. it investigated matters relating to prices and incomes as they were referred to it. Moreover, although its powers of investigation enabled it to produce exhaustive studies considerably exceeding the specific requirements of an incomes policy, it was unable to enforce its judgements except through the mobilisation of public opinion. The inclusion of prices within the purview of the Board and the extension, in 1968, of the government's power to enforce its recommendations indicated the main practical difficulty of an incomes policy, *viz* that in the incomes–prices leapfrog it is incomes which push up prices but people are unwilling to accept curbs on their incomes until prices have been brought under control. This is the link with monetary policy. As we shall see, a proper control over the supply of money can be used to put a brake on prices and thus provide a suitable climate for initiating an incomes policy. Whether or not one comes into being depends on non-economic factors such as the readiness of trade union leaders to adopt a new approach to wage determination and the establishment of confidence between government, the unions and employers.

Fiscal or budgetary policy is considered in Chapter 11 and it is sufficient in this context to emphasise that it aims primarily at controlling aggregate monetary demand. Thus in times of inflation the objective is a budget surplus to contract the circular flow of income and, by contrast, in times of general unemployment a budget deficit to expand incomes has been the criterion. Trouble arose when, first of all, inflation could only be contained by halting growth and when, later, inflation and considerable unemployment co-existed. The link between monetary and fiscal policy may well be that in this circumstance, the former can be used to hold inflation in check whilst the latter encourages demand. Our discussion so far suggests that an incomes policy would be a stabilising factor without which it would be most difficult to maintain that nicety of balance between fiscal and monetary measures, not always by any means working in opposite directions, necessary to attain the goal of full employment and economic growth without inflation.

The supply of money

It has become customary to divide the money supply into M_1, M_2 and M_3 which were defined in the *Midland Bank Review* of November 1970 as follows: "M_1: notes and coins in circulation and sterling current accounts held by the private sector. M_2: M_1 *plus* deposit accounts of the private sector with the deposit banks and discount houses only. M_3: M_2 *plus* sterling deposit accounts with other banks, all non-sterling deposits of the private sector and all deposits of the public sector." One of the problems of monetary policy has been that it has tended to concentrate on controlling M_1, with some extensions to include M_2 but with little attention to M_3. This failure to be comprehensive has been largely responsible for the failure of traditional monetary measures to control the economy although it is appropriate to note a point that will be considered later, *viz* that monetary and fiscal policy in Britain in the twenty-five years after the Second World War often pulled in opposite directions and so the apparent failure of either one of them only indicated that its effects were being swamped by those of the other.

Traditional monetary policy in Britain has aimed at controlling the credit created by the commercial banks together with, on some occasions, restrictions on hire purchase credit. However, there was no real control over the volume of money which is essentially a function of the Bank of England's operations in the course of managing the national debt and of fulfilling its objective of meeting the requirements of the public. Thus attempts to limit lending by the commercial banks were often largely negated by purchases by the Bank of England of government bonds in order to keep up their prices and therefore keep down their interest rates thus making redemption and conversion exercises less expensive to the government. The cost of servicing the National Debt was, by the same token, kept down and this can be considered desirable in its own right in that it reduces the burden of taxation.

The Radcliffe Report

The apparent inadequacy of open market operations used in conjunction with variations in Bank Rate to deal with Britain's persistent post-war inflation led to the introduction of additional physical controls, e.g. directives which often fixed ceilings on the amounts which banks could lend and special deposits which directly influenced their cash bases.

In 1959 the Radcliffe Committee reported on the working of Britain's monetary system and drew attention to the necessity of switching attention from just the cash bases to the overall liquidity of the banks. This latter is directly affected by the debt management operations of the Bank of England and, as this factor was taken as given, the answer seemed to the committee to lie in direct controls of the banks in conjunction with other specific measures such as limiting the down payments and the repayment periods associated with hire purchase finance. This "package deal" concept must be counted an advance towards a wider appreciation of the full meaning of the term "the money supply". Unfortunately, the report distracted attention from the basic weakness of British monetary policy, *viz* the Bank of England's automatic support of the gilt-edged market and it was not until 1971 that a step, discussed on page 153, was taken which seemed to recognise this point.

The Quantity Theory of money

The Quantity Theory of money can be expressed by the Fisher equation, *viz* $MV = PT$. This states that the quantity of money (M) multiplied by the velocity of its circulation (V) must equal the average price level (P) multiplied by the number of transactions (T). The theory makes the point that if V and T remain unchanged it follows that a change in M must initiate an equal proportionate change in P. Even in this crude form the Quantity Theory does not get us very far towards understanding the whys and wherefores of general price changes. Moreover, since it merely states that the amount spent during a given period (MV) must equal the value of what is sold (PT) it does not even provide a sound base for assuming that a change in the quantity of money does *cause* changes in price levels. We can only deduce that P and M must move together.

The assumption that V and T remain unchanged is the most damaging aspect of the theory from a practical point of view. T could only remain unchanged in a permanent state of full employment. The number of transactions (the amount of business done) increases during the reflationary and inflationary phases of a trade cycle as purchasing power expands faster than the output of goods and services. During the disinflationary and deflationary phases T declines. Nor does V remain stable; it is somewhat less open to generalisation than T but it tends to increase during inflation as money is losing its purchasing power and to decrease in deflation when people increase their demand for money, i.e. their liquidity preference, both as a safety measure against the uncertainties of future employment and income and because it is sound policy to hold on to money when prices are falling so that goods can be bought when they have become cheaper.

Has, then, the Quantity Theory anything of value to offer? Neo-Keynesians, as we may call them, have tended to deny that it has. Keynes was concerned with the heavy unemployment between 1918 and 1939 when the lowest general unemployment rate recorded was 9·7 per cent and when it never fell much below 20 per cent in the older industrial areas. Under these conditions, treating M as the prime mover in line with Quantity Theory thinking, Keynes considered that increasing the supply of money by government purchases of securities in the open market and the lowering of Bank Rate was unlikely to have any reflationary effect. Who would borrow money for commercial purposes when markets were depressed and declining? This point of view has passed into the conventional wisdom of our science. It has also become widely accepted that restricting the supply of money can have a negative effect in curtailing an inflation but that it is a "blunt instrument", striking indiscriminately at whatever firms are at the head of the queue for finance when it is used.

These considerations have been the basis of neo-Keynesian opposition to the idea of using variations in the money supply to control inflation. One may well wonder what Keynes's own reaction would have been. Would he have had the same doubts about control via the money supply in times of inflation as he had in times of depression? Did he see his

"General Theory of Employment, Interest and Money" as *general* in all conditions or only in depressed conditions which he attributed largely to a chronic tendency to over-saving? In a letter to *The Economist* of May 29th, 1971, Mr. William Wallace—who worked with Keynes in the period 1927–29 during which, with Keynes' backing, he wrote "We can conquer unemployment"—quotes Keynes as saying "Well, Wallace, we have given them a formula to meet deflation: one day they will ask us for one to meet inflation." As Mr. Wallace wrote: "Sadly, he died too soon."

The Chicago School

In the 1960's Professor Milton Friedman in Chicago conducted studies of statistics relating to the period 1881–1967 which showed such a close correlation between changes in the supply of money and, after a time lag, movements in income and the general level of prices that he concluded that there must be a causal relationship between them. The Quantity Theory was re-instated in that variation in money supply had been allotted a positive role in income and price fluctuations. It is important to note that the arguments of the Chicago School are based primarily on observed correlations and still lack that adequate analytical explanation which can give them the status of acceptable theory. Nevertheless, they have made sufficient impact to lead to the introduction of a new relationship between the Bank of England and the banking system designed to give fresh emphasis to controlling money supply.

Competition and credit control since 1971

Probably the most important aspects of the new regime are that i) credit control extends to all banks (not just the six London Clearing banks) and also to Finance houses and ii) the Bank of England no longer supports the market price of government stocks with more than one year to maturity. The former spreads the net of control over most of the range of credit, the latter can secure control of money supply proper.

Credit control is now exercised by means of Special Deposits, a matter which may detract from the effectiveness of the overall policy because it makes it possible for the government itself to avoid the stricter discipline implicit in depending on open market operations. However, *all* banks must now maintain a minimum ratio of 12½ per cent of eligible reserve assets to eligible liabilities. Reserve assets are: money at the Bank of England (excluding Special Deposits), money at call and short notice, bills discounted (Treasury Bills and local authority and commercial bills eligible for discount at the Bank of England), company Tax Reserve Certificates (whilst still in use), and government stock with one year or less to maturity. The last mentioned item is included because such stock is always saleable at close to its face value and is, therefore, rightly considered a liquid asset. Eligible liabilities are the net sterling deposits of the banks and include sterling certificates of deposits which can be readily bought and sold in the special market which has grown up. These certificates are acknowledgements of deposits of large sums and circulate as money in their own sphere in much the same way as those goldsmiths' receipts which were the precursors of bank notes.

Finance houses are subject to a 10 per cent minimum ratio of eligible reserve assets to eligible liabilities and the latter excludes amounts borrowed from the banks thus avoiding the double application to the same funds of the liability to hold reserve assets and make Special Deposits. The calling of Special Deposits will usually be the same for banks and finance houses but the Bank of England may, in certain circumstances, call them at a higher rate from the finance houses. Nevertheless Special Deposits and total reserve assets may not represent a higher proportion of eligible assets for finance houses than for banks. It is anticipated that many finance houses will acquire the full status of banks now that there is so little difference between the treatment of the two types of institution.

The new pattern of control is intended to provide uniform treatment of all banks and finance houses and it is hoped that greater efficiency can be secured by encouraging more genuine competition between them. Most banks have, in recent years, extended their interests into the realms of hire-purchase finance, unit trusts, investment trusts and, recently, Barclays have led the way into merchant banking. They have competed in trying to offer their customers a widening range of services but, until the autumn of 1971, they had not competed as regards the rates of interest charged on their loans. Each bank determines its own base rate and adjusts its rates on deposits and advances in relation to this. Whether or not there will be any consistent divergence in the base rates of different banks seems rather uncertain. It is just conceivable that greater efficiency might be stimulated but there are only a few banks and tacit agreement not to "rock the boat" would seem more likely.

The Discount Houses' role has also been modified a little to fit the new framework. They continue to apply each week for a sufficient amount of Treasury Bills to cover the amount on tender and they maintain a minimum of 50 per cent of their funds in defined categories of public sector debt. On the other hand, they no longer tender for Treasury Bills at a price agreed among themselves which means that they could be competing with one another by offering different rates of discount.

Thus, in principle, interest rates throughout the financial system are free to respond to changes in the supply of money. In the last quarter of 1971, money supply increased as a result of more bank lending, heavier public sector borrowing and an inflow of foreign exchange and so interest rates moved downwards. The hope was that investment and business in general would respond to lower interest rates and so halt the rising trend of unemployment. In fact all that happened was that some aspects of consumer demand increased, thus, if anything, aggravating the condition of "stagflation".

Summing up

We should not be surprised by the above noted sluggishness of industry. No one could claim that the performance of the British economy since 1946 has been such that confidence in the future can be created as easily in the hearts of businessmen who have had to battle with the vagaries of fortune as in the rather gullible minds of politicians whose interest is riveted on popularity ratings. Moreover, there is no reason to doubt the conventional economic wisdom that interest rates do not play much part in investment decisions and that monetary policy is more effective in curbing than in stimulating an economy. There is, clearly, a great deal more to be learned about the response of economies to fiscal, monetary and other measures before we can be certain about the right mixture to use in any given circumstance.

If this is so, how can one explain the often bitter debate between Friedmanites and noe-Keynesians? The *Lloyds Bank Review* articles of Anna J. Schwartz[1] and Nicholas Kaldor,[2] respectively averring and denying the validity of the Chicago School's arguments were marked by an acrimony not usually associated with economic discussion. Economists have tended to range themselves pro-Keynes or anti-Keynes and, whilst disagreement is entirely wholesome, one may be forgiven in suspecting that the whole truth lies in neither camp.

One interesting casualty of this debate is the Radcliffe Report of 1959 to which reference has been made earlier. This report has tended to be dismissed as very pro-Keynesian because it doubted the efficacy of monetary policy. If, however, one reads the report as an account of how the monetary system was working and not as a generalisation about monetary policy, it seems fairly reasonable for it to deduce that governments would have to rely on fiscal policy. The Bank of England worked on the principle that it must buy government securities in the open market in order to prevent interest rates from diverging from its own view of the underlying trend and also in order to maintain gilt-edged prices at levels "consistent with the underlying long-term objective of preserving market conditions favourable to maximum official sales of government debt",[3] and so it was reasonable to doubt the efficacy of what passed for monetary policy in Britain. The Radcliffe Report diverted attention from the cash basis to the overall liquidity of the banks and to the wider aspects of credit control enshrined in its suggestion for "package deals". Its acceptance of the Bank of England's debt management policy as a fact of life

[1] October, 1969: *Why Money Matters.*
[2] July, 1970: *The New Monetarism.*
[3] *Bank of England Quarterly Review*, March, 1969.

would explain the deduction that reliance for controlling the economy would have to be mainly on fiscal controls. Such a conclusion would also seem feasible at a time when governments were still contravening the dictum of Keynesian analysis to counter inflation with a budget surplus. Even when budget surpluses began to be achieved, after 1967, the Bank of England continued to "lean on interest rates". At a time when money supply was being increased by a favourable balance of payments and by the Bank of England's debt management policy, it is not to be wondered at that partial credit restriction and a budget surplus failed to secure their objectives.

Not only is it unwise to discard Keynesian ideas because they didn't work in the circumstances indicated above but also it is worth considering British experience in 1969 before leaping into the arms of the new monetarism. During the first nine months of that year the supply of money was held down to $1\frac{3}{4}$ per cent compared with annual increases of over 10 per cent which had become the general experience. There was some "shake-out" of inefficient labour, a number of weaker firms closed down and share prices weakened but inflation was not eliminated. This may have been due to lack of time but it seems equally probable that the economic problem in Britain is too complex for it to be solved by one group of measures alone. In order to promote growth, maintain full employment and advance social justice fiscal, monetary and incomes policies all seem to have a part to play and, as yet, economic analysis is unable to give clear, unqualified guidance for any particular situation.

QUESTIONS

What do you understand by "monetary policy"? Discuss its use to control phases of trade cycles.

Discuss the relative merits of monetary and fiscal policies as means of controlling the economy.

What is the Quantity Theory of money? Appraise it critically.

In what ways is it suggested that keeping a tight control of the supply of money would have helped Britain in the 1960's?

Are the views of J. M. Keynes and Milton Friedman necessarily incompatible?

Collect the current figures for   i) budget out-turn
                                 ii) supply of money
                                 iii) retail prices
                                 iv) average earnings
and consider them critically in the light of Keynesian and monetarist theories.

REFERENCES AND FURTHER READING

V. Anthony: *Banks and Markets* (Heinemann, 1972)

B. Griffiths: *Money and Monetary Policy* (Longmans and I.E.A., 1971)

D. R. Croome & H. G. Johnson: *Money in Britain 1959–69* (Oxford, 1970)

Bank of England Quarterly Bulletin: *Key Issues in monetary and credit policy*, June 1971

Bank of England: *Reserve ratios and Special Deposits*, December, 1971.

13 The balance of payments

A country's balance of payments is a record of its financial transactions with the rest of the world over a period of time, usually a year. It therefore indicates whether, over a run of years, we are paying our way in the world or not.

The Balance of Payments statement

Table 1[1] contains a summary of the U.K. Balance of Payments from 1963 to 1969. The 1969 figures are analysed in more detail in Table 2.[2] It must first be pointed out that the presentation in these two tables is relatively new (it was first introduced in September, 1970) and that it represents the third revision since the Second World War. However, we shall use the current form as shown in these tables and draw attention where necessary to the changes which have been made.

The Current Balance is perhaps the most important sub-total. It shows the country's position in day-to-day dealings with the rest of the world. Visible Trade concerns our exports and imports. The monthly trade figures show this balance of visible trade, that is the total value of exports less the total value of imports. For the U.K. this figure is usually, but not necessarily, negative, indicating that her imports of goods customarily exceed her exports of goods in value.

Britain's normal deficit on the trade balance is usually counterbalanced by a surplus on the invisible account. This concerns the export and import of services; for example shipping, banking, insurance, tourism and so on. The most important positive item here is the receipts from investments abroad. The most important negative item is Government expenditure overseas, for example, in maintaining military bases abroad. If the trade balance is in deficit the surplus on invisibles may more than cover it, so that overall the current balance is in surplus. This was the case (see Table 1) in 1963, 1966, 1969 and again in 1970 when the current balance was plus £631 millions.

Items 2, 3, 4 and 5 in Table 2 make up the "long-term capital account" which used to be separately distinguished. These four items correspond roughly to British Government loans to other countries, official loans to the British Government, investment by foreign companies in British industry and investment in overseas companies by private industry here.

[1] Page 160.   [2] Page 161.

The separate presentation of the capital account used to make it liable to misinterpretation as being a statement of how the favourable or unfavourable current account was "balanced", i.e., it is argued, it gave insufficient weight to the independent nature of many long-term capital movements. In 1964 in the U.K. a current account deficit of £395 millions existed in conjunction with an *outflow* of £363 millions of long-term capital

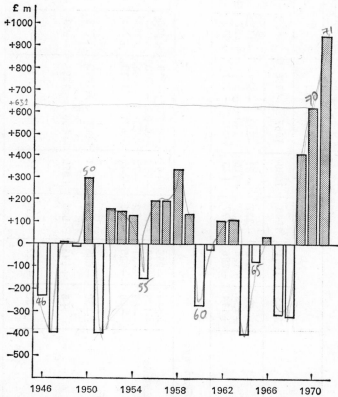

Fig 13.1 U.K. Balance of Payments on Current Account 1946–1971

and in 1968 a similar situation existed when the respective figures were £319 millions and £142 millions. A form of accounting which gave due weight to both sources of drain on the reserves would have an obvious advantage and it became the practice to show "Monetary Movements" as a separate account. This new account included short-term capital movements as well as changes in reserves and was, therefore, largely a statement of how the "*basic balance*"—the sum of Current and long term Capital Accounts—had been financed. These monetary movements are

Table 1

The U.K. Balance of Payments, Summary 1963–1971

£ millions

Current Account

	1963	1964	1965	1966	1967	1968	1969	1970	1971
Visible Trade	−80	−519	−237	−73	−552	−643	−141	+7	+297
Invisibles	+194	+124	+160	+116	+240	+324	+557	+604	+655
Current Balance	+114	−395	−77	+43	−312	−319	+416	+611	+952

Currency Flow & Official Financing

	1963	1964	1965	1966	1967	1968	1969	1970	1971
Current Balance	+114	−395	−77	+43	−312	−319	+416	+611	+952
Investment & other Capital Flows	−103	−289	−308	−564	−560	−1010	+48	+562	+1847
Balancing Item	−69	−11	+32	−26	+201	−81	+279	+114	+429
Total Currency Flow	−58	−695	−353	−547	−671	−1410	+743	+1287	+3228
S.D.R. Allocation								+171	+125
Gold Subscription to I.M.F.								−38	
Total of above	−58	−695	−353	−591	−671	−1410	+743	+1420	+3353
Financed as follows:									
Official borrowing drawn (+) repaid (−)	+5	+573	+599	+625	+556	+1296	−699	−1295	−1817
Official reserves (drawings on + additions to −)	+53	+122	−246	−34	+115	+114	−44	−125	−1536

itemised in Table 2 (Items 6 to 21, except the totals and item 14). If the basic balance was in deficit, the U.K. could borrow money from the I.M.F. or from other sources, or it could run down the reserves. If the basic balance was in surplus, the U.K. could repay debt or build up the reserves.

Table 2   Total Currency Flow and Official Financing 1969

		£ millions
1	Current balance	+416
	Investment and other capital flows	
2	Official long-term capital	− 98
3	Overseas investment in U.K. public sector	+ 63
4	Overseas investment in U.K. private sector	+621
5	U.K. private investment overseas	−617
6	Euro-dollar borrowing in London for investment overseas	+ 70
7	Import credit	+256
8	Export credit	−333
9	Balances (gross) of sterling area countries	+258
10	Balances (gross) of non-sterling countries	− 50
11	Foreign currency transactions of U.K. banks	−106
12	Other short-term flows	− 16
13	Total investment and other capital flows	+ 48
14	Balancing item	+279
15	Total currency flow	+743
16	Allocation of special drawing rights	—
17	Gold subscription to I.M.F.	—
18	Total—rows 15 to 17	+743
	Official financing Net drawing from (+) or net repayments to (−):	
19	I.M.F.	− 30
20	Other monetary authorities	−669
21	Drawings on (+) or additions to (−) official reserves	− 44
22	Total Official Financing	−743

However, the distinction between long-term and short-term capital movements was never very clear. Many short-term flows have a profound effect on our overall position. Others are translated into long-term flows through sophisticated international capital markets such as the Euro-dollar market. The new presentation takes all capital flows and lists them together. Added to the current balance they show the *total currency flow.* If this is a surplus, it shows the total amount which the Government has added to the reserves or used to pay off debt. If it is a deficit, it shows the amount which the Government has had to find. In 1968, for example, the total currency flow outwards was £1410 millions. This was the sum the government had had to find, by borrowing or by running down the reserves. In 1969, however, the currency flow was £743 millions inwards. In 1970 this figure rose to £1287 millions. These surpluses enabled the government to pay off international debt and to add to the reserves. The methods of financing adopted are shown in items 19, 20 and 21 in Table 2.

One small item which may puzzle the reader is the "Balancing Item" (Item 14). In some countries' accounts this item is called "errors and omissions". It indicates the difference between a) the total of items 1 to 12 which are often inaccurate because of the difficulties in recording transactions and because of variations in timing, and b) the amount of foreign currency which the country has in fact gained or lost (item 15) which is recorded precisely by the Bank of England. The Balancing Item indicates how accurate (or inaccurate) the records are. The key figure is the Total Currency Flow which is accurate.

Some notes on the revised Balance of Payments presentation

Item 6. Euro-dollar borrowing. This flow represents borrowing by British subjects and institutions from the large pool of Euro-dollars deposited in London.

Item 7 and 8. We give credit on exports and receive credit when buying imports.

Items 9 and 10. Overseas countries and their private citizens and firms add to or withdraw from the bank balances they hold in the U.K.

Item 11. This item represents the lending and other dealings in foreign currencies of U.K. banks.

Items 16 and 17. In some years there is a gold subscription to the I.M.F. The receipt of Special Drawing Rights from the I.M.F. (when appropriate) will also affect the total currency flow (see Table 1, 1970 and 1971).

Items 19 and 20. These show borrowings from or repayments to the I.M.F. and to other overseas institutions (central banks, etc.) reflecting the direction of movement of the total currency flow.

Item 21. This represents the movement in the reserves for the year in question.

Movements in the Balance of Payments

In recent decades Britain has consistently sought a current account surplus for a number of reasons. She desired to invest overseas, to help underdeveloped countries and to build up investments which were run down during the Second World War and which bring in income to the Invisible Account (as Profits, Interest and Dividends from Overseas Investment). She had to repay debt; debt incurred during the war, particularly to

Sterling Area countries, debt incurred immediately after the war to the U.S.A. and to Canada, and debt incurred since then to the I.M.F. and to other international groups. She has needed to build up her reserves, which were too low to cope with expanding world trade and particularly to take the strain of the whole Sterling Area. For all these reasons, Britain has needed not merely a current account surplus but also, ideally, a positive total currency flow. We shall later see that she has usually failed to achieve these objectives.

An unwanted result of a balance of payments surplus is that it tends to be inflationary. In the circular flow of income, net exports represent an injection into the flow. And if to this we add all currency flowing in, a positive currency flow may well be inflationary, depending on the employment position in the country and how the currency inflow is used. Consequently, a country for which a surplus is not imperative may well prefer a nil net currency flow in order to keep the economy stable rather than to encourage inflation or deflation. What might be called a "balanced" payments position tends to be neutral. Money is neither flowing into nor out of the country.

Why then should a country ever seek a balance of payments deficit? There are a number of possibilities. An underdeveloped country may be impelled to import goods which cannot be balanced by exports in order to keep economic growth going. Such a country may also receive vast amounts of aid in the form of capital investment to assist its economy. On the other hand, a country like West Germany may adopt a similar policy for completely different reasons. Her deficits become other countries' surpluses, so that in this way she could help deficit countries to get their payments position in order. Furthermore, just as a surplus on the balance of payments is inflationary, so a deficit will be deflationary. Money is flowing out of the country, rather than in. This is one way of combating an inflationary tendency at home and of taking the heat out of an economy.

It is customary to regard a balance of payments surplus as good and a balance of payments deficit as bad. But one country's surplus is another country's deficit; and it is just as necessary for surplus countries to reduce their overall surpluses and so give the deficit countries a chance to remedy their situation, as it is for the deficit countries to reduce their overall deficits. Both types of country have responsibilities, to themselves, to their neighbours and to world trade in general.

Curing an imbalance in the Balance of Payments

The terms "a favourable balance of payments" or "an adverse balance of payments" refer strictly only to the current account and if we wish to talk about the net effects of the current account and long-term capital movements we must refer to a favourable or unfavourable overall or basic balance. This is rather confusing when, at the same time, we know that the total account must balance. A more subtle terminological problem arises out of distinguishing between i) a neutral balance and ii) one involving significant financing either officially or by changes in the reserves. Obviously we cannot talk of balancing in the first case and not balancing in the second. What we do is to call the second case one of "imbalance".

a)   *Changing the level of aggregate demand.*

One of the results of the level of aggregate demand rising faster than in the economies of a country's trading partners is that imports tend to rise. Furthermore, home produced goods tend to be bought at home instead of being released for exports. If the rising demand gets beyond the full employment level of national income (or even near to it), prices will begin to rise and, with prices, incomes. The resulting rise in prices will accentuate the decline of exports, which become relatively less attractive to overseas buyers, and will encourage the growth of imports, which become relatively more attractive to home consumers. Rising aggregate demand, therefore, produces a balance of payments deficit, particularly if it leads to inflation. In contrast, falling aggregate demand tends to produce a balance of payments surplus, particularly if it leads to deflation.

One way in which a balance of payments deficit can be cured is therefore by deflation. Aggregate demand is cut back, by increased taxation and reduced government spending. These fiscal measures are reinforced by reductions in the supply of money and rises in the rate of interest through monetary measures. As a result demand falls; incomes fall; prices fall or at least remain stable. In consequence, imports are cut back, resources are released for export, and prices move in such a way that exports are encouraged. Exports should rise, imports fall, and the deficit should be wiped out.

On the other hand, a balance of payments surplus can be cured by inflation (or, in times of unemployment, by reflation). Here the reduction of taxation and the increase in government spending raises aggregate demand. The money supply is increased and the rate of interest lowered. Credit may be further extended by direct action on hire purchase controls. In consequence, imports increase, and home resources are drawn into home consumption. If prices rise, exports are further discouraged because they become relatively less attractive to foreign buyers. Imports should rise, exports fall, and the balance of payments surplus should disappear.

b)   *Changing the exchange rate*

Before we consider the various conditions which limit the application of the above theoretical approach in practice, let us look at the second method by which an imbalance in the payments position can be corrected. The exchange rate is the rate at which, under the I.M.F. rules, one country's currency exchanges for another. For example, £1 = 4·03 dollars. Devaluation is the lowering of this exchange rate by deliberate action. In 1949, for example, the U.K. exchange rate was lowered from £1 = 4·03 dollars to

£1 = 2·80 dollars. (The word "deliberate" is included to distinguished this process from depreciation, the falling of the exchange rate through market forces of supply and demand). Revaluation is the reverse of devaluation. It means the raising of the exchange rate by deliberate action. For example, the German deutschmark was revalued in 1961 and again in 1969.

When a country devalues, its goods become cheaper in terms of other currencies, whereas imported goods become dearer in terms of the home currency. Cheaper exports and dearer imports should mean more exports and fewer imports, so that a balance of trade deficit should be reduced. In the case of revaluation, a country's goods become dearer in terms of other currencies, and foreign goods become cheaper in terms of the home currency. Cheaper imports and dearer exports should mean more imports and fewer exports, so that a balance of trade surplus should be reduced.

Devaluation will not work in this way, however, unless certain conditions are fulfilled. Let us deal first with the elasticities of demand. It is true that a fall in the price of exports will cause the volume of exports to increase. However, it is the value of exports which is important. In order to benefit, the country which devalues must secure a greater revenue from exports than before. This means that the elasticity of demand for exports must be greater than 1. In algebraic terms, $p_2q_2 > p_1q_1$ where p_1 and p_2 are the prices, and q_1 and q_2 are the quantities of exports sold before and after devaluation respectively. In diagrammatic form:

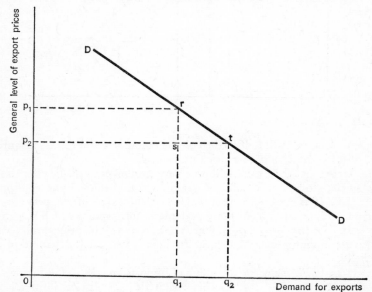

Fig 13.2 Demand for exports

Referring to Fig 13.2 the total revenue from exports before devaluation was $p_1 \times q_1$ represented by the area of the rectangle Op_1rq_1. Total revenue after devaluation was $p_2 \times q_2$, represented by the area of the rectangle Op_2tq_2. For devaluation to be successful, i.e. to increase revenue from exports, it is necessary that rectangle stq_2q_1 is greater in area than p_1rsp_2.

The same argument will apply to deflation, at least in as far as a relative fall in price is expected to produce a favourable movement in the balance of payments. It is true, of course, that deflation, by acting directly on

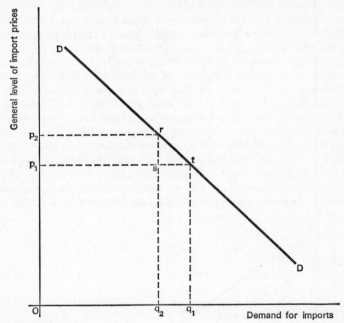

Fig 13.3 Demand for imports

aggregate demand, will reduce the volume of imports and release resources for export irrespective of any price movements.

The argument for imports follows a very similar pattern. For the rise in import prices to be beneficial, it is not enough that the volume of imports should fall. It is necessary also that the total value of imports should decrease. This entails an elasticity of demand for imports which is greater than 1. In this case, $p_2q_2 < p_1q_1$, where p_1 and p_2 are the prices and q_1 and q_2 are the amounts bought of imports before and after devaluation respectively.

Referring to Fig 13.3, for the value of imports bought to fall it is necessary that $Op_2rq_2 < Op_1tq_1$ i.e. that rectangle p_2rsp_1 is less in area than rectangle stq_1q_2.

It thus appears that for a successful devaluation or a successful deflation (insofar as this depends on relative price movements) the elasticity of
demand for exports must be greater than one and the elasticity of demand
(E_d) for imports must also be greater than one. But supposing E_d exports
is 2 and E_d imports is less than 1? Or supposing E_d exports is more than 2
and E_d imports is 0? The net effect obviously depends on the combined
effect of the two elasticities of demand. The Marshall–Lerner condition
for successful depreciation (or devaluation) states that the sum of the
elasticities of demand for that country's exports and imports must be
greater than one. Since our previous reckoning would produce a sum
greater than two, we must look a little more closely at the Marshall–
Lerner condition.

We will first consider the effects of a devaluation in the local currency,
e.g. a U.K. devaluation in terms of sterling. If, in the extreme case,
elasticity of demand for exports was zero, receipts from exports in (e.g.)
sterling would be the same as before. Now the Marshall–Lerner condition
says that the sum of the elasticities must be greater than 1. Hence, the
elasticity of demand for imports must be greater than 1. In this case, the
value of imports in sterling will fall, and the combination of the same
receipts from exports plus less expenditure on imports will improve the
balance of payments.

Take another extreme case, when the elasticity of demand for imports
is zero. In this case imports will rise in sterling value by the full amount of
the devaluation—let us say, by 10 per cent. The Marshall–Lerner
condition then indicates that the elasticity of demand for exports must be
greater than 1, so that the value of exports will rise by more than 10 per
cent (perhaps by 15 per cent). The 15 per cent rise in export revenue
allied to the 10 per cent in import expenditure will improve the balance of
payments.

The same argument can be pursued in foreign exchange (let us say, gold).
If the elasticity of demand for exports is zero, then the gold value of
exports will decline by the full extent of devaluation (say by 10 per cent).
However, if the elasticity of demand for imports is greater than 1, the gold
value of imports will decline by more than 10 per cent (perhaps by 15 per
cent) and, the fall in the value of import value being greater than the
fall in the value of exports, the balance of payments will improve.

If, on the other hand, the elasticity of demand for imports is nil, then
the gold value of imports will remain unchanged. The elasticity of demand
for exports must be greater than 1, so that the gold value of exports will
rise, if the balance of payments is to improve.

These extreme cases, in either domestic or foreign currency, do not
prove the Marshall–Lerner condition, but they do indicate its validity
well enough. For a significant improvement in the balance of payments, of
course, the sum of the elasticities might need to be considerably greater
than 1—perhaps 3, 4, or 5.

Revaluation

All the arguments applied to devaluation can be applied equally well to revaluation. The raising of the exchange rate will increase imports and lower exports. The balance of payments will deteriorate provided the sum of elasticities of demand for exports and imports, reckoned in terms of either domestic or foreign currency, is greater than 1. Since the object of re-valuation is to reduce a payments surplus, such a deterioration will fulfil the aim of the exercise.

Conditions necessary for the success of a devaluation

We have already considered in detail the Marshall–Lerner condition, indicating that for a devaluation to be successful, the sum of the elasticities of demand for imports and exports must exceed 1. Other important factors are:

1   the country which is devaluing must not inflate; or, at least, it must inflate at a lower rate than its competitors in world trade. Inflation will reduce the price advantage secured by devaluation. It may be so damaging as to counteract entirely this advantage. If a country inflates, but at a lower rate than other countries, the slower rise in home prices will add to the advantage secured by devaluation.

2   it must be possible for the devaluing country to increase its exports to meet any expansion in the demand for them. This requires either that there is already some slack in the economy or that the home market is squeezed to release resources to the export industries. The latter is the most likely requirement because over-valuation is frequently associated with inflation. In this case the restriction of the home market is also import-ant to prevent the expansion of export output from driving up costs and prices and thus, ultimately, slowing itself down.

The British Balance of Payments since 1960

1   *The General Picture*

In Table 1[1] there are details of the U.K. Balance of Payments position between 1963 and 1971. The general picture of the 60's was as follows.

In 1960 and 1961 there were current account deficits, accentuated in 1960 by a large capital outflow. In 1962 and 1963 there were current account surpluses, but in 1964 a very large deficit on both current and capital accounts. The deficit was reduced in 1965 and turned into a small current surplus in 1966. But in 1967 there was another large current account deficit, followed by a similar deficit in 1968. By 1969 this had been turned into a large surplus, which gave way to an even larger surplus in 1970 and 1971.

[1] Page 160.

A persistent factor in Britain's balance of payments problem has been the inadequacy of her foreign exchange reserves. These reserves act as a buffer against fluctuations in payments and receipts, much in the same way as a family's cash holding does but with one vital difference: if they

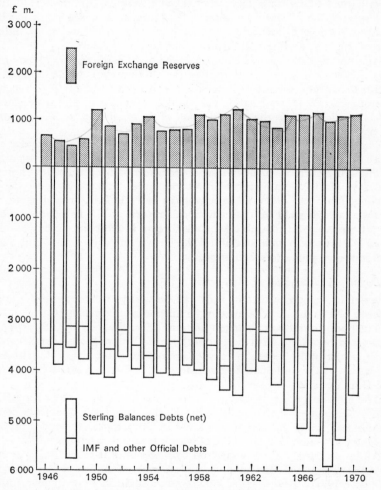

Fig 13.4 U.K. Reserves and Short-term Liabilities 1946–1970

are inadequate this fact induces speculative pressures on them. The adequacy of reserves is judged against i) the normal fluctuations in trade and ii) the country's short-term liabilities to foreigners. Britain's position in this latter respect is depicted in Fig. 13.4. Fortunately the foreign held balances are fairly stable due to the usefulness of the pound as a reserve currency for various Sterling Area countries. But if the reserves are weakened by a chronic overall deficit the owners of the balances are bound to question the advisability of holding reserves threatened by devaluation. At a certain stage, when it becomes apparent that devaluation is very probable, a one way option offers itself to speculators. It has become impossible to lose and quite likely that they will enjoy a windfall gain if they sell sterling and buy, say, dollars and convert back later.

Another source of speculative pressure on the reserves is "leads and lags": British importers, nervous of devaluation, accelerate their payments to foreigners while exporters, hoping to benefit, delay their receipts from abroad. Such speculation may add to a country's difficulties but it is not pernicious: it is the natural result of the combination of inadequate reserves and a weak balance of payments.

The reason that various post-war governments did not make the increasing of reserves a priority may well have been that they preferred to allow the current surplus in good years to finance foreign investment, which yields Britain a high rate of return, rather than use it for paying off sterling liabilities, whose interest cost is relatively low, or adding to the reserves, which yield no direct financial return at all. In retrospect one might question the advisability of this foreign investment strategy, which often left Britain in such an illiquid foreign payments position, and made the pound so prone to speculation.

2 Deflation and the Balance of Payments

The deflationary measures in 1961 can be taken to illustrate those taken in each of Britain's ten balance of payments crises since 1946.

The background was a current account deficit in 1960 of £265 millions, reinforced by a long term capital outflow of £192 millions. Furthermore, short term funds began to leave London in February, 1961, to take advantage of the anticipated revaluation of the German deutschmark and the Dutch guilder.

The measures taken in July, 1961 included a raising of Bank Rate from 5 to 7 per cent; a further call for special deposits (from 2 to 3 per cent); an increase in expenditure taxes; a cut in Government expenditure; and a call for a "pause in the growth of wages, salaries and dividends".

Although Bank Rate was lowered by stages until it reached $4\frac{1}{2}$ per cent in April, 1962, the Budget of that year was essentially a "no-change" budget, with few new changes in taxation, a slight increase in government spending, and an overall Budget surplus remaining virtually unchanged.

The Balance of Payments improved in the second half of 1961 and current surpluses were recorded in both 1962 and 1963. Undoubtedly the July 1961 measures had some effect, so that in this case deflation seems to have worked. But there were other factors—for example, a relatively high level of unemployment, which persisted through 1962; a low level of industrial production; and, on the other hand, rapid rises in wages and in prices which would tend to counter some of the effect of the deflationary package.

3 Devaluation and the Balance of Payments

There have been two devaluations of the pound sterling since 1945. In September, 1949, the pound was devalued from £1 = $4.03 to £1 = $2.80 and in November, 1967, the exchange rate was lowered to £1 = $2.40.

The background to the second devaluation was a rapidly worsening balance of payments position from a current account surplus in 1966 to a large deficit in 1967, leading to widespread speculation on the foreign exchange markets against the pound. In fact the pound had been showing signs of over-valuation as early as 1962–3, had been seriously weakened by the 1964 crisis and had had to be supported by heavy borrowings from European central banks and the I.M.F. During the lull of 1965–6 further I.M.F. loans were used to fortify the reserves but inflation continued largely unabated. In 1967 the precarious balance was upset by a series of shocks: a slow down in business in Europe reduced British exports, the Suez canal was blocked, and strikes brought the London and Liverpool docks to a standstill in September. In the background the relaxation of "the wage freeze" and the ending of the 1964 import surcharge scheme combined to weaken the balance of payments. Then, to cap it all, the strong speculation in favour of the German deutschmark caused a drain on Britain's reserves. Possible devaluation was hawked around the corridors of foreign governments and the I.M.F. so that a veritable flood of speculative swaps out of sterling had reduced Britain's reserves to a parlous state by November 18th when the official announcement of devaluation from $2.80 to $2.40 was made.

Essentially, then, the 1967 sterling devaluation was the consequence of a long period of inflationary pressure. During much of the period 1959 to 1966 wage costs per unit of output had been rising much faster in Britain than in most other industrial countries. This in turn had caused the export prices of British goods to rise substantially, though by less than the increase in labour costs.

This suggests that Britain's export sector was at a double disadvantage: with steeply rising costs, the rise in the price of British goods was *too little for exports to remain profitable, and too much for them to remain competitive* against foreign products. This was the reason for the failure of the fiscal and monetary restraints imposed at various times in the early and middle 1960's to have much effect in shifting resources into exports; and the reason why it had become necessary to run the economic machine with "the brakes on" more and more often. Thus the long-run strategy of the 1967 devaluation was to resolve this dilemma by making British exporting both competitive and profitable.

The act of devaluation was reinforced by severe deflationary measures: a crisis Bank rate of 8 per cent; restrictions on bank lending; and tighter hire purchase terms. All this was followed by a March budget in 1968 which increased taxation by almost £800 millions and produced a Budget surplus of almost £1,400 millions. These measures were the price that had to be paid for a further loan from the I.M.F.: clearly indicative of the extent to which a series of crises had destroyed confidence not only in the pound but in the country's ability to rectify matters.

In the event the balance of payments deficit of 1967 was followed by a current account deficit of £319 millions in 1968. The prices of imports rose some 10 per cent but increased consumer expenditure and re-stocking by industry pushed up their volume by 10·5 per cent so that their value increased by about 21·6 per cent. On the other hand, many exporters preferred to maintain the foreign currency prices of their goods and to take the benefits of devaluation in the form of higher sterling prices (and profits). The average price of exports rose by some 8 per cent, volume by 13·5 per cent, and value by 22·6 per cent. Devaluation had yielded no appreciable gain to the balance of payments.

However, the second quarter of 1969 saw a change in Britain's fortunes, and evidence that the 1967 devaluation was at last working. The rise in the value of imports halted whilst that in the value of exports continued. A surplus on current account materialised and was sufficient to finance the now much reduced outflow of long-term capital and to enable some repayment of the massive short-term debts. There was, at last, some resurgence of confidence in sterling and some improvement in the reserves.

The 1969 turn around was achieved against a backcloth of rising world trade the effect of which more than counter-balanced that of continuing inflation in Britain. Exports of manufactures rose by 15 per cent between 1967 and 1968, and by a further 17 per cent in 1968–69. At the same time, however, Britain's share of the world's export of manufactures fell from 12·2 per cent to 11·2 per cent, so that our expansion of exports did not keep pace with the overall expansion of world trade, despite devaluation. This would suggest that inflation in Britain did in fact have a harmful effect on our export trade.

A factor which assisted the 1967 devaluation was that most other industrial countries did not devalue. This gave Britain an advantage which was not immediately eroded by competitive devaluations by other industrial countries. Moreover, during 1969, the deutschmark was revalued upwards by 9 per cent and this added to the price advantage of competing British goods.

Finally, it tends to be overlooked that the improvement in the balance of payments after 1968 was assisted by a strong independent rise in Britain's invisible earnings. Conversely, the weak pre-devaluation situation reflected not only inflation but also low and declining invisible earnings. As Fig. 13.5 shows, this downward trend concealed two distinct elements: a slow improvement in private earnings, and a marked worsening in government payments abroad, especially for military purposes. In the late 1960's, on the other hand, private invisible earnings, particularly

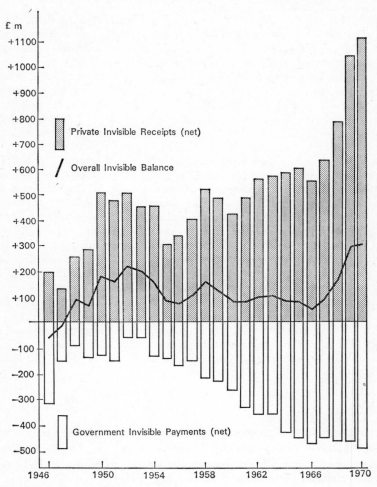

Fig 13.5 U.K. "Invisibles" 1946–1970

from foreign investments rose substantially, whereas government payments abroad levelled off as Britain cut down her foreign commitments. Hence the improvement in Britain's invisible balance, which reinforced the long-term effects of devaluation.

The dilemma of the seventies

During 1970 and 1971 large current account surpluses enabled Britain to repay the short-term debts incurred in past crises and to strengthen her reserves substantially.

However the very size of these surpluses highlighted the difficulty for Britain of how to combine growth, full employment, and balance of payments equilibrium. It is true that a reduction in inflationary demand pressure had eventually brought about an export recovery after the 1967 devaluation of sterling. But the cost of financial restraints was a slow down in production and investment spending, and increasing unemployment touching one million by 1972. If, instead, a full employment policy had been pursued the rise in demand and output would certainly have led to higher imports and a smaller payments surplus—perhaps even a deficit. And so the apparent strength of the balance of payments around 1970 was not only spurious but actually a sign of a failure of economic policy.

At the same time, the increasing pressure of wage-cost inflation continued to threaten the long-run competitiveness of British goods and services. This is bound up with the fact that productivity grows more slowly in Britain than in most other industrial countries, whereas money wages grow at a similar rate. Thus to combine growth, full employment and payments equilibrium it is essential to restrain the pace of inflation. Also it will probably be necessary for Britain to exercise reasonable freedom over her exchange rate so as to avoid the possible straitjacket of one day having to defend an over-valued pound. Since the 1971 dollar crisis there have been signs of greater flexibility in the field of exchange rates e.g. the floating of the pound in late 1971 and again in mid-1972.

All this suggests the need for an economy running at rather less than top speed. Whether the combination of price stability and cautious expansion at a level below extreme full employment is a practical policy will remain to be seen.

QUESTIONS

"Britain's balance of payments difficulties in the 1960's were the result of mismanagement of the economy." Comment.

What measures have British governments taken to cope with balance of payments crises? How successful have they been?

What have been the effects of the 1967 devaluation on Britain's balance of payments?

Discuss the long-term and the short-term factors causing Britain's balance of payments difficulties in recent years.

Compare devaluation and deflation as measures for dealing with balance of payments crises.

To what extent have Reserve Currency considerations aggravated Britain's balance of payments problems?

Are the monthly trade figures a good guide to Britain's balance of payments position?

REFERENCES AND FURTHER READING

F. W. Paish: *How the Economy Works* (Macmillan, 1970)

B. J. Cohen: *Balance of Payments Policy* (Penguin, 1969)

J. F. Nicholson: *Contemporary Problems of Foreign Exchange and Trade* (Ginn, 1971)

A. R. Prest: *The U.K. Economy* (Weidenfeld and Nicholson, 1970)

P. Donaldson: *Guide to the British Economy* (Penguin, 1971)

Board of Trade: *Reports on Overseas Trade* (H.M.S.O. Monthly)

Board of Trade: *Trade and Industry* (H.M.S.O. Weekly)

14 International monetary affairs

If international specialisation and trade are to develop, and allow the world's living standards to improve, two important conditions must be fulfilled. The first of these is that countries should feel able to resist the temptation to use controls, subsidies and tariffs to protect their home industries against each others' exports. The second condition, which is the subject of this chapter, is that there should be an efficient medium of exchange between countries; that is to say, an efficient international monetary system. Moreover, if the world's monetary system is sound it is less likely that countries will feel it necessary to use tariffs and other restrictions on trade.

The need for "good-neighbour" policies

An important ingredient of international economic stability is that the various nations co-operate in pursuing mutually consistent policies. Take the case of a country, A, which either accidentally, or in order to improve its balance of payments, pursues a policy of recession and unemployment resulting in a large fall in its imports. Since one country's imports are another country's exports, A's trading partners will be "infected" with recession originating in their export sectors and spreading via the multiplier effect through their economies. In addition to this, the loss of foreign exchange reserves of these other countries may by its impact on their banking systems and money supply reinforce the recessionary tendencies. The effect of this fall in income will be to make their imports from A (A's exports) fall also; and so on. The final result will be a new equilibrium in which all the countries find themselves worse off with lower levels of income and employment.

Suppose, though, that one of the other countries, B, takes active measures to protect its own employment situation. If B seeks to do this by restricting its own imports it will intensify the recession not only in A but also in other countries, since under the G.A.T.T.[1] rules B is prevented from discriminating against A. This generates further harmful 'feedback' effects, including possibly retaliation, on its own export and employment situation. On the other hand if B tries to end its recession with monetary and fiscal policies aimed at expanding home demand, its imports will increase and its balance of payments and foreign exchange reserves suffer.

[1] General Agreement on Tariffs and Trade.

The same sort of harmful chain reaction can occur in the opposite direction. A country experiencing inflation but holding large foreign reserves may seek to absorb excess demand by reducing its exports and increasing its imports. The reader will be able to analyse how this could lead to inflation being 'exported' to other countries.

A sound international monetary structure

Broadly speaking, a sound international monetary system under fixed exchange rate arrangements, such as the post-war I.M.F.[1] adjustable peg

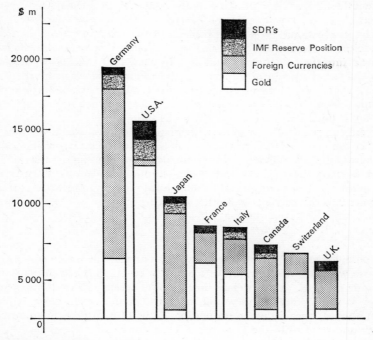

Fig 14.1 World Reserves 1971

system, implies two things. First, each country's central bank needs to hold a large enough reserve of foreign exchange (gold, S.D.Rs[2] and foreign currencies) to be able to finance not just seasonal trade fluctuations, but any *temporary* balance of payments deficit, while the root cause of that deficit—for example inflation—is being tackled. It is also important that the country's reserves should be large enough, relative to its short-term liabilities abroad, to sustain confidence at home and abroad in its currency and so deter speculation.

[1] International Monetary Fund.   [2] Special Drawing Rights.

Secondly, the world's money system needs to contain an arrangement to permit the exchange-rate of a country with a *fundamental* balance of payments disequilibrium (that is, one which could be reversed only by severe deflation or reflation over a period of years) to change its exchange rate so as to help a return to equilibrium.

Fixed exchange rates

In 1947 the International Monetary Fund was set up to aim at international monetary equilibrium. The economists who designed the Fund were influenced in their thinking by the monetary problems of the pre-war world.

The international economic problems of the 1920's were related to the Gold Bullion Standard. This was a fixed exchange rate system in which the home currency of a country could be converted at an official specified rate into gold and foreign currencies on the foreign exchange market, e.g. before 1931 a British firm exporting to the United States could be sure of turning its dollar earnings back into pounds (with which to meet its home costs of production) at a rate of £1 = $4.86.

From the point of view of international trade fixed exchange rates are very convenient. Unfortunately, against this must be set a possible drawback from the point of view of any particular country using the system. This drawback arises essentially from how the authorities in a country answer the question, "At what official exchange rate (parity) shall our currency convert into the currencies of other countries?"

Too low a rate

Suppose, for example, a country decides on an exchange rate which is (in a sense we shall now examine) "too low". To take an extreme instance, imagine the U.K. at the present time (1972) deciding on an exchange rate of £1 = $1. Evidently this would make the pound worth more at home than abroad, because without question £1 will buy a greater quantity of goods and services in the U.K. than $1 in the U.S.A.

What would be the effect of choosing this 'wrong' exchange rate? Firstly, British firms selling in, for example, the U.S. market, would find their export prices in dollars much lower and more competitive than those of many American products; while American firms selling in the U.K. would in many cases find their products over-priced in terms of pounds. As a result there would be a strong tendency for Britain's exports to the U.S.A. and other countries to rise, and her imports to fall.

If Britain's economy was at or near full-employment the extension of demand for exports and import-substitution would, if large enough, trigger off, or intensify, inflationary pressures and rising prices. Moreover, the higher home prices of imports would quite likely set off claims for higher wages which would lead to a further inflation of costs and prices. An inflationary process of this kind probably occurred after 1949 when sterling was devalued by 30 per cent against "hard" currencies like the dollar.

Similar developments could occur in a country whose foreign exchange rate is initially "correct" but which finds the purchasing power of its currency, say because of falling costs, becoming greater at home than abroad—in many ways the position of the West German economy in the 1950's and 1960's, when it was twice necessary for the mark to be revalued upwards on the Foreign Exchange market in line with its increased domestic value in order to check inflationary pressures and ease the balance of payments problems of its trading partners. However, in recent years, Japan has demonstrated that a country can secure the foreign trade advantages of an artificially low foreign exchange rate for quite a long time as long as it is prepared i) to maintain strict disinflationary controls over its economy and ii) to ignore the problems created for other trading nations.

Too high a rate

Take on the other hand the case of a country deciding on an exchange rate which turns out to be "too high": many of its exports will be over-priced and uncompetitive, while imports into it from other countries will be low-priced and competitive. The level of output, incomes and, perhaps, prices will fall and the country concerned will find itself faced with i) rising levels of unemployment and ii) economic stagnation as was the case in the U.K. during the 1920's. Nevertheless, artificially high exchange rates have often been defended as pertaining to national prestige!

Recent background history

1   *The International Monetary Fund*

During the Second World War most of the world's monetary system was in effect "frozen". During this period discussions were started which culminated in the decision in 1944 at Bretton Woods in the U.S.A. to set up a new monetary regime which would overcome the disadvantages both of a rigid gold standard and of an unstable floating rate system.

After much negotiation between the British and American delegations, led by Keynes and White respectively, final agreement was reached, mainly along the lines of the White plan, and the I.M.F. was set up in 1947. In simple terms we can regard it as a club, consisting of most non-communist nations. Like any club, the I.M.F. has benefits and rules.

The main benefit is that any member country can, in a time of *temporary* balance of payments weakness, draw on the I.M.F.'s supply of gold and foreign currencies in order to supplement its reserves while it is taking measures to strengthen its balance of payments. In return, each member on joining the I.M.F. makes available as an "entrance fee" a quota, one-quarter of which is gold and three-quarters its own currency. The size of this quota depends on the trading importance of the member concerned. Normally a member may only "purchase", i.e. draw on, foreign currencies to the extent of 25 per cent of its quota in any twelve-month period; and drawings must stop altogether when the Fund's holdings of the member's own currency reach 200 per cent of its quota. Interest of $\frac{1}{2}$ per cent is charged and an extra progressive charge is made on drawings which exceed 100 per cent of a member's quota.

The main rule of the I.M.F. is that each member country must undertake to make its currency convertible into gold (and other currencies) at a declared exchange rate which will thereafter remain generally fixed (pegged) within an overall band of two per cent of its parity. This band was increased to $4\frac{1}{2}$ per cent in 1971. Devaluations and revaluations of over 10 per cent may, however, be made with the approval of the Fund in the case of a country with a *fundamental* payments disequilibrium. Hence the term "adjustable peg". The I.M.F. is therefore designed to combine the advantages of the gold standard (freely convertible currencies at stable exchange rates) with the advantages of floating exchange rates (full scope for full employment policies) whilst avoiding the drawbacks of each.

In the early years it soon became evident that the I.M.F.'s pool of gold and currencies was too small. In the period from 1947 to 1957 world production and international trade increased dramatically, yet the resources of the I.M.F. remained fixed at a value of about $9000 m. There was a risk that countries using the I.M.F. monetary system, like the gold standard before it, would come to suffer from an increasing shortage of reserves, and have to live with persistently deflationary measures to protect their currencies.

To counter this the I.M.F. introduced in 1952 a system of "stand-by credits" which enables it to advance currencies to any member anticipating a crisis and a fall in its reserves, but which does not wish actually to draw the funds unless absolutely necessary. In effect it allows an extended and more economic use of the I.M.F.'s limited supply of exchange. The first major use of stand-by credits was by Britain in 1956.

2   Gold, dollars and pounds

Gold is still the main single element in world foreign exchange reserves. However, to-day, as earlier in the century, the supply of gold for monetary use has failed to grow as fast as international trade, so that a smaller and smaller part of most countries' foreign exchange reserves has consisted of gold. The cause of the shortage is partly that some gold output is sold for industrial and ornamental uses; but mainly it is due to the unprofitability (under existing conditions) for the main gold-producing country, South Africa, of increasing gold output substantially, and the unwillingness of another gold producer, the Soviet Union, to accept trade arrangements that would lead to any large export of gold to the West. Moreover the scarcer gold becomes the more there is a tendency for a kind of international "Gresham's Law" to operate—for gold to be hoarded privately and centrally and go out of international circulation.

The role of the *dollar* as the main reserve currency began when the post-war dollar shortage was accommodated by means of a massive injection of dollar aid from America to Europe under the Marshall Plan in the years 1947 to 1952. Next, in the late 1950's the U.S.A. itself moved into payments deficit and this caused a further outflow from her reserves of first gold and later dollars. There were several reasons for this payments deficit. It was due to 1) the international competitive difficulties of American goods as a result of home inflation and the 1949 European devaluations, 2) the outflow of American business investment and foreign aid, 3) increasing military expenditure culminating in the escalation in the late 1960's of the Vietnam War, which not only bore directly on the balance of payments, but also aggravated inflationary pressures at home.

Just as in the case of gold, though for different reasons, there is a limit as to how far the dollar can be used as a reserve currency. This limit is set by how far the American authorities can tolerate a continuing payments deficit and increasing foreign debts; and how far foreign countries will be prepared to accept debts against the U.S. in the form of dollars rather than receiving gold. The gold crisis of March 1968 showed that this limit of confidence had already been reached.

Up to that time the central banks had, by intervening when necessary in the gold and foreign exchange market, successfully maintained a buying and selling gold price of $35 per ounce. The idea behind this stabilisation policy was that changes in the price of gold, on which the whole world system of credit is based, can set off dangerous inflationary and deflationary pressures. However as the United States deficit got bigger, confidence in the dollar declined, with the result that early in 1968 the run on the dollar, and the demand for gold, became so heavy that the official gold price could not be held. A "two-tier" system was introduced consisting of an official $35 central bank market, and a free private market which is responsive to the forces of supply and demand. This removed the possibility of a dollar crisis draining off official gold stocks into private hands. However there remained the possibility of speculative movements out of dollars into other national currencies and in the 1971 crisis this materialised on an enormous scale.

Sterling has long been used as an international reserve currency. An important route by which the pound found its way into the reserves of other countries was through sterling balances arising out of wartime and post-war borrowing by Britain from Sterling Area countries. These foreign holdings of sterling became useful to their holders in two stages: first in the late 1940's and early 1950's as they were released ("unblocked") from wartime controls and made available as foreign exchange for use inside the Sterling Area; and secondly, after 1958, when the pound became convertible into dollars and other currencies and was, in principle, as "good as gold". This was true, however, only as long as Britain's balance of payments seemed secure enough to allay fears that the pound might return to inconvertibility, or be devalued against gold and the dollar. From 1964 to 1967 these fears did become increasingly justified and the status of the pound as a world currency became questionable.

In spite of the use of the dollar and the pound, (and since 1970 S.D.R.s), the post-war international monetary system has remained essentially gold-based. Not only do member countries of the I.M.F. have to contribute part of their I.M.F. quotas in gold; but the international acceptability of the dollar and the pound has rested in the last resort on their being convertible into gold. The present "adjustable peg" system differs however from that of the 1920's in that there are now two world reserve currencies, instead of one; and that there now exists the I.M.F. to manage an expandable international supply of foreign exchange and S.D.R.s, and aim for stable but flexible exhange rates.

3 The 1961 currency crisis

The closing of the Suez canal in 1956 set off speculation against the pound because it was widely believed that Britain's economy would be vulner-able to an interruption of Middle East oil supplies. To protect its reserves Britain made use of the 1952 I.M.F. provision to obtain a large stand-by credit. In this way the Fund was successfully used to counter the effects of speculation on a major international currency, the devaluation of which would have provoked a world-wide re-adjustment of exchange rates. In 1957 Britain obtained a further stand-by credit to support the pound.

Nevertheless, it was becoming clear that if the Fund was to continue to be used successfully it would have to be enlarged to keep up with the growth of world trade. In September 1959 the I.M.F. adopted a scheme to increase members' quotas and hence the size of its foreign exchange drawing facilities by 50 per cent. This increased the Fund's value from $9000m. to about $14 000m. Moreover by this time the convertibility of the pound and other West European currencies had increased the effective scope of the Fund's resources: previously many of the Fund's currencies had only been paper assets of little use for drawing on by members to protect their reserves. In 1966 there was a further increase in quotas, enlarging the Fund to over $20 000m. In 1970 the size of the Fund was again increased, to about $30 000m.

A searching test of the I.M.F. came in 1961 and arose largely from a weakening balance of payments in Britain, following the election inflation of 1959, and the emergence of large balance of payments surpluses in West Germany and Holland. The strong position of Germany and Holland had in fact been a feature of the 1950's, and was the result of a combination of, on the one hand, rapidly improving productivity and efficiency and, on the other, austere monetary and fiscal policies preventing inflation; both these factors led to German and Dutch production costs and export prices becoming increasingly competitive at the expense of, for example, exports from Britain where productivity was growing slowly and inflation was not under control.

In March, 1961 the German mark and the Dutch guilder were revalued upwards by 5 per cent, and this sudden shock showed how vulnerable the pound was to speculation. With widespread fears of a further revaluation of the mark and the guilder, or a devaluation of the pound, a flood of speculation set in as speculators sold sterling and rushed to buy marks and guilders. Britain's foreign exchange reserves came under heavy pressure, particularly now that sterling had become convertible and could be bought and sold fairly freely on the foreign exchange market.

There were two international responses to the dangerous 1961 situation. The first was the "Basile Club rescue operation", which was arranged in the midst of the crisis to counter the speculation and which, though it took place outside the I.M.F., involved the leading I.M.F. member nations. The essence of the operation was that their central banks agreed to "swap" each others' currencies so as to defeat speculation and protect each others' reserves.

In the 1961 crisis central bank swaps protected the pound successfully up to July, when the British government introduced disinflationary monetary and fiscal policies which eventually brought about some strengthening in the balance of payments. At the same time the U.K. obtained a support of $1900m. from the I.M.F.

By the end of the year inflationary pressure was falling and speculation against the pound was subsiding. The 1961 crisis was over. Apart from a rumble of speculation against sterling in 1963 and some sporadic pressures on the U.S. dollar, the next two years saw a fair degree of stability in the international monetary system.

The second response to emerge from the 1961 crisis was the setting up of a kind of "Inner-I.M.F." Club consisting of leading industrial and trading member countries ("the Group of Ten"), which agreed to make available to one another total supplementary credits of $6000m.—amounting in effect to a second I.M.F. "kitty", which could be used in times of emergency by any member of the "ten" to protect its reserves against speculation while it was taking steps to restore its competitive position.

4   The 1971 Dollar crisis

Weaknesses in the system were revealed by the 1971 dollar crisis. As early as May the United States payments deficit had led to speculative dollar sales on such a scale that the West German and Dutch governments, threatened by a huge inflow of unstable reserves, had allowed their currencies to "float" upwards on the foreign exchange markets. The American payments position continued to weaken and on August 15th the U.S. government announced, first, that the dollar would no longer be freely convertible into gold and other reserve assets; and secondly, that a temporary extra 10 per cent tariff would be imposed on dutiable imports. The purpose of these actions was probably to serve as a bargaining counter (especially against Japanese policies) by means of which an arrangement could be reached, mainly within the "Ten", to revalue upwards the main currencies against the dollar, so as to allow a recovery of the U.S. balance of payments. For under the adjustable peg it is virtually impossible to devalue the "central" currency, the dollar, unilaterally against all other currencies.

The effect of these measures was that when the European foreign exchange markets re-opened on August 22nd the central banks were unwilling to support fixed parities against an inconvertible dollar. They therefore allowed their currencies to float, partly stabilized, alongside the mark and the guilder. Japan later followed suit. Meanwhile the I.M.F. looked sheepishly on at the collapse of the fixed exchange rate system.

In the event it took several months for a dollar devaluation, and a partially restored and slightly modified fixed rate system, to be negotiated, and at one time there was a very real risk that countries would follow protectionist policies and perhaps precipitate a major world recession. This short period also of course provides a fascinating case study on the workability of floating rates.

International monetary reform

The experiences of the 1960's, the dollar crisis of 1971, and the floating of the £ sterling in 1972 had shown the world economy to be at a cross-roads; nations would have to accept the need to co-operate to reform the system, or else be prepared for a continued succession of monetary crises and the eventual likelihood of international economic collapse.

There have been three main groups of proposals for reform, namely: 1) the restoration of a "strong" gold standard, 2) the introduction of a system of centrally (I.M.F.) created reserves consisting of "artificial", unbacked, "fiat currency", 3) the replacement of the present fixed exchange rate system by one of more flexible, perhaps even floating, exchange rates, so as to make it unnecessary for countries to hold such large reserves of gold or foreign exchange.

1   Restoration of the gold standard

This is a proposal which has often been advocated by, among others, the French. Given a fair chance the introduction of a "strong" gold standard would, it is said, have important advantages over any of the alternatives. This could be done by drastically revaluing upwards the world (central bank) price of gold which was from 1934 to 1971 pegged at an artificially low price of 35 dollars per ounce. Raise the price of gold by international agreement to, say, 70 dollars and three beneficial effects, it was held, would follow:

a) existing gold stocks would double in value, thus greatly increasing the value of most countries' reserves;

b) a higher gold price might make it possible for Asian governments to encourage successfully the "dishoarding" of gold from private sources there, which would in the end be sold to central banks and find its way into monetary reserves;

c) a higher gold price would stimulate the mining of new gold for monetary purposes. Thus an adjustable gold price would enable the benefits of gold standard stability to be retained, while the drawback of the 1920's—gold scarcity leading to beggar-my-neighbour policies— would be avoided. Against it, however, we must set a number of drawbacks, some political and others economic:

i) a higher price for gold would help the gold producers, South Africa and the Soviet Union which, in varying degrees, are viewed unsympathetically by the "Western world";

ii) there is the likelihood that proposals for a higher gold price would set up massive speculation to buy gold and sell currencies like pounds and dollars which would become virtually unacceptable. On the other hand if the U.S. raised the dollar price of gold without warning and alone, i.e. devalued the dollar unilaterally, this too would give a bad jolt to the world economy;

iii) there is the problem of the cost of operating a gold standard: the resources needed for example to mine the ore and refine it.

2 *Centrally created reserves of fiat currency*

Inside most countries gold has long been replaced by token money such as bank-notes and bank deposits which, though no longer backed by gold, are generally accepted as a medium of exchange for internal trade and business. Government-issued token money which is legal tender, is called "fiat currency". The use of this made it possible for a central bank to control and regulate the money supply inside a country according to the needs of the level of economic activity.

A proposal for world monetary reform has therefore been that countries should co-operate through the I.M.F. to introduce an *international* fiat currency, consisting of a new paper money, or of specially created I.M.F. deposits. This centrally created fiat currency would become available to form an increasing part of countries' foreign exchange reserves. Moreover, the supply of this "super-currency" could be regulated to grow in line with the needs of world trade—in contrast to the present use of gold, which is in scarce supply, and which is supplemented by unstable national currencies.

Perhaps the best known and most radical proposal along these lines was that put forward by Professor Triffin. Essentially *the Triffin Plan* envisaged the transformation of the I.M.F. into a powerful "super" central bank which could manufacture deposits of a fiat currency which—following the name invented by Keynes in his war-time proposals for such a currency—

we may call "bancor", and which member nations would agree to accept as an international reserve currency.

Under this scheme the I.M.F. would use "open market operations" to buy gold and national currencies on the world's foreign exchange markets. The central bank of a country whose currency had been thus purchased would find itself credited with an I.M.F. deposit of bancors which it could now use as part of its foreign reserves. In this way the I.M.F. could in principle create fresh reserves of fiduciary bancors to grow in line with the needs of an expanding world economy.

The reason why the Triffin plan has never been put into operation is probably that it would give the I.M.F. supra-national powers over the central banks, e.g. to limit irresponsible inflationary policies. Moreover the I.M.F. would have some freedom of action to decide which member countries at any given time were most "deserving" of further bancor supplies. In July 1966 an I.M.F. report rejected Triffin-type reform, which was put on the shelf indefinitely.

Under the 1968 *Rio de Janeiro agreements* the I.M.F. was for the first time enabled to issue a centrally created reserve of fiat money to be called Special Drawing Rights—S.D.R.s. The purpose of S.D.R.s is to add to a country's reserves so as to reinforce them against speculative pressures while it is adjusting its balance of payments position. I.M.F. members will receive periodic issues of S.D.R.s, based on the size of their quotas, which they will own and will not need to repay at any later date. Unlike present I.M.F. drawing and credits S.D.R.s will constitute a net permanent addition to world liquidity: i.e. to use Professor Tew's term, "liquidity-in-the-black", as opposed to temporary borrowed credits and drawings, "liquidity-in-the-red".

The first issue of $3400m. of S.D.R.s, sometimes called "paper gold", in 1970 was an historic event in post-war international monetary policy. Even so, there are possible weaknesses in the S.D.R. system, and indeed any other system of centrally created fiat money. The first is that there may be no direct economic pressure on debtor countries to strengthen their payments positions but that, on the contrary, their access to fresh reserves of fiat money may enable them to postpone the adoption of disinflationary and other adjustment policies. In fact in the S.D.R. system this risk has to some extent been lessened by two features: a) any member must continue to hold a balance of 30 per cent of the total S.D.R.s it has been allotted by the I.M.F.; b) sellers of S.D.R.s pay a small rate of interest to the I.M.F., whereas members accepting S.D.R.s receive interest.

The second possible weakness of a central fiat system is that it may exert little pressure on *creditor* countries to adjust *their* balance of payment positions. Keynes had proposed at Bretton Woods that creditor countries, like debtors, should be required to *pay interest* to the world monetary authority, as an incentive to modify their balance of payments: in the event the I.M.F. has never included any such creditor penalty, though it has charged interest to debtor countries drawing currencies from the Fund.

3   *Flexible exchange rates*

One school of thought argues that all the ingenuity and effort displayed in the support of a system founded on fixed rates has been essentially misplaced and unnecessary: that the shortage of liquidity has resulted from the need, under the I.M.F. rules, to defend those fixed exchange rates; and that if a different international system of exchange rates had been adopted the difficulties of world liquidity and stability, culminating in a series of crises, need never have occurred. If instead, the argument goes on, our fixed exchange rate system were replaced by one of floating rates the world liquidity shortage, and the problems connected with it, would disappear.

The post-war system of fixed exchange rates has also failed to provide an adequate mechanism of balance of payments adjustment. An important aim of the I.M.F. system has been to free countries from excessive balance of payment restraints in order that they could pursue policies of full employment and economic growth. Given this, many governments have erred on the side of inflation so that changes in domestic costs, prices and incomes have not been used, except in times of crisis, to bring about balance of payments equilibrium. Unfortunately, mainly for political reasons, the "safety valve" of exchange rate changes has not been used sufficiently early or quickly in practice to regulate excessive payments surpluses or deficits. This "stickiness" of exchange rates has been quite contrary to the spirit of the I.M.F. rules, which is that exchange rates should be stable but not rigid and should, when necessary, and after consultation, be changed as appropriate.

In short neither of the two possible balance of payment adjustment mechanisms, changes in internal prices and incomes, and changes in exchange rates, has been fully in action since the war. Nor is it likely that a country would be prepared to change its exchange rate more often than, say, once a decade on average. Yet serious and fundamental balance of payment pressures can easily occur over much shorter periods, e.g. in the case of a primary producer country which is vulnerable to changes in the terms of trade and in foreign investment flows.

One of the worst effects of fixed rates is the damage done by currency speculation, as Britain has found in several sterling crises. Once a currency falls under suspicion speculators are quick to sell it and move into other currencies, even though the suspect currency may not necessarily always be basically weak. The speculators are in a "heads I win, tails you lose" position against the monetary authorities of the deficit country: if the currency is not after all devalued the speculator can at worst buy it back at only the slightly extra cost due to interest charges on his speculative borrowings and, perhaps, a slight appreciation of the market exchange

G

rate. At best, if the currency is devalued, the speculator makes a handsome profit at the expense of the government of the deficit country.

To what extent would *floating exchange rates* provide a better alternative to fixed rates? One important point is that a foreign exchange market with floating rates will determine an exchange rate which will in principle assist the adjustment of the balance of payments to equilibrium. For example, a movement of the balance of payments into deficit would by reducing

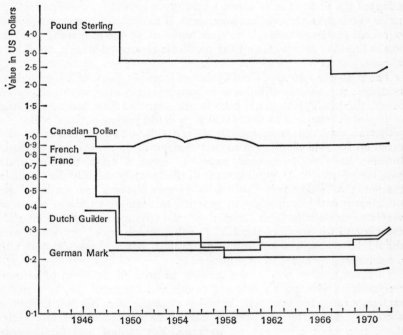

Fig 14.2 Changes in Key Currencies 1946–72

the foreign demand for the home currency make the exchange rate fall. This depreciation would make the country's exports cheaper abroad in foreign currency, and thus more competitive. Similarly its imports would be dearer at home in home currency and, thus, less competitive. This in turn would stimulate the volume of exports and retard the volume of imports so that, assuming a sufficiently elastic demand for them, in accordance with the Marshall–Lerner condition,[1] the value of exports would in time increase relatively to the value of imports until the balance of payments was once again in equilibrium. In this way market forces would

[1] See page 167.

bring about equilibrium exchange rates between currencies, making it unnecessary for a country to run the risk of defending a "wrong" parity, at the cost either of deflation and unemployment or of inflation. Secondly, floating exchanges would make much smaller demands on a country's foreign exchange resources which would need to be used by the central bank only to "smooth out" exchange rate fluctuations. A fixed exchange rate, such as the gold standard or the I.M.F. adjustable peg, needs to be defended with much greater reserves.

Table 1   Types of exchange rate systems

1 The gold standard.	
2 An adjustable peg with a "narrow band".	Fixed exchange rates.
3 An adjustable peg with a "wide band".	
4 A sliding parity ("crawling peg").	
5 A "smoothed" floating rate.	Flexible exchange rates.
6 A freely fluctuating rate.	

Problems of floating rates

What then of the serious criticisms which were levelled at floating rates after the experience of the 1930's? We can consider these in turn.

i) One objection is that floating rates may fluctuate wildly and disturb trade and foreign investment. Apart from the factor of speculation, this is largely a matter of elasticities, particularly the price-elasticities of demand for exports and imports: the less elastic these demands the more the exchange rate will have to vary in order to adjust any balance of payments disequilibrium. In fact where the sum of the two elasticities is less than unity changes in exchange rates could theoretically be de-stabilising, making the payments disequilibrium larger rather than smaller. However, there is now a lot of statistical evidence that most countries' imports and exports are fairly responsive to changes in exchange rates. In any event it is possible for traders to insure against exchange rate fluctuations by carrying out purchases or sales on the "forward" exchange market. Also long-term foreign investment and the long-term prospects for trade are in any case just as vulnerable to sporadic devaluations and revaluations under fixed exchange rates as they are to smaller short-term fluctuations in rates. Again, smaller countries can "peg" their currencies at a fixed rate on to a major currency. Lastly, a "smoothing policy" can be used by the central bank.

It was to "iron out" exchange rate fluctuations that the Bank of England in April 1932 set up the Exchange Equalisation Account. The E.E.A.'s job is to smooth out sterling's exchange rate by buying foreign exchange when the rate is high, and selling foreign exchanges when the rate is low. After some initial mistakes, when it misjudged the underlying "trend" of sterling, the E.E.A. became a formidable operator, and its interventions were so successful, that by the middle 1930's speculators were leaving sterling well alone. This leads us to the next point.

ii) This is the problem of speculation. Here it is difficult to see that the risks are in fact as serious under floating rates, because the speculator is exposed to the discipline of losing if he guesses wrong, because the exchange rate is free both to appreciate and depreciate. There are no "one-way options"; one successful speculator makes his profit mainly at the expense of another unsuccessful speculator, and this tends to make exchange rates more stable.

The experience of late 1971 suggests that floating exchange rates may fluctuate quite widely, even with central smoothing, but that this need not damage trade or investment. Many companies "insured" themselves by using the forward market in the major currencies, in which it is possible to buy or sell foreign exchange at a known rate ahead of requirements; on the other hand this is not possible in the minor currencies where there is no forward market. In the case of the really big traders and investors there is such a spread of business that exchange fluctuations in foreign earnings and payments tended to cancel out.

iii) Another criticism is that floating rates permit unscrupulous governments to promote exports and retard imports by means of competitive currency depreciation. It is true that this could happen—as it did in the 1930's (although nowadays there is no comparable need to export unemployment). But in any case it can and does also happen under the present system when a country with an undervalued currency resists revaluation, as in the case of Japan in 1971. The solution to this problem lies in achieving greater international co-operation and responsibility under the aegis of international organisations like the I.M.F.—whatever exchange rate system may be in use.

iv) A final criticism is that nowadays, when most countries are pursuing full-employment and rapid economic growth, a free rate system may increase the dangers of domestic inflation. Consider the case of a country pursuing full employment which develops a deficit in its balance of payments and which therefore finds its currency depreciating on the foreign exchange market; suppose too that (as in the case of Britain) it imports large amounts of foodstuffs and raw materials, for which the demand is fairly inelastic. Then the effect of the fall in the exchange rate will be that much of the imports will continue to be imported at the higher price. This increase in raw material costs will drive up prices of finished goods and this will lead to claims for higher wages. In this way cost-inflation may be set off, causing a further fall in exports, and a continuing balance of payments deficit. This will in turn cause the exchange rate to depreciate further, and import prices to rise once more, thus giving another turn to the cost-inflation spiral. Unless an effective disinflationary policy is introduced an extremely dangerous hyper-inflation could quickly develop. So it would be a mistake to infer that under floating rates a country can throw sound internal policies to the wind. On the contrary, if anything, a consistent anti-inflationary control over the growth of internal prices and incomes, by means of fiscal, monetary and other weapons, is more than ever necessary.

Floating rates do not, any more than fixed exchange rates, provide a panacea for the world's payments problems, nor any magical substitute for sound and consistent economic policies at home and abroad. Nevertheless there is considerable scope for future reform in the direction of increased exchange rate flexibility leading to greater payments stability and an easing of the world liquidity shortage and recent attention has been turned to wider bands and sliding parities.

Wider bands

Greater flexibility came with a new monetary agreement[1] in December, 1971, when the permissible margin of fluctuation either side of the new I.M.F. parities was increased from 2 per cent to $4\frac{1}{2}$ per cent. Sterling's new rate was $2.6057 (inside a ceiling of $2.6643 and a floor of $2.5471.) This was a revaluation of 8·6 per cent against the dollar, but in terms of all currencies, and also of gold (now priced at 38 "new" dollars) it left the pound on balance roughly unchanged. The U.S. dollar itself became effectively devalued by 9 per cent. Secondly the negotiations probably helped to weaken the sanctity of rigidly fixed rates and provoke a greater readiness to adjust unrealistic parities in the future. The principal benefit of wider bands is that some of the pressure is taken off each country's reserves, adverse movements in the balance of payments do not demand such instant action and this itself makes the life of speculators more hazardous.

Table 2 The December, 1971 Parities as a percentage of those of May, 1971

Currency	Against the dollar, %	Against all currencies, %*
United States	—	−9·0
Britain	+8·6	+0·8
France	+8·6	−0·5
Germany	+13·6	+6·0
Italy	+7·5	−1·0
Belgium	+11·6	+2·5
Netherlands	+11·6	+2·5
Canada	+1·5	−1·8
Japan	+16·9	+12·5
*weighted according to pattern of trade.		

[1] Known as the Smithsonian Agreement.

Sliding parities

Another proposal for greater flexibility is through sliding parities, sometimes called "moveable bands" or "crawling pegs". This would allow each country periodically to adjust its official exchange rate up or down by a moderate amount—say 3 per cent annually—with two possible practical advantages. First it would be supported by many who at present would reject floating rates, which it might in the end pave the way for. Secondly, it would suit the E.E.C. and other blocs aiming at a common currency. The main problem could be that the degree of rate adjustment might be insufficient always to allow balance of payments equilibrium: in this case there might well be severe speculative and reserves pressures leading to eventual devaluation or revaluation. Thus sliding parities might suffer the worst of both worlds by providing neither the stability of fixed rates nor the flexibility of floating rates.

It might have seemed that the advent of Special Drawing Rights, which are relieving the world liquidity shortage, would have driven a nail into the coffin of floating exchanges. On the other hand the increasing international willingness to reform and experiment including S.D.R.s, augers well for the introduction of a more flexible system in the future.

QUESTIONS

To what extent has the I.M.F. been successful in dealing with problems for which it was designed?

What is "a world liquidity crisis"?

Consider the arguments for and against fixed exchanges rates.

Is it true that floating exchange rates would encourage speculation and be harmful to trade?

What are S.D.R's? Why have they been called "paper gold"?

"Most international monetary problems would be solved by the establishment of a single world currency". Is this true?

Why did Keynes suggest creating a form of world money, "the bancor"?

REFERENCES AND FURTHER READING

B. Tew: *International Monetary Co-operation 1945–67* (Hutchinson, 1967)

H. G. Johnson: *The World Economy at the Crossroads* (Oxford, 1965)

K. B. Drake: *International Economic Relations* (Longmans and I.E.A. 1970)

J. F. Nicholson: *Contemporary Problems of Foreign Exchange and Trade* (Ginn, 1971)

W. M. Clarke and G. Pulay: *The World's Money, How it works* (Allen and Unwin, 1970)

S. Brittan: *The Price of Economic Freedom* (Macmillan, 1970)

15 Free Trade and economic blocs

Both the effectiveness and the ineffectiveness of economic thought are displayed clearly in the matter of Free Trade. Generations of students of economics have lapped up the invincibility of the theory of comparative costs in terms of two countries and two commodities but acquaintance with their answers in public examinations establishes beyond doubt that they relegate it, in their minds, to the fairyland of economics textbooks. The same duality of thought is characteristic of the world at large: Free Trade, it is said, "is a fine ideal but it would be disastrous to adopt it in our imperfect world". Therefore the countries of the world play at moving towards Free Trade through negotiations under the auspices of the General Agreement on Tariffs and Trade (G.A.T.T.) and raise their hands in horror if any other country infringes the Agreement whilst, at the same time, they set up trading blocs surrounded by the trade barriers or justify with "special reasons" their own particular forms of protection. Such confusion is not unusual in human affairs. Those whose special interests in protection run counter to the general interest of the community in free trade are unlikely to realise this conflict. They identify the good of the community with what is best for themselves. Others see "patriotism" as a "right little, tight little island" concept and cannot accept that the economic welfare of the community may not fit their picture. On the other hand, ardent Free Traders have often claimed non-economic benefits as the automatic accompaniment of the removal of protection. "Free Trade, Peace, Goodwill among Nations" runs the motto at the foot of a certificate of membership of the Midhurst and District Free Trade League, founded in 1904. The theory of comparative costs does not establish anything other than that communities will achieve the highest possible standard of living when they specialise in producing those goods and services in which they have a comparative cost advantage and freely exchange their surpluses for the produce of other communities.

Free Trade as a policy requires international goodwill; it requires some sort of international Development Area policy to help communities unable to cope with the pace of change; it requires flexible domestic economic policies, the free movement of people and capital and a general acceptance of full-employment as an object of policy. It may still produce better standards of living for most countries than severe restrictions on trade even without these conditions but its consequences will tend to be haphazard.

Arguments for protection

If countries are suspicious of one another and want to live in a constant state of *preparedness for war* they might be foolish to opt for Free Trade which involves dependence on others. On the other hand, the wealthier a country the more likely is it to be able to arm itself adequately. The interaction of the economic and political considerations of defence policy are much more sophisticated than is usually assumed.

A very common argument is that a country will prosper if it develops the production of goods which at present it imports. This is the *"infant industry"* argument which can be extended to cover the whole of an economy in the *"underdeveloped country"* argument. It does seem reasonable to suggest that temporary barriers to trade could enable new industries to grow in strength to the point at which they could compete freely with industries in other countries. The basic advantages of Free Trade are not being denied. In fact, it is being suggested that these advantages cannot be reaped fully because established industries elsewhere are preventing the development of new industries in areas to which they are equally or more suited. This apparently sensible thesis is not, however, borne out by the facts: protected industries never seem to grow up and this is probably because they base themselves on artificial market conditions. One doesn't blame a hot-house plant for wilting when moved out-of-doors!

Thus protection seems only to serve particular interests and not the welfare of the community as a whole. What then should be done about the promoting new industries or lessening the impact of the decline of existing localised industries? As regards the former, self-help out of very limited resources is unlikely to produce anything politically acceptable and the most satisfactory way of developing the production of goods in which the country has a comparative advantage is by securing the help of foreign capital. This can be private investment by foreign firms and individuals or it can be international investment through some agency such as the World Bank. In the present day the latter is probably preferable as it does not carry with it the taint of exploitation and the returns on investment do not have to be either as immediate or as high as when private capital is involved. Bereft of outside help poor countries have to turn to some form of protection for new ventures, having neither the means nor the expertise to launch them in direct competition with large, established and probably aggressive industries in more advanced countries. In this case, subsidies seem preferable to tariffs in that they permit development in face of realistic market prices and the cost of support is obvious. On the other hand, political lobbies are just as impassioned about maintaining subsidies as about keeping up tariffs so it does not seem to matter very much which path is chosen—neither leads automatically to an efficient industry.

The economic argument is more clear when we turn to the *protection of declining industries*. If protection accompanies a clear programme of resource re-allocation it is justified by the fact that immobility of factors makes rapid adjustment difficult, even impossible. Unfortunately the process of decline is so painful that people think of protective measures as designed to halt decline, e.g. the British coal and cotton industries. When this does not happen the cry is for more protection—not quicker adjustment. In view of the protraction of decline and local hardship which seem inseparable from this line of action, one can hardly give it much support especially when it is realised that the continued misallocation of resources lowers the standard of living of the whole community.

The use of tariffs and quotas to deal with *general unemployment* may seem rather farcical to those brought up in the post-Keynesian era but it would seem safe to assume that if there was ever a recurrence of a trade depression like that of the 1930's, the political arena would echo again to demands to keep out imports and to exhortations to U.K. citizens to "buy British goods and give work to British workmen". Of course, this argument ignores the fact that when we cut imports, incomes in our export markets fall and therefore we create unemployment in our export industries—which, already, will probably be suffering from the world-wide effects of the depression. The political call for protection can thus have disastrous effects however well-intended and the economist must point to reflationary measures on an international scale as being the path out of this dilemma.

Economic blocs

The basic economic argument for the U.K. or any other advanced nation being a member of an economic bloc is the impact of a large market on specialisation, investment and the scale of production. If we lived in a Free Trade world in which there was also complete freedom of movement for capital and labour there would be few additional *economic* benefits of being a member of the E.E.C., apart from such as might spin off from political developments. However, in spite of the General Agreement on Trade and Tariffs, we still live and look like continuing to live in a world of economic blocs. The more outward-looking these blocs are the better will it be for all concerned but those who find themselves outside in the cold are likely to have a very thin time of it, especially if their existing standards of living depend on trade in the products of scale-intensive industries. Thus one should reflect not only on the probable economic advantages of membership of the E.E.C. but also that exclusion would mean not just foregoing those likely benefits but even experiencing positive disadvantages. We have to assess the unfolding situation of a relatively small community *vis-à-vis* the surging economies of powerful blocs such as E.E.C. and the U.S.A.

The Common Market

When future generations study the history of the twentieth century they are certain to pause with wonder at the strange debate about Europe which ebbed and flowed through British politics for so many years. The basic idea which generated such a plethora of speeches, pamphlets, resolutions, car stickers and what-have-you has been that the countries of Europe should proceed by means of first a customs and then an economic union together with the adoption of common social policies, towards some sort of political union the nature of which will be determined when the time is ripe. In short, this is an experiment to see whether the old and often warring states of Western Europe can come to live together as members of one political unit.

From the very start European institutions have been set up and a common secretariat dealing with economic and social affairs has grown yearly in importance. Thus we have on our doorstep one of the greatest political developments the world has ever seen. The essence of serious discussion of this matter should be the weighing of political, social and economic pros and cons. Thus a person who considers the political dangers exceed the possible benefits of such an experiment will expect to anticipate economic gains considerably in excess of costs before he favours participation. Equally a person who finds the political balance favourable will be in favour of joining unless the economic costs seem very much greater than the expected benefits. The job of economists is to marshal the probable costs and benefits in such a way that people can judge as wisely as possible, if they so wish.

A formidable problem facing people trying to understand the arguments for and against joining the Common Market is the differences in the estimates of the effects of staying out or going in. As the reasoning behind each estimate is usually too specialised to be generally understood there is a natural danger of each person seizing on those statistics which seem to support his own predeliction and ignoring those which don't.

In this chapter we shall not try to compare the various "guesstimates" of benefits and costs because any attempt to quantify these is bound to be out-of-date as soon as it is made. Moreover, either one projects present trends on the assumption of *ceteris paribus* or, acknowledging the dynamic aspects of the matter, one must build a model based on some more or less plausible forecast of the course of change. The approach adopted here will be the simple one of discussing the evolution of the E.E.C. in terms of basic economic concepts.

Large-scale production

The benefits of large-scale production, of specialisation according to the law of comparative costs and of the free movement of resources to where they can be used best for the satisfaction of wants are commonplace in elementary economic theory. In the U.K. to-day the leading or growth industries are technically advanced ones such as electrical engineering and electronics, chemicals, engineering, plastics, synthetic fibres and motor cars. The technical advantages of scale are so great in these industries that they could not be achieved by firms competing in as small a market as the U.K. on its own. "The Ten" (the original six plus U.K., Norway, Denmark and Eire) form a wealthy market of some 250 millions offering full scope to modern production techniques. It might be argued that if the U.K. followed the sort of policy that seemed at one time to be being followed by the defunct Industrial Reorganisation Commission *viz* the encouragement of mergers so that one large firm emerged in place of a number of smaller ones, then the advantages of scale could be enjoyed outside the E.E.C. Technically this might be possible in some cases but where would such firms *sell* their goods?

The size of a market is determined by the population of an area and, most important, its wealth. In Figs 15.1 and 15.2 nothing could be more marked than the contrast between the markets for British goods a) if the U.K. is on its own and b) if it is one of "the Ten". In the latter case it finds itself in what is, at present, the second largest market for advanced industrial goods in the world. On its own it could not even match Japan and to those who ask "why, if Japan can prosper on its own, couldn't the U.K. do the same?" the answer must be that it might be able to, but it would have to accept the same rigorous economic discipline at home, the ruthless eradication of economic inefficiency by bankruptcy, the pruning of all research which only produces results which can be "borrowed" from other countries, and the curbing of the home market so that firms can only survive if they succeed in exporting their products to such tough markets as the U.S.A. The Japanese economic "miracle" has not been achieved with fine words, fair shares and social security. Could Britain follow along this very painful track?

The U.K. market on its own would be too small for achieving maximum efficiency of output. A very large market is necessary for industries which have to spend vast amounts on research and development. Where markets are small these costs have to be spread over a smaller output and higher average costs reduce the competitiveness of manufacturers. This seems to apply particularly at the moment, to computer firms, makers of office equipment, manufacturers of drugs and aircraft producers. In the third quarter of this century there have been many examples of excellent aircraft some of which never went into production, some of whose production was started but then halted, some of which were produced in such small quantities that they earned no profit and others that only went ahead because of governmental co-operation in bearing the development costs.

There are many advanced projects which are unlikely to get off the ground without initial government support and as any return on such

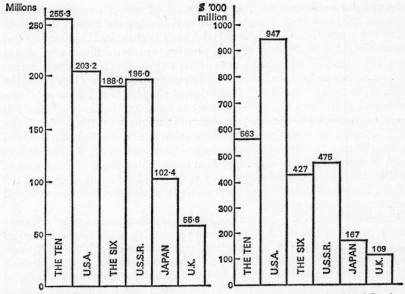

Fig 15.1 1970 populations

Fig 15.2 1970 Gross National Products

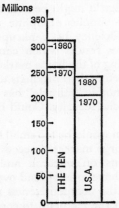

Fig 15.3 Comparative populations in 1970 and 1980

ventures is directly related to the size of the market they become increasingly "uneconomic" in a market as small as the U.K. on its own.

Another advantage of membership of a really large market is that there is scope for giant firms to emerge in competition with one another. In a smaller market there would, at best, be room for only one firm. In so far as oligopoly is more likely to struggle for efficiency than is monopoly, the more competitive conditions of a large market can benefit consumers.

Investment and growth

The U.K.'s economic growth rate has lagged behind that of other industrial nations in recent decades. Growth, measured in terms of G.N.P. per head, depends primarily on industrial investment. This in turn depends on the expectations of returns and, in the U.K., for the decade before entry into the E.E.C. there was considerable uncertainty about the future.

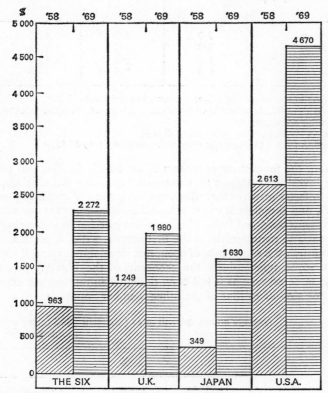

Fig 15.4 Gross National Product per head in 1958 and 1969

In consequence, investment was sluggish. As a result the U.K. growth rate remained low whilst that of the "Six" tended to improve.

Fig 15.4 and Table 1 illustrate the extent to which the U.K. failed to share in the E.E.C.'s experience of growth with the result that its average standard of living had fallen below that of "the Six" by 1969. In themselves these figures prove nothing nor should one read from them the assumption that being in the E.E.C will automatically result in similar growth in the U.K. However, our analysis, based on specialisation, exchange, large-scale

Table 1   Investment: annual averages 1955–69*

	% growth		
	1	2	3
	G.D.P.	Investment	Investment Ratio
Britain	2·7	5·3	13·3
France	5·4	8·6	16·3
Germany	5·3	6·6	18·9
Italy	5·4	5·3	14·3

Col. 1 shows in real terms the average percentage growth in G.D.P.
  „ 2 shows in real terms the average percentage growth in fixed investment (excluding housing).
  „ 3 shows investment as a percent of G.D.P.
  * (Selection from a table in *The Economist* February 5th, 1972)

production, the market requirements of modern industries and the prospects for investment suggest that membership of the E.E.C. should open the way to faster growth; statistics seem to confirm that this happened to "the Six", and therefore it seems reasonable to assume that our analysis is consistent with observed facts. If it is, we are justified in suggesting that if Britain reacts to membership as the first members did, if the E.E.C. continues on much the same lines of economic development and if the world economic scene (particularly the economy of the U.S.A.) proceeds in much the same pattern as it has been doing, then our growth experience will become similar to that of the other member countries.

Table 2   Average annual growth rates (constant 1963 prices and exchange rates)

	%		
	1952–58	1958–65	1965–70
Belgium	2·6	4·8	4·2*
France	4·5	5·6	5·8
Germany	7·1	6·0	4·5
Italy	5·5	5·6	6·0
Netherlands	4·8	5·5	5·0*
Britain	2·8	3·6	2·0
Japan	7·0	10·5	12·1
U.S.	2·2	4·7	3·2

From *The Economist* June 26th, 1971.   *1965–69.

At this stage it is tempting to join those who say that there are too many "ifs" to justify such a portentous political step, but any path into the future is full of equal uncertainties. Britain cannot order her affairs with disregard for what is happening in the rest of the world.

Economic union

Protagonists of the E.E.C. would claim that such benefits as have accrued so far from moving closer together are likely to be dwarfed by those which they expect from complete harmonisation in the decades ahead.

The community began life by working towards a customs union and had removed all tariffs between its members by 1968. From then onwards members aligned their external tariffs to establish a common external tariff which has emerged, on average, as the lowest of all industrialised countries. A parallel development has been to introduce the free movement of labour, services and capital throughout the community. Not only do workers have equal legal status in all member countries but they also retain their social-security rights when they move from one member country to another. In a wide range of services *viz* petroleum exploration, real estate, mining, gas and electricity production, wholesale and retail trade, cinema film production, re-insurance, and some aspects of agriculture and forestry, restrictions on the establishment of firms were abolished by the end of 1970 and discussions were to be carried out to remove them in an equally wide range of professional services. The free movement of capital has presented a somewhat more intractable problem because of the part played by the taxation and control of capital in the control of national economies. Nevertheless many capital movements have been freed and eyes are now set upon the formation of an unified capital market for the community.

Gradually, the community countries are moving towards common policies for industry, agriculture, finance, transport and energy which will turn the union of markets into a single, indivisible market. This process of harmonisation includes a common approach to restrictive practices, taxation, transport and regional development. An attempt to deal adequately with the immense amount of work that has been done in these spheres cannot be encompassed within a single chapter but the spirit of the community can be well illustrated by the tentative steps taken towards monetary union.

Monetary union

The establishment of a common European currency excites both strong support and vigorous opposition .To some it is indispensable for the success of harmonisation, to others it represents the final divestment of authority from the national governments. That a common monetary policy will emerge in due course from the existence of economic union would seem to be perfectly logical but it is rather doubtful whether its early imposition would attain the desired objective of preventing the currency crises which, as in 1969 and 1972, have been the result of disparate economic performances. The changes in exchange rates which have taken place have been the result of different stages of development, different rates of growth and different inflationary of deflationary movements. Such differences are likely to persist for some time and until there is a much closer political union, allowing a more thorough-going regional policy than that at present evisaged, movements in exchange rates can provide that bit of "give" needed to ease the growing together of the various economies.

Nevertheless, monetary union appears to have secured a top rating in community policy objectives and, after an abortive attempt in 1971 to move towards a rather rigid form of union, a more flexible, more realistic outlook emerged. This new approach recognised the necessity of adjustments in exchange rates during the "growing together" period as well as the advantage of a central banking nerve centre to co-ordinate national policies and, ultimately, exercise control over all the community.

The narrowing of the band within which the community currencies are to be allowed to swing against each other is conceived as the first, tentative step towards ultimate fixed rates and the emergence of a common currency. However, this process is not spelt out in detail and is to be eased by allowing a widening of the band within which the community band as a whole can swing against the dollar. Thus we have increased flexibility against the outside world but a tightening up within the market.

This exchange rate business is probably less important than the wider harmonisation moves and the creation of institutions to make community policy effective. Neverthelesss, the narrower exchange rate bands will necessitate closer co-operation between the central banks when intervening in the foreign exchange markets and will also restrict the liberty of the central banks to act in the field of interest rates and liquidity policy at home. They will be driven towards a common policy requiring the evolution of a central community monetary authority.

The first step towards such an authority could be the establishment of a permanent committee of central bank governors with the power to make recommendations about monetary policy to the central banks and even to take its own decisions in spheres such as exchange rate policy. The emergence of a strong monetary authority in Europe could exercise a steadying influence on world monetary and economic affairs in a way which can never be open to the authorities of the constituent nation states.

Industrial union

It is, perhaps, too easy to discount the economic benefits of monetary union because they are probably mainly psychological but the economies of scale which are expected to emerge from industrial union seem much more concrete. A single market means the removal of legal, fiscal and political barriers so that multinational European firms can come into being. Common policy will range over technological co-operation, company law, financing industrial development, the role of nationalised industries, government credit to industry and regional policy. Extend this list to include common policies on energy, traditional and atomic, social conditions and vocational training and the magnitude of the project begins to unfold so that it can be realised that the full experience of the benefits of membership is a matter for future generations.

Problems for members

Having postulated that most of the benefits of being a member of an economic bloc such as the E.E.C. derive from the size of the market, we must pause to consider difficulties involved. Most of these are problems of adjustment but loom large in people's minds because of the uncertainty surrounding them.

To begin with, what about the effect on the U.K. balance of payments? This has been subjected to intense statistical study but no very clear picture emerges unless one makes the assumption that other things will remain the same. If we just add up the costs of payments into the community fund to support agriculture and the inroads likely to be made into our markets by firms in "the Six", we can produce quite a fearsome picture. However, if we include possible gains from trade and growth, the balance of payments position appears quite manageable. Furthermore, if we take into account the provision in the Treaty of Rome for help to any member threatened by a serious balance of payments crisis, the concern for this adjustment cost is considerably reduced.

Some industries and the regions in which they are located may find their difficulties aggravated by our membership. This is an effect of speeding up the country's growth rate. As yet no very successful solution has been found to this problem in the U.K. or anywhere else but one thing is certain and that is that as the E.E.C. grows in wealth it will be more able to tackle this problem than would the U.K. on its own. The community is very alive to regional problems, all its members have them, and a community regional policy exists and is developing.

The cost of living may rise during the transition period of five years allowed for "getting into line". This could result from the move from farm subsidies for keeping down the price of domestically produced food to external tariffs for keeping up the price of foreign food. To imagine that this would make a very great difference would be to over-estimate the food price differences at the time of entry. Over the years inflation in the U.K. has undermined the truth of the traditional picture of cheap British food. Moreover, the expected 0·5 per cent per annum rise in the price of U.K.

food during the transitional period fades into insignificance against the 6 per cent per annum or greater increases attributable to inflation in the late sixties and early seventies. Some food prices will rise, some will fall and their overall impact on the cost of living may quite probably be offset by the falling prices of manufactured goods. In this context, of course, we are referring to the rise or fall of prices attributable to transition. Inflation may well convert all falls into increases and thus make it impossible to portray, for the general public, a clear picture of what is happening.

A quasi-economic cost of entry is its effect on existing traditional trading partners, especially in the Commonwealth. Most of the African and Asian members will, if anything, gain from associating themselves with the E.E.C. On the other hand, New Zealand, and perhaps, Canada and Australia may face fairly acute problems of adjustment. One has to weigh these difficulties which, being temporary, can be overcome with suitable arrangements against the improved prospects open to those countries when trading with a thriving "Ten", albeit across the common external tariff, as compared with a probably stagnating, isolated U.K. Norway's decision (1972) not to join the E.E.C. reduces "The Ten" to "The Nine" but does not affect the material argument for and against Britain's entry.

The most heated opposition to membership of the E.E.C. is generated by political factors. Many people resent the apparent loss of national sovereignty and loss, perhaps, of their personal "empires" with the nation-state. The vision of a political union, whilst grasped by some as "devoutly to be wished", strikes others with horror. This is not an argument to be followed here. In the decades ahead there will be many disagreements between member countries and decisions taken will be no more universally wise than in nation states. There is no final guarantee that the experiments will succeed—that will depend on the will and ability of the peoples involved to forge common outlooks to replace their traditionally divisive nationalisms.

Economics and politics

Where does Economics end and Politics begin? Having considered the economic forces involved in membership of the Common Market we have been led to trace their evolution through the unfolding of new policies and we have had to conclude in terms of vision, will and ability to see these through. Economic analysis does not produce a conclusive argument in favour of or against any line of action; what it does do is to provide material which is important to anybody concerned with reaching a realistic, informed opinion about the likely effects of any particular policy.

QUESTIONS

Why do most countries pursue protectionist policies when economic analysis points clearly to the benefits of Free Trade?

Should Britain impose quotas and import duties on textiles in order to help Lancashire?

"Our Development Areas can only receive proper attention if we keep out of the E.E.C." Comment.

Are there any sound economic arguments for Britain joining the E.E.C.?

Discuss the likely effects on Britain's main industries of the removal of all barriers to the movement of goods and factors between Britain and the other countries in the E.E.C.

For what economic reasons do countries seek to protect their domestic industries against competition from other countries? What are the relative merits of the methods of protection which are used?

Comment on the statement that "Britain is already over-populated and is, therefore, bound to suffer from joining the E.E.C. because of the free movement of people which membership involves".

i) "Britain cannot compete with goods produced by the highly skilled, highly paid workers of the U.S.A."
ii) "Britain cannot compete with goods produced by the unskilled, poorly paid workers of India". Comment on these two statements.

REFERENCES AND FURTHER READING

J. Viner: *International Trade and Economic Development* (Oxford, 1953)
G. Myrdal: *Economic Theory and Underdeveloped Regions* (Duckworth, 1957)
J. M. Livingstone: *Britain and the World Economy* (Penguin, 1966)
D. Swann: *The Economics of the Common Market* (Penguin, 1970)
Britain in Europe (Reprint from *The Economist*, 1971)

16 Population and food supplies

The Malthusian argument

The Reverend T. R. Malthus had a profound effect on the political and economic thinking of his time. He is often placed, along with such figures as Ricardo, at the head of classical economics. Unfortunately, there is considerable disagreement as to what Malthus did say. He tended to be unsystematic, often hiding profound remarks in footnotes or in the middle of long, perhaps irrelevant arguments. We are concerned here with his teaching on Population, as found in his *Essay on Population* of 1798.

Before Malthus, there seemed to be little awareness of the dangers from either overpopulation or depopulation. He wrote at a time when the growth of population, previously relatively slow, suddenly accelerated. His warning of pending catastrophe was sounded in a relatively calm atmosphere.

Malthus argued that population would always tend to outrun the means of subsistence available. The natural law of population was that it would increase in Geometrical Progression, while food supplies would, at the most, increase in Arithmetical Progression. The gap between the two would inevitably widen until humanity was driven back to a mere subsistence level. At this level, famine would cut back the population; infant mortality would be high, and the high death rate would keep the population within bounds. Unfortunately, any rise in living standards, as a result of better methods of food production, would result in larger families and thus an increase in the size of the total population. The same cycle would begin, and inevitably the population would sink again to subsistence level.

From this vicious circle there were only two basic ways out. One method by which the number of people could be confined within the limits imposed by the available food supply was the operation of what Malthus called positive checks. Examples were disease, famine and war. We have already seen how famine might keep the population within bounds. Disease and war would have a similar effect in maintaining a high average death rate.

The other method offered a way in which people themselves could prevent the population from expanding with undue speed. People could operate preventive checks. Malthus argued that earlier marriage and a consequent higher birth rate caused much of the problem. Preventive checks were thus designed to keep down the birth rate. One such check was the postponement of marriage. "It is our duty to defer marriage till we can feed our children." Later marriages would mean fewer children. Another preventive check was moral restraint: strictly defined as "the restraint from marriage which is not followed by irregular gratifications"[1]

Malthus's theories foreshadowed much contained in modern population theory. But before we apply his doctrine to the present day, we must first consider some facts about population and changes in population.

The growth of population in the U.K.

The Report of the Royal Commission on Population[2] contains a great deal of information about population growth in the U.K. Some of its main findings are summarised here.

Between 1700 and 1950 the population of Great Britain rose from 7 millions to 49 millions. Until 1700 the rate of growth was very slow, but then began to increase, owing apparently to a fall in death rates. During the nineteenth century the population grew very rapidly, from $10\frac{1}{2}$ millions at the beginning of the century to 37 millions at the end.

Table 1	Population of the United Kingdom
1841	20 183 277
1861	24 524 971
1881	31 014 828
1901	38 236 898
1911	42 081 927
1921	44 027 196
1931	46 038 357
1939	47 761 700
1951	50 225 224
1961	52 719 604

Source: Census Report of 1961.

However, since the end of the century the rate of population growth has fallen rapidly, because of a fall in the rate of natural increase. There has been a great fall in death rates, particularly at younger ages, as a result of advances in sanitation, medical knowledge and living standards, but there has been an even greater fall in birth rates. There were nearly three million fewer births in 1931–41 (6·9 millions) than in 1871–81 (9·8 millions) despite the much larger population. This is due to a much smaller average family size, falling from 5–6 in the mid-Victorian era to around 2 in the 1920's. The spread of deliberate family limitation is certainly the major factor making possible a much smaller family. The

[1] Second Essay Vol I. p15.   [2] June, 1949

motives for limitation are very much more complex, but probably include the changing economic role of the family, the spread of compulsory education, and the improved status of women.

The steady fall in birth rates and the consequent slower rate of population growth have been interrupted in recent years. In the 1943–48 period births were well above the pre-war average, explained partly by the making up of births postponed in the early years of the Second World War but also by a tendency for couples to marry at a younger age. The pattern of higher birth rates was repeated in the late 1950's, again due largely to earlier marriage and the tendency to have children earlier in married life.

While these fluctuations in birth rate have been appearing, death rates have remained predictable. It is the erratic behaviour of the birth rate which makes projections of the future population of Britain so unreliable. Forecasts made in recent years have given figures ranging from 68 millions to 74 millions for the year 2000, the differences being explained largely by different assumptions about birth rates. On the one hand, early marriages and the concentration of child bearing in the early years of marriage will tend to increase birth rates, if only by lowering the age gap between the generations. On the other hand, the increasingly wide use of safe contraceptive methods, and economic pressures, are likely to act in the opposite direction. The decline in the birth rate in the early 1970's would seem to confirm this.

The growth of world population

While European countries have tended, broadly, to follow the British pattern, the growth of world population has been very different.

Table 2	Estimated world population at selected dates millions
1850	1250
1950	2500
1980	4000
2000	6–7000

Such figures show not only a rapid increase but also a rate of increase which is growing fast. In rough terms, the world population doubled in the century 1850–1950. It is expected also to double in the period 1960–2000.

Available sources suggest that primitive agricultual societies tend to have very high birth rates (between 35 and 50 per 1000) and also very high death rates, which are normally lower than the birth rates (30 to 40 per 1000). This gave a slow rate of growth in normal times, perhaps between 0·5 and 1 per cent per annum. But there were recurrent sudden peaks when, through war, disease, or famine the death rate would become

150, 300 or even 500 per 1000. The frequent occurrences of these peaks—it was common for one-fifth of the population, or even more, to be wiped out—combined with a very high infant mortality controlled the size of agricultural societies.

As societies become undustrialised, the normal death rate falls rapidly (perhaps to 15 per 1000). Infant mortality is drastically reduced, and the recurrent peaks due to disease and famine are eliminated by the spread of knowledge, better transport, and progress in medicine and sanitation. War remains uncontrolled and may, of course, wipe out large numbers. But the key factor in population control now becomes the birth rate. Often, in industrialised societies, this falls also to 25 per 1000 or below. But if a backward agricultural community is aided, so that death rates fall rapidly, while the birth rate remains high, a population explosion is inevitable. Examples are afforded by Ceylon, whose death rate fell from 22 to 12 per 1000 in the seven years 1945–1952, and whose natural rate of increase in 1948 was 27 per 1000, as compared with under 5 per 1000 in the 1870's; and also by Malaya, with a rate of increase of 24 per 1000 and the Philippines, with a rate over 20 per 1000.

Such changes are reflected in the increasing rate of growth of world population. Between 1650 and 1750, the rate was perhaps 0·3 or 0·4 per cent per annum. With the industrialisation, the rate increased rapidly. Between 1850 and 1900, world population was growing at a rate of 0·7 per cent per annum; between 1900 and 1950, the rate had increased to 1 per cent per annum. The figure now is 1·7 per cent per annum, meaning an annual increase in world population of over 40 millions. Such a rate of increase would cause world population to double in 40 years, and this would pose a most difficult problem. It seems clear that the "exploding" countries must try to bring their birth rates down to a manageable level, or death rates will tend to rise.

The problem is not general. Europe, North America and Russia have reached at any rate temporary demographic equilibrium, with low death and low birth rates. But at the same time Asia, S. America and Africa are expanding rapidly with a population growth of 1·5 to 2·5 per cent per annum. Such growth is the result of an "industrial" death rate combined with "pre-industrial" birth rates.

Until quite recently it was considered in some circles both possible and useful to produce annually a single figure for each country which would summarize all the main factors affecting the future natural increase of the population. This was the *Net Reproduction Rate*. When the Reproduction Rate was greater than 1, the population was more than reproducing itself. When it was less than 1, the population was failing to reproduce itself.

However, no single figure can act as a reliable measure of the ultimate replacement of the population because of the inevitable year to year fluctuations in the factors involved.

Life Expectancy figures, indicating how many years the average person can expect to survive from birth, provide a convenient way of summarizing the mortality experience of all age groups of a population. They are also useful for making comparisons, over time or between countries.

The economic consequences of population changes

Before we consider the relevance of Malthus's doctrine in the modern world, it is necessary to formulate some of the economic consequences of changes in population.

a) Increases in population

The first obvious result of a rising population is that labour as a factor becomes more plentiful in relation to other factors of production. This may have the effect of depressing living standards in accordance with the doctrine of diminishing returns. This will happen only if the factors are combined already in the optimum proportion. If a country is under-populated then an increase in population will result in higher returns to labour and so a higher standard of living. What is more certain is that the increasing population will increase the relative scarcity of other factors, notably land, and this is likely to result in higher rents.

If the scarcity of land becomes absolute rather than relative, a second result is likely to be a growing food shortage. For less land will be available for growing food, and at the same time the rising population will demand more food. This will mean less food per head and declining standards of nutrition unless the shortage of food is counteracted in other ways. The pressure on space—on land area rather than on land produce—will become more acute. More land will be needed for housing, for roads, for factories and for recreation, and this will create problems of congestion and overcrowding as well as the reduction in the land area left over for food production.

Other consequences of an increase in population are not so serious. If we assume, not simply that population growth makes for greater scarcity of other factors, but that it also facilitates better use of and a growth of, these other factors, then the increase may be highly beneficial. A third consequence may well be a rising demand which promotes economic expansion. For the increase in population will create an expanding market and this will encourage firms to produce more, to invest more and to sell more. This is particularly true in those circumstances where the increase is concentrated in the lower age groups. If the number of young people in a population is expanding rapidly, the growth in the market will be accentuated and economic expansion will be encouraged.

The fourth consequence follows. Change is facilitated in a situation of rising population. It is easier for workers to flow into new, expanding industries as the working force is rising all the time. The introduction of new techniques, new methods, new ideas, is assisted when the wealth created by an ever expanding population is available.

The last two points suggest that economic growth is facilitated by a rising population. An expanding market encourages investment. Change is a function of new technology. And both increased investment and new technology promote economic growth. In consequence we should expect that a fifth result of population increase will be economic growth, and the history of Europe in the nineteenth century strongly supports this argument.

A sixth consequence of increased population may not be so desirable. An increasing demand at home will pull in more imports. As population expands, so also do imports. This may have unfortunate consequences on the balance of payments. But of course the increased imports may be counterbalanced by increased production and increased exports from the rising labour force.

On balance, the advantages of a rising population will outweigh the disadvantages if faster economic growth is possible; but if the main pressure is on land and food supplies, and if economic growth is slow or is in its early stages, the disadvantages will be more noticeable. We have concentrated on economic consequences, but, of course, population increase brings social problems too, such as overcrowding and pollution.

b) *Decreases in population*

The first consequence of a decrease in population is that other factors become more plentiful in relation to labour. This may well increase the earnings of labour and decrease, for example, rents. This depends on the extent to which other factors' output is affected by the reduction in the labour force. It is also necessary to bear in mind that the original reason for the decrease in population may have been low living standards, i.e. low standards forced the decline rather than the decline promoting higher standards. It is likely, however, that a decrease in population will ease the pressure on available food supplies, and to this extent such a change could be beneficial.

On the other hand, decreasing population will mean that some of the advantages of scale will be lost. The market, far from expanding, will be declining and this will discourage investment and be conducive to stagnation. If it is true that one of the major factors causing greater economic growth is a growing population then it must also be true that a declining population will hold back future economic growth. It may of course, happen that the fall in population eases the pressure on imports and so helps the balance of payments position.

One further result is likely. A declining population is basically an ageing population. The number of births is insufficient to replace the population and the average age of the population will be rising. This means a less mobile population and one which is less adaptable to change.

H

The older population is likely to be less healthy and a greater financial burden on the diminishing working population.

In summary, a declining population is usually disadvantageous. The only possible advantage is the relief of pressure on food supplies and land space.

Table 3   Age Structure of the Population of England and Wales

	1931		1966		2001 (Estimated)	
	Number	%	Number	%	Number	%
Under 15	9 520 000	23·8	11 057 000	22·9	18 666 000	28·1
15–64	27 469 000	68·8	31 210 000	64·8	40 187 000	60·5
65 & over	2 963 000	7·4	5 922 000	12·3	7 570 000	11·4
Totals:	39 952 000		48 189 000		66 423 000	

Source: Registrar General's returns.

c) *The effect of migration*

Migration is essentially a two-way traffic. Immigrants moving into a country have certain well defined economic effects. Emigrants leaving a country will produce quite different results.

If the net migration is inwards it may add significantly to the total size of the population if this is not increasing rapidly for reasons of natural growth. This effect was marked in Britain during the early 1960's. Consequently, the first effect will be to add to the working force, particularly since most immigrants will come from the younger age-groups. The consequences we have noted of an expanding population will apply here. The younger average age of the population will mean that the working force is more mobile and more adaptable to change. If the immigrant population has a birth rate markedly greater than the home population, the result will be a relatively more rapid expansion of the labour force and of the immigrant section of the population. If the immigrant population has an average standard of life lower than the home population, the effect may be to depress the average level of wages. Certainly there will be greater pressure on housing, and social problems may arise in integrating the two communities. Overall, if the immigration is to a country already overpopulated, the disadvantages of overcrowding, pressure on land, and shortages are likely to outweigh the benefits of economic growth and an expanding market. But if a country is underpopulated immigration will be almost entirely beneficial.

On the other hand, net migration outwards from a country will have a very different impact. The working force will decline and the average

age of the population is likely to rise. This will hold back economic growth and restrict the mobility of the population. However, it may be beneficial if a country is overpopulated or has a low standard of living. In such a case, emigration is likely to ease the pressure on resources and help to raise living standards.

We must also consider the later effects of such movements of population. An immigrant population may send money back to the home country and this will harm the balance of payments. An emigrant movement may improve the balance of payments by encouraging a movement of funds the other way. It may also develop sources of material and open up markets for the mother country. Emigration from Britain during the nineteenth century helped to develop the Empire for British trade.

The nineteenth century answer to Malthus

In Britain, population in the nineteenth century expanded very rapidly and yet the standard of living rose. The Malthusian problem of diminishing food supplies per head of population did not arise. For this there were two very good reasons.

Firstly, new sources of food supply were opened up. Britain did not continue to feed the bulk of her population. The proportion actually fed from home production fell steadily during this period, but new countries took over the role of supplier. The vast wheatlands of North America supplied wheat; the grassland of Argentina became an important source of meat; Australia, New Zealand and South Africa all played their part in improving Britain's food supplies. The invention of the refrigerated ship was a major breakthrough, enabling meat, for example, to be shipped round the world to feed Britain.

Secondly, agricultural methods underwent a revolution. The discovery of new root crops made new rotations possible, providing fresh nutrients for the soil and incidentally winter feed for the cattle which could now be kept alive. The invention of new machinery greatly increased production and made for greater yields from the available acreage. The cultivation of new strains, both of crops and of livestock, also made for increased productivity. The whole face of agriculture changed, and the new technology produced such an expansion in output as Matlhus could not have dreamed of.

In addition to these factors causing a rapid improvement in food supplies, there was a sharp fall in the birth rate in Britain at the latter end of the nineteenth century. As people's living standards improved, they had fewer, not more children. The population grew, but not as rapidly as Malthus had feared. Food resources expanded very rapidly; the population growth slowed down; and the combination of these two movements was sufficient to raise, not lower, living standards and lay the Malthusian bogey, at least in Britain.

Malthus in the modern world

The population explosion

We have already noted (in Table 2 page 208) how rapidly the world population is growing. It has been estimated[1] that the rates of increase of world population have been themselves rising rapidly, as shown in Table 4.

Table 4   Rate of Increase of World Population

1650–1750	16·8%
1750–1800	24·4%
1800–1850	29·2%
1850–1900	37·3%
1900–1950	53·9%

The margin of error in forecasting population growth is decreasing, and the accuracy of census figures is increasing. The first census held on modern lines in China, in 1953, gave a population figure over 25 per cent higher than the previous estimates. We can anticipate a world population of 4000 millions by 1980 and of between 6000 and 7000 millions for the year A.D. 2000. Declining mortality rates are likely to continue, while in countries with high birth rates there is little likelihood of a decrease in the near future.

Table 5   The time taken to evolve each 1000 million people World Population

The first 1000 m.	A.D. 1830
The second ,,	1930
The third ,,	1960
The fourth ,,	1975
The fifth ,,	1987
The sixth ,,	1995
The seventh ,,	2000

Source: Article in *The Times*, January 12th, 1972

World population is thus growing very rapidly. Is the Malthusian prophecy to be fulfilled during this century?

World food supplies

An average calorie intake for a healthy diet would perhaps be between 2400 and 2700 per day. The Food and Agricultural Organisation of the

[1] L. Dudley Stamp: *Our Developing World* (Faber and Faber).

United Nations publishes tables of calorie intake for the principal countries of the world. These show that 60 per cent of the people surveyed in 1949–1950 were below the minimum of 2000 calories per day; and this was a substantial increase on the pre-war figure. It is important also that the diet should be balanced. But since the great majority of mankind lives on cereals, what is the value of the average cereal intake for the world of 430 grammes per day? The calorific value is 1550 which is well below the minimum. And the problem is getting worse. In India, population in 1918 was 315 millions, with an average of 560 grammes of food grain available per head. In 1945, with a population of 400 millions, the average per head was 420 grammes. Between 1945 and 1952, the average diminished further. Famine, stressed by Malthus as one of the positive checks, caused the death of one million Indians in 1942 when the rice crop failed in Bombay. Although, looking at the world as a whole, food production is keeping pace with rising population, there are countries where the problem is acute. India, with 5 million extra people each year, requires an extra acre every six seconds just to keep up. In Pakistan, the reclamation of two acres a minute would hardly enable the country to keep pace with rising population.

Can food supplies be increased?

World food production is currently increasing at a slightly faster rate than world population. But this trend is not uniform throughout the world. Whereas in Eastern Europe food production per head is 40 per cent or more above the pre-war level, in Latin America, Africa and the Far East it is probably slightly below the pre-war level.

Even if it is true that average consumption in the less developed countries is slightly above the very low pre-war level, we need to ask whether food output can keep pace with the accelerating growth of world population; and to attempt to make good existing deficiencies in diet. By 1980, for example, assuming a world population of 4000 millions, cereal production would need to go up by one-third and the output of animal products by at least 100 per cent. By the year 2000, these figures would be 100 per cent and more than 200 per cent respectively. The present slow growth of world output will not meet these requirements.

Although world food surpluses from the developed countries are very considerable, and already provide invaluable aid to the less-developed areas they cannot be a long term solution to the world food problem. The only effective long term solution is to secure the necessary increases in food production within the less developed countries themselves. From the physical and biological aspects there is no reason why food production in the less developed areas should not be expanded to the extent necessary to meet the world's needs at least till the end of the 20th century. Yields of wheat and rice, for example, in Africa, Latin America and the Far

East are well below Western Europe's standards. Animal production figures show differences which are even larger.

Such high yields in the developed countries are largely attributable to modern techniques. Adequate resources must be devoted to increasing the supply of food.

Governments must assist small farmers by generous expenditure on research, irrigation, drainage, roads and to provide agricultural credit. In Asia, land reform is a precondition of economic development. In many rural areas of the poorer countries, the rate of interest (seldom below 50 per cent) precludes borrowing for capital improvement.

Scientific advance could revolutionise the world food picture. Already we have scientific fish farming, and "miracle rice". But even existing scientific knowledge, applied to the problem, could produce a spectacular increase in food supply. The area under cultivation could be extended; crops could be given more water through irrigation projects, and more nourishment through fertilisers. More productive crop varieties and animal breeds could be introduced. Old fashioned techniques could be modernised, and the use of existing crops and animals could be made more effective. Among possible immediate practical measures are:

1)   Giving crops enough nitrogen, phosphorous and potassium, and so increasing not only yields but protein consumption by humans.
2)   Supplying electric pumps for drainage, reclamation and irrigation.
3)   Developing equipment for use on the land. It is arguable that, at the present stage of development in many countries, a simple plough drawn by a bullock may be of more immediate use than a tractor.
4)   Making more effective use of food supplies, for example, by preventing waste and spoilage, and using a greater proportion of available plants. Control of disease and vermin is also a high priority.
5)   Improving transport and developing means of preservation such as deep-freeze plants or canning factories.

By applying existing agricultural knowledge in Britain we could increase our own food production by 50 per cent or more. In underdeveloped countries the increase would be far greater. Greatly increased food production could take place in many countries if existing cultivated areas were adequately farmed, and if uncultivated land, the sea, and inland waters were brought into production. It is not shortage of available scientific and technical knowledge that is the obstacle. The extreme slowness with which existing knowledge is applied is caused by political, psychological and social factors.

Population control

It is often argued that the better method of raising world standards of nutrition is to control population growth rather than to increase food supplies. Investment in birth control will solve the problem for a smaller capital outlay by reducing the birth rate. Underdeveloped countries, as we have seen, combine a pre-industrial birth rate with an "industrial" death rate. The argument sounds attractive. An all out campaign to spread birth control would bring population and resources into equilibrium. Rapid economic and social development, such as is essential for rising living standards, would be much easier if population increases were smaller.

In Japan, the legalising of abortion cut the birth rate by 50 per cent. In India, an all-out campaign to educate and inform, and to produce a cheap, effective contraceptive has been in progress for some years. But even if such campaigns succeed in their prime objective of sharply reducing birth rates, pressing problems will remain. Decreases in mortality may be even sharper than forecast, so that the reduction in birth rate merely restores the status quo, and the growth of population continues.

The age distribution of the population in the underdeveloped countries, where, on average, 40 per cent of the people are under 15 years of age, rules out any sudden improvement. The problems of finding an easily used, acceptable, effective contraceptive remain. There is the problem of communication where literacy is low and the population is widely scattered and predominantly rural. Opposition to a national birth control policy may come, not merely from religious elements, but from belief in virility and national pride.

To name such problems is to indicate that it is not enough to limit population growth. The rapid increase in food production must be pursued vigorously at the same time. Rising standards of living are likely to assist, ultimately, in the decline of the birth rate. They are, of course, highly desirable for their own sake, and the steady but slow progress now being made must be maintained and, if possible, quickened. Even so the problem is likely to remain with us for the rest of the twentieth century.

QUESTIONS

Make out a case in favour of emigration to the U.K. from underdeveloped countries.

Should we stop child allowances and tax rebates and instead subsidise people who have no children?

Do you think the expression, "the population explosion", is misleading?

Professor Paul Ehrlich has argued that Britain's population should ideally be 30 millions.
a)   Do you agree?
b)   How could Britain's population be reduced to this figure?

Is Britain's population problem "too many old people"?

"Britain should encourage emigration rather than immigration." Comment.

"Malthus may have been wrong in his predictions for nineteenth-century Britain but his analysis is right for the twentieth-century world." Discuss.

Would birth control solve the problem of world hunger?

"The spread of higher education must be counterbalanced by later retirement if the burden of the working population is not to become unbearable." Comment.

Is an ageing population preferable to a declining population?

REFERENCES AND FURTHER READING
T. K. Robinson: *The Population of Britain* (Longmans and I.E.A., 1968)

P. Sargent Florence: *Atlas of Economic Structure and Policies*, Vol. 2 (Pergamon, 1970)

J. H. Lowry: *World Population and Food Supply* (Edward Arnold, 1970)

The Report of the Royal Commission on Population, June 1949.

Report of the Select Committee on Science and Technology, Vol. x

L. Dudley Stamp: *Our Developing World* (Faber and Faber, 1969)

R. K. Kelsall: *Population* (Longmans, 1967)

The British Association: *Hunger—can it be averted?* (1961).

17 Economic planning

"Planning" is one of those words which flow into and out of fashion and generate a great deal of heated argument. To some people planning means any departure from *laisser faire* however modest, to others it means the detailed, centrally administered control of every aspect of economic activity and there is an infinite variety of interpretations of the word between these extremes. Complete central planning is sometimes referred to as *normative* by contrast with *indicative* planning which involves "the collection, processing and distribution of information to others responsible for policy making and executive action".[1]

We can also categorise planning according to its purpose. A community may plan for military strength or for economic growth or for full employment or to build up its reserves of foreign exchange. In all these cases planning will span the whole community, i.e. we are dealing with macro-economic planning. Then again plans may be organised in particular sectors of an economy, large sectors such as regions giving us regional planning,[2] small sectors such as industries or even firms giving us just the sort of planning which we would expect to find even in what might be called a completely "unplanned" economy. A community may view planning as a means of avoiding the effects of the market forces of supply and demand or it may, on the other hand, use it to release those forces from monopolistic restrictions.

Command economies

A command economy is one in which decisions about what to produce and how much of each commodity to produce are taken centrally, i.e. an economy directed by an overall plan. There is something basically appealing about the idea of "the experts" getting together and pooling their knowledge to produce a blue-print for success. One feels that this should eliminate all the waste which seems inevitable if there is no plan for people to work to and that it should minimise any risk of failure. In this thinking it does not seem to matter very much whether the objective is military strength, economic self-sufficiency or economic growth, although the simpler the objective and the less related it is to complex ideas such as "raising the standard of living of the individual members of a community",

[1] A. Gilpin: *Dictionary of Economic Terms* (Butterworths).
[2] Discussed in Chapter 10.

the more reasonable does planning become. This is because the planners can know fairly exactly what things are wanted and in what quantities for some time ahead when dealing with, for example, military strength. Even here, of course, the development of a new weapon either at home or by another nation can result in considerable waste, particularly if the planning machinery is at all inflexible. Planning in the U.S.S.R. has been successful in enabling a relatively poor country to attain and maintain military parity with the incomparably wealthier U.S.A. Market forces could not be expected to satisfy the technical requirements of the armed forces nor could they be expected to deflect goods from consumers to the government. Thus planning in this sense is really technical rather than economic.

When we postulate an economic objective such as "raising the standard of living" we immediately run into the difficulty of being unable to say exactly what things people will want and in what quantities they will want them in the future. Some committee of planners must pretend to clairvoyance in this respect before any plan can take shape and thus the whole framework is based on assumptions which are most unlikely to turn out to be accurate. The next stage is to decide on the relevant inputs of factors for each productive activity. Only too often discussions about planning concentrate exclusively on the determination of outputs but this is much the easier part. If it is decided to produce 10 000 units of a particular product per year then it must be decided *where* they are to be produced and in each location there must be correct inputs of capital, components, raw materials and labour together with a planned distribution network. The same will be true of each component and raw material and in all cases labour with the right skills will have to be directed to the plants. It gradually becomes clear that the whole process must be exceedingly complicated and authoritarian if there is to be any resemblance between the plan and what really happens.

The factory managers in such a system are in a most unenviable position. It is they who must operate the plan and therefore bear the brunt of the failure of the necessary inputs to be available in the quantities necessary to produce the stipulated targets. In the absence of market forces there is little they can do to influence the supply of factors, nor have they any criteria other than quantitative targets as regards output. The result tends to be a concentration on quantity rather than quality of output because, after all, the problem of disposal of the output lies with other agencies than the manufacturers. An interesting by-product of central planning is the customary view that it is a good thing for a factory manager to exceed his target. If, however, the plan is right, the exceeding of targets will throw it out of gear, creating unwanted quantities of certain goods and, if the surpluses have been produced by an unplanned diversion of factor inputs to the products in question, there must be unintended scarcities of others. It is problems like these that have been leading the U.S.S.R.

towards limited experiments in methods which that country has hitherto despised as the inefficient instruments of "capitalism".

The ownership and control of capital does not seem to provide any useful base for distinguishing between economic systems. One can have an authoritarian command economy with either publicly or privately owned capital although in the latter case the ownership would be likely to be concentrated mainly in the hands of a few people. On the other hand a market economy can co-exist with either form of ownership although it may be more difficult for public industries to submit to it than private ones.

Market economies

The market for any commodity consists of the interaction of the relevant conditions of demand and supply. Supply takes place in accordance with producers' past experience or their expectations of the market. If more is being supplied than buyers will purchase at prices judged adequate by the suppliers, some of these latter, in response to sub-normal profits, will try to cut back on production. On the other hand if the prices fetched by a commodity exceed the expectations of producers these latter will enjoy super-normal profits and will be encouraged to step up production.

An increase in the production of any commodity involves an increased demand for the necessary factors of production. Those already employed in this line will tend to enjoy quasi-rents since higher marginal revenue productivities will tend to raise earnings. Higher earnings will serve to persuade units of the factors to transfer from their present occupations. Thus, at any given time, a rise in the output of a commodity will tend to raise its unit cost and will only be undertaken in response to a rise in the amount per unit that people are prepared to pay for it. In the long term, of course, increased output may enable a firm to lower unit costs by adopting more efficient methods of production. However, the short-term rise in the price of a commodity reflects its opportunity cost, i.e. the cost to the community in terms of other goods which the transferred factors had been or could be producing.

A fall in demand for a commodity resulting in sub-normal profits will cause the marginal revenue productivity of the factors involved to diminish, demand for them will fall and so will their earnings. Consequently marginal units of these factors will transfer to other occupations. Thus the price mechanism is operated by the interplay of consumers' choice and producers' profits, of the opportunity costs of commodities and the transfer costs of factors, and the earnings of factors are determined by their contributions to the satisfaction of the constantly changing wants of consumers. This chain of control is sometimes referred to as "consumers' sovereignty".

Planning defined

This complex mechanism cannot be left to work on its own any more than a car can be left to drive itself along a road. The immobility of resources, the inequalities of wealth and income, the restrictive practices of monopolies and the inability of consumers to contend with unbridled sales promotion tactics require careful controls of the mechanism. Do we classify such controls as planning? If we are taking precautions to see that the economy is running in accordance with social, economic and political targets then it would seem right to include such measures as part of the planners' armoury. So it would seem that there can be no clear distinction between planned and unplanned economies, there are just degrees of planning with authoritarian command economies at one extreme and free market economies at the other. It would seem to be a permissible use of the word "planning" to distinguish between a piecemeal approach to normal economic policy objectives, i.e. a collection of unco-ordinated plans, and a comprehensive attempt to keep them all in view and taking careful note of the areas of conflict and incompatibility between them.

Planning for growth

By "economic growth" we mean the change in any community's real income per head. Real income is income in terms of what it will buy, i.e. national income at constant prices. One has to be careful about taking any growth figure at its face value because the national income figure on which it is based can include many items an increase in which it would be hard to describe as "growth". Thus if the National Coal Board in the U.K. is producing coal which nobody wants and which, therefore, has to be stored in disused quarries and the like, the taxpayers pay for this coal which is included in the national income as satisfying collective wants. Similarly if taxpayers subsidise uneconomic railways lines or the produce of agricultural commodities surplus to the amounts which can be sold without support on the market, growth can appear to take place through what is really a waste of resources. When there is a drive to re-arm, the increased production of munitions and weapons may result in a rise in the national income but this can only be interpreted as growth in any meaningful way if it is assumed that the people of the country consciously prefer more armaments to more consumers' goods. This is a subjective problem which cannot be solved by devising superior methods of measurement and we cannot just sweep it into a corner without losing sight of the whole purpose of our study. It is very important to look carefully at figures for average real income per head or any other measures before interpreting them too literally.

The increased ability of any community to produce goods and services depends primarily on the twin process of specialisation and the accumulation of capital. The development of new techniques of production requires investment in new fixed capital, in research and in the training of new skills. Any plan for economic growth must therefore include measures to stimulate investment which, in a free market economy, is undertaken in response to the expectation of profit. There are certain positive actions which can be taken by the government on this score. It can, by good government, create an atmosphere of stability, of diminished uncertainty so that the risks of production seem less and the chances of an adequate return on investment more likely. It can by legislation foster financial institutions so that the raising of credit is simplified. It can itself undertake investment in the infrastructure, an area not characterised by high rates of return on the capital employed. It can implement measures to increase the mobility of labour so that growth in one industry is not partially offset by the wastage of idle resources in another. Measures to free international trade from protective barriers widen industry's markets and encourage expansion, they also weed out the inefficient firms which are holding on to resources which could be better used elsewhere. Measures to free the domestic market from the restrictive practices of manufacturers, traders and trades unions make for closer links between efficiency and rewards and thus help to direct investment and labour into those channels most conducive to growth. On the negative side, a government can remove any fiscal barriers to investment which social reasons or just plain convenience tend to throw up. The removal of special taxes on profits and a general shifting of the burden of taxation from companies to individuals will tend to brighten firms' prospects. Increasing the rate at which the cost of new investments can be deducted from revenue in calculating the tax basis of firms encourages keeping capital equipment up-to-date.

This pattern of measures is not what most people would think of as "economic planning". Of course, if we added figures relevant to any given moment in time they would look more impressive, more factual, but they would still be a far cry from the blue-prints of a "five-year plan". Nevertheless, if carefully designed and integrated policies are adapted to meet changing circumstances we have in fact a much more flexible and, probably, more fruitful plan than if we are always having to work to predetermined input–output figures.

Indicative planning

During the 1960's it became popular to point to France as an example of a successful new type of planning for growth. This all began with the Monnet Plan in 1946 which has been succeeded by a series of four-year plans. The French technique has been i) to select a target growth rate for each main industry, ii) to make preliminary estimates of the probable resulting expenditure on capital goods, of government expenditure on goods and services and of exports of goods and services and to treat the amounts available for personal consumption as residual, iii) to break down these preliminary estimates into industrial production estimates by separate industrial commissions, iv) at the same time for five commissions to study general matters such as finance, manpower, changes in productivity, research, and the location of industry, and v) to use the results from iii) and iv) to produce a revised plan. This final draft may vary from the original not only in detail but also as regards the target average growth rate itself.

It is claimed for this sort of planning that it infuses a new efficiency into industry because both management and labour are stimulated by a sense of purpose given by the overall plan and the prompt achievement of targets. The planning itself is held to reduce the likelihood of specific shortages halting the process of growth. In particular, the co-operation of management is said to follow from the knowledge that other firms are working on the same lines and from participation being voluntary. Flexibility is held to be the keynote to indicative planning and this together with its voluntary nature and its apparent early success gave it a temporary vogue in the U.K. in the 1960's—the years of N.E.D.C., N.I.C. and the 1965 Plan. However, the Federal Republic of Germany succeeded better than France in promoting growth and without planning of this type. Moreover the other countries of the E.E.C. have all achieved quite respectable growth rates and it would seem that participation in the E.E.C. provides a better explanation of France's success than planning does.

Many particular doubts arise from a consideration of indicative planning in France. It shares with all detailed planning for as far ahead as four years the inability to take proper note of change in the techniques of production and in foreign trade. Consultation tends towards accepting majority views and these are not necessarily those of the most enlightened managers. Whenever the government interferes in industry it tends to listen most carefully to big firms and all firms tend to form alliances so as to speak with one voice. The competitive edge of industry is dulled as market sharing and investment sharing develop. What begins as an exercise in government and individual firm co-operation is likely to foster cartels and although these are not inconsistent with expansion, the driving out of small firms and of individualistic firms seems likely to rob the economy of sources of many innovations. An overall doubt about the wisdom of this way of organising an economy must develop from the failure of French governments to avoid the strong tide of inflation and balance of payments difficulties in the middle and later nineteen sixties.

"Planning by consent"

The British version of indicative planning originated with the establishment of the National Economic Development Council in 1961, with the express purpose of planning to increase the country's rate of growth. N.E.D.C. draws its members from government, industry and trades unions and has pursued its studies of society through a number of Economic

Development Committees. The terms of reference of these committees is that *"within the context of the work of the N.E.D.C. and in accordance with such working agreements as may be determined from time to time between the Council and the Committee, each Committee will:*

i) *examine the economic performance, prospects and plans of the industry and assess from time to time the industry's progress in relation to the national growth objectives and provide information and forecasts to the Council on these matters;*

ii) *consider ways of improving the industry's economic performance, competitive powers and efficiency and formulate reports and recommendations on these matters as appropriate."*

That the industries served by an E.D.C. have been provided with material which could lead to an improvement in efficiency goes almost without saying. Studying and reporting on the weaknesses of industries and of official policies affecting those industries particularly in so far as they hinder expansion and their capacity to compete with foreign products both at home and in overseas markets, must also have had beneficial effects.

Perhaps a less valuable aspect of their work has been the study of imports with the rather mercantilist attitude that they indicate by their very presence that something is wrong. It is imagined that increasing the efficiency of management, removing some of the restrictive practices of labour, speeding up technological development and improving market structures should reduce imports. If we really do seek growth we must pursue efficiency with the widest possible vision of world markets, and this will mean a ready acceptance of imports and not looking on them as undesirable.

In view of the growth target of 4 per cent per annum which N.E.D.C. adopted in 1962 it would, perhaps, be kindest to draw a veil over the subsequent lean years which brought the country to stagnation by 1970. Not that there was any lack in further aids to planning. From 1964 a Department of Economic Affairs, primarily concerned with economic growth and planning, stood guardian over six years of deceleration. During the same period a super-ministry, the Ministry of Technology, sought to infuse planned progress into the newer "scientific" industries. In 1965 came the National Plan which was really a little more than a forest of targets and predictions needed for and resulting from an intended maintenance of an annual growth rate of 3.8 per cent. The abysmal weakness of the whole episode was the failure to adopt those directional policies which would have enabled this growth rate to be achieved. Investment, the source of growth, doesn't just happen because it has been "planned": it results from comparing the prospects of profit with the risks involved and, in Britain, the combination of high direct company and personal taxation diminished the former whilst uncontrolled inflation, inadequate reserves of foreign exchange, and uncertainty about Britain's relationship with the E.E.C. all contrived to increase uncertainty.

Planning for stability

Let us return to the more general type of controlling the economy which was implicit in our earlier consideration of means to stimulate growth through increased investment. Increased investment will generate inflationary pressures which will cause prices to rise unless there is a state of some general unemployment or unless other measures soak up the additional income created by the investment. This can be illustrated by reference to the circular flow of income depicted in Fig 17.1.

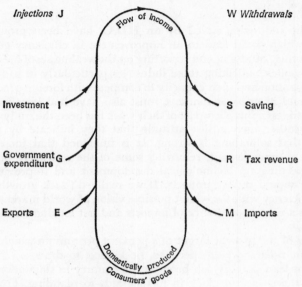

Fig 17.1 The circular flow of income

An increase in investment (I) can be seen as an injection (J) into the circular flow of income. Some of this income drains off into saving (S), imports (M) and government revenue from taxation (R), the remainder passes on through the purchase of domestically produced consumer goods which invokes the multiplier mechanism. If the government remains passive, the rise in imports is likely to be accompanied by a fall in exports as goods are deflected from foreign to home markets, attracted by the high domestic prices: a balance of payments crisis develops and has to be dealt with by severe fiscal and monetary measures which curb consumer spending and industrial investment. Growth is halted until reserves of foreign exchange have sufficiently recovered to entice the government into removing its controls and the cycle begins again. This is the process which used to be popularly known as "stop-go". It can only be prevented if action is taken right at the start of the cycle to prevent rising investment being inflationary.

Fiscal and monetary measures can be used to keep consumer and government expenditure within the bounds of the rising flow of production resulting from the increased investment. Consumer and government expenditure must be kept in check for long enough for investment to result in the extra capacity and output which would allow aggregate demand to increase safely. An incomes policy can be used to restrain the cost-push elements of inflation. The general direction which the economy should take is usually fairly clear to see and there are a sufficient number of alternative pathways to allow for flexibility. What is important is that there should be a large measure of agreement concerning the direction in which the economy should be moving at any given time.

For the attainment of stability it is also necessary that there should be a general acceptance of the real meaning of "full employment" and some understanding of the factors determining at any time the maintainable minimum level of unemployment. There are functional relationships between "full employment" on the one hand and the rate of growth and the immobility of factors on the other. The stimulation of investment merely because there is an "unacceptable" level of unemployment in a country does not mean that growth will follow. The unemployed factors have to be ready to move to growth areas and to acquire the skills needed in the growth industries before i) the latter can expand and ii) the level of unemployment can fall without there being inflation.

Stability is not something which results automatically from the free working of market forces nor can it be achieved by the unco-ordinated actions of individual firms. We may call the necessary exercise of controls by the name of "planning" but we must note that there is no innate incompatibility between this type of planning and the existence of a market economy.

Planning in poor countries

It can be argued that, irrespective of the merits of economic planning in advanced economies, it is essential in poor countries which are still struggling to accelerate the early stages of growth. In some ways the problems of such countries are not really economic in that it is parity of esteem with rich countries that is desired above all else. This results in an attempt to modernise and industrialise at a rate greatly in excess of that warranted by the existing ability to save. It is very difficult for people living at subsistence level to save anything.

On the other hand, investment projects in a poor country are all likely to be of types that add little to the output capacity of the country in the immediate future. The first steps from poverty for any nation must be such things as communications, transport, river control, schools and housing. These steps provide the basis for increasing output but they play only a very indirect part in it themselves.

The equilibrium growth rate, i.e. the maintainable growth rate of any community can be expressed as

$$\frac{s}{g} = \frac{\Delta y}{y}$$

where s represents its *average propensity to save*, g its *capital-output ratio*, y its *real income*, and, therefore, Δy *a small change in its real income*. A poor country will have a low average propensity to save but a high capital-output ratio, i.e. a large input of capital will only produce a small increase in output. Therefore the rate at which real income can increase in such a community is low. Attempts to speed up this rate by investing at a faster rate than people are planning to save will create an inflationary state of affairs which will cause the familiar pattern of rising prices, shortages, balance of payments difficulties and loss of business confidence all leading to a period of stagnation and, in a weak economy, collapse.

In this situation governments can seek foreign aid to finance investment or encourage foreign firms to undertake investment directly on their own account. This path is not devoid of stumbling blocks. To be effective, foreign aid must be contractual because it is impossible to work to any scheme of development if its finance is likely to be disrupted at the convenience of the financier. However, the governments of rich countries usually want to stipulate certain conditions for aid, to commit themselves only for a short period of years and to withhold the right to reduce their commitments if either conditions at home or in the country to which aid is being given seem to warrant it. Such conditions would never be acceptable between countries of equal wealth, how much more must they appear an affront to the dignity of states which are poor and which, in many cases, have only just emerged from colonial status? Nor is it much use offering the governments of these countries loans on conditions and rates of interest applicable to financial dealings between wealthy communities. As we have already seen, the first jobs to be tackled will yield little or no return to the investor immediately or at any time, and therefore cannot generate of themselves the income out of which to pay interest. Even interest-free loans are unsuited to the situation because it is impossible to predict with any certainty the emergence of any ability to repay the debts and then only so slowly, over such a long period of time, that they will ultimately serve only to distort the patterns of world trade and exacerbate international relations. Long-term, guaranteed gift projects are the only reasonable and mutually beneficial ways in which the governments of rich countries can aid those of poor ones.

Private investment by firms is another matter. This still runs into the problems of a dislike of patronage and the ensuing political uncertainties about being left to carry on business freely. It is difficult for the governments of poor countries to realise that the political and economic risks of working in their lands make the profit required by any enterprise very high. If a sense of grievance at foreign firms earning high profit amidst domestic poverty results, as is quite likely, in punitive taxation or threats of sequestration these firms will tend to reduce their scale of operation and, more important, new investment will dry up.

In poor countries, in particular, economic planning cannot be dissociated from politics. It involves directing investment into the most urgent requirements of the infrastructure, securing overseas investment capital, restraining inflation, maintaining a sound balance of payments and, at the same time, creating an adequate sense of achievement in order to establish reasonable political stability.

The role of planning

In this chapter we have looked at a few aspects of economic planning and our conclusion must be that the part which planning can play in attaining the economic objectives of any society is limited by the extent of our present knowledge and methods of analysis. In future years greater understanding of economic relationships and superior techniques of forecasting may enable detailed planning to be successful where now it cannot hope to be.

At present the economist must point to the fact that success in attaining the objectives of growth and stability has been just as great and perhaps greater in countries which have used as sensitive and flexible measures as they can devise to guide their economies in response to events as they have arisen, as it has been in countries which have adopted fairly rigid plans. Moreover, inflation, balance of payments crises and low growth rates have been as much associated with planned economies as with others. It would seem that we must conclude that planning should be limited to such areas as those in which we have sufficient understanding to give a reasonable chance of being more successful than market forces and that, in general, the concept of planning that we should adopt is one of directing and moulding those forces so that they work towards the goals we have in mind. It may be wiser to concentrate on making sure that we are going in the right direction and watching the immediate twists and turns of the road than to pretend that we know how to adjust our route through the unknown hazards extending far ahead of us.

QUESTIONS

What would be the economic implications of replacing the price mechanism by rationing?

What economic arguments are there for government supervision of the price mechanism?

"The price mechanism may not be fair but it is effective." Is this true?

To what extent, if any, is Britain a planned economy?

Compare the methods of normative and indicative planning.

"Planning for growth may be good for planning but is bad for growth." Comment.

Are there any reasons to think that central planning of the economy would enable Britain to achieve a higher growth rate?

"Under-full employment involves a waste of resources. Over-full employment involves a wasteful use of resources. Both therefore impede economic growth." Discuss.

To what extent is planning essential for the development of poor countries?

REFERENCES AND FURTHER READING

T. Wilson: *Planning and Growth* (Macmillan, 1965)

G. Herbert: *The Management of the Economy* (Ginn, 1971)

G. Polanyi: *Planning in Britain* (Longmans and I.E.A., 1967)

S. Shenoy: *Underdevelopment and Economic Growth* (Longmans and I.E.A., 1970)

F. Oulès: *Economic Planning and Democracy* (Penguin, 1966)

W. A. Eltis: *Economic Growth* (Hutchinson, 1966)

In conclusion

You will have probably disagreed with some of the deductions made in this book. You may even doubt whether the facts presented are all accurate or whether the theories used are sound. If so, you are well on the way towards achieving that scientific approach to economic affairs which it has been our prime objective to evoke. The important thing is that you should now follow up your doubts and disagreements and check on them for yourself so that you either come to agree with us or formulate a definite alternative view based on analysis. This, of course, is a counsel of perfection for those coping with a number of subjects at A-level, Intermediate level, Higher National level, etc. Nevertheless, you can be aware that uncritical acceptance of our conclusions is not expected and also that shrugging them off just because you don't like them is an inadequate response.

The division between economic theory and applied economics is artificial and only exists in study because real life problems are usually too complex for analysis by beginners. Therefore, we have to build up a considerable body of theory before we can apply any of it with any advantage. When studying theory it is very important to bear in mind all the time that the objective is its application. When you turn to applied economics it is equally important to realise that you are applying theory and not just "making up" opinions.

Finally, economists always have to remember that their science, though vital to Man's attempt to control society, is only one of a number of social sciences. In some matters it may have more to offer than other studies, in some cases less. In no case can the considered comments of economists or any other social scientists be lightly dismissed if we are seriously concerned with advancing the purposes of Man. To all social scientists it remains a matter of deep concern that communities continue to value the lightly held, unsubstantiated views of the man-in-the-street equally with the fruits of their own studies. As civilisation develops the problems of living together become increasingly difficult to solve and it becomes ever more important that more people should understand those problems and that the rest should recognise that the commonsense approach to them involves giving due weight to the finding of genuine students.

Appendix

Value Added Tax

In April, 1973, the U.K. will replace Purchase Tax and Selective Employment Tax by a Value Added Tax (VAT). In essence, VAT is a multi-stage sales tax whereas Purchase Tax is a single stage sales tax. While Purchase Tax has been levied in the U.K. at the wholesale stage only, VAT will be levied on the "net value added" at each stage of the production of goods and services. The calculation of VAT will be based on the selling price—a manufacturer, for example, selling a commodity to a wholesaler for £10 will pay VAT on that £10, but relief will be granted from tax already borne. If, for example, the manufacturer paid £5 for his raw materials, and this £5 included 50 pence in VAT, he can claim back this 50 pence in calculating his total tax liability. Although the tax is collected from traders at each stage it is, in its final effect, a tax on consumers' expenditure.

VAT has the great merit of being broadly based. It is levied on a very wide range of goods and services. In the U.K., certain items will be *exempt* from VAT, for example postal services, education and insurance. Small businesses (with turnover less than £5000 a year) will also be exempt. A trader whose goods or services are *exempt* will not have to keep records nor account for any tax to Customs and Excise. On the other hand, he cannot reclaim any tax he has paid on his purchases; therefore, VAT is likely to result in increases in the prices of exempt goods and services.

In addition, food, water, books, news services, fuel and power, construction of buildings and several other categories will be *zero-rated*, which means that such items will not be taxed although rebates can still be claimed by traders on any tax already paid. In spite of such exceptions the yield from a 10 per cent VAT is expected to equal or exceed the present yield of the two taxes which it replaces.

The rate at which VAT is levied can be uniform or varied for different categories of goods. The U.K. proposal is for a single uniform rate of 10 per cent, the only exception being exempt and zero-rated items. Such a system will simplify the tax structure, since there are several different rates of purchase tax (all, incidentally, higher than 10 per cent).

Although rationalisation of the tax structure is one important objective, the main reason for the introduction of VAT is that the E.E.C. countries are adopting a standard VAT and that Britain must conform when she joins the Common Market. The present Six and the three other applicants (apart from the U.K.) have all introduced VAT in recent years. Rates are generally higher than the proposed U.K. rate of 10 per cent and several countries have different rates for different categories of goods and services.

The effects of VAT can only be estimated from other countries' experience. The number of "tax-points" is likely to increase very considerably. Prices of goods and services taxed for the first time will tend to rise, but this should largely be counteracted by a fall in the prices of other items. We must note, however, that continuing inflation may well swamp any VAT effect in this respect. One very desirable effect is that VAT should assist our exports. All exports will be zero-rated, and an exporter can therefore reclaim any "input tax" already paid by him. His exports will thus be entirely tax-free.

Finally, the government will be able to vary VAT between Budgets by Treasury Order by up to 20 per cent of the ruling rate. In this way VAT could prove a valuable regulator of aggregate demand.

Index